JAGGER

JAG

GER

REBEL, ROCK STAR, RAMBLER, ROGUE

MARC SPITZ

Gotham Books

GOTHAM BOOKS
Published by Penguin Group (USA) Inc.
375 Hudson Street, New York, New York 10014, U.S.A.

Penguin Group (Canada), 90 Eglinton Avenue East, Suite 700, Toronto, Ontario M4P 2Y3,
Canada (a division of Pearson Penguin Canada Inc.); Penguin Books Ltd, 80 Strand, London
WC2R 0RL, England; Penguin Ireland, 25 St Stephen's Green, Dublin 2, Ireland (a division
of Penguin Books Ltd); Penguin Group (Australia), 250 Camberwell Road, Camberwell,
Victoria 3124, Australia (a division of Pearson Australia Group Pty Ltd); Penguin Books India
Pvt Ltd, 11 Community Centre, Panchsheel Park, New Delhi—110 017, India; Penguin
Group (NZ), 67 Apollo Drive, Rosedale, Auckland 0632, New Zealand (a division of Pearson
New Zealand Ltd); Penguin Books (South Africa) (Pty) Ltd, 24 Sturdee Avenue, Rosebank,
Johannesburg 2196, South Africa

Penguin Books Ltd, Registered Offices: 80 Strand, London WC2R 0RL, England

Published by Gotham Books, a member of Penguin Group (USA) Inc.

First printing, September 2011
1   3   5   7   9   10   8   6   4   2

Photo research by Hal Horowitz

Gotham Books and the skyscraper logo are trademarks of Penguin Group (USA) Inc.

LIBRARY OF CONGRESS CATALOGING-IN-PUBLICATION DATA

Library of Congress Cataloging-in-Publication Data

Spitz, Marc.
Jagger : rebel, rocker, rambler, rogue / by Marc Spitz.—1st ed.
p.   cm.
Includes bibliographical references.
ISBN 978-1-592-40655-5
1. Jagger, Mick.   2. Rock musicians—England—Biography.   I. Title.
ML420.J22S65   2011
782.42166092—dc22
[B]   2011009851

Printed in the United States of America

Set in Electra
Designed by Sabrina Bowers

For Brendan Mullen,
who loved a good argument

Contents

INTRO "Brenda"   1

1 "I Dig to Sing"   17

2 "Preaching the Blues"   29

3 "Stone of Hope"   45

4 "As Tears Go By"   61

5 "We Piss Anywhere, Man"   71

6 "Under the Influence of Bail"   81

7 "I Went Down to the Demonstration"   105

8 "So, Remember Who You Say You Are . . ."   119

9 "All My Friends Are Junkies"   137

10 "The New Judy Garland"   155

CONTENTS

11 "Infamous"   167

12 "The Ballad of a Vain Man"   181

13 "The South's Answer to the Rutles"   193

14 "Punker Than Punk, Ruder Than Rude"   203

15 "It's Nice to Have a Chick Occasionally"   213

16 "State of Shock"   223

17 "Look in My Eyes, What Do You See?"   237

18 "An Evil Face"   253

19 "The Red Devils' Blues"   263

20 "A Knight of the Realm"   271

21 "Who Wants Yesterday's Papers?"   279

EPILOGUE "Onstage with a Cane"   287

Acknowledgments   293

Bibliography   295

Index   303

JAGGER

INTRO

"Brenda"

Most people don't remember "Rock Against Yeast." As far as *Saturday Night Live*'s musical parodies go, it's not nearly as iconic as John Belushi's Joe Cocker impression or the Christopher Walken–anchored Blue Oyster Cult *Behind the Music* send-up (known to all simply as "More Cowbell"). Still, within this mostly forgotten sketch, which aired during the show's February 17, 1979, episode (hosted by the teen idol and television star turned country rocker Rick Nelson), you will find the basis for this book. "Rock Against Yeast" perfectly articulates the current Mick Jagger Problem: Can we continue to worship and desire a man whom we don't really like anymore? The Mick Jagger Problem leads us to question whether we ever really did like him. If the answer is no, then how did this guy remain a constant presence in popular culture for fifty years and not, for one instance in that half century,

1

seem like . . . our pal? After all, his songwriting partner, business partner, and sometime nemesis Keith Richards has been everyone's cool older brother since Lyndon B. Johnson was president of the United States.

Back to "Rock Against Yeast." In this sketch, the late Gilda Radner portrays Candy Slice, a Patti Smith manqué with a rooster shag haircut, white tank top, black stick legs, sneakers, unshaven armpits, and a chemically ruined equilibrium. She is participating in a superstar benefit concert featuring Bob Marley (Garrett Morris), Dolly Parton (Jane Curtin), Olivia Newton-John (Laraine Newman), and a fat and thin Elvis tribute band known as the Elvii (John Belushi and Dan Aykroyd), as well as Nelson himself. Bill Murray, as his recurring rock industry, satin-baseball-jacketed sleazeball Jerry Aldini (of "Polysutra Records"), pulls a beer-swigging, belching Candy out of her oxygen tent long enough to participate in the above-mentioned benefit concert, where she debuts, along with her band, the Candy Slice Group, a garage rock number entitled "Gimme Mick." It's a complicated ode to both her attraction and repulsion to a then thirty-six-year-old Mick Jagger. "Mick Jagger, if you're out there, this is for you," Candy slurs.

"Gimme Mick! Gimme Mick!" she later shouts in the chorus. "Baby's hair, bulgin' eyes, lips so thick! Are you woman? Are you man? I'm your biggest funked-up fan. So rock and roll me till I'm sick," Candy raps. The group soon takes it to the bridge, where Candy, having confessed her attraction to Mick, launches into a Patti Smith—esque stream of consciousness that seems to equivocate it. "You, Mick Jagger, actually continue to perform at a concert where someone got knifed and killed during the '60s," she raps, dredging the specter of the then decade-old concert at the Altamont

Speedway in San Francisco where eighteen-year-old fan Meredith Hunter was killed by a furious Hells Angel while the Stones performed "Under My Thumb," bad acid raged in thousands of nervous systems, and the love era supposedly ended (more on that later).

"You, Mick Jagger, are English and go out with a model and get an incredible amount of publicity!" Jagger had recently stolen the willowy Texan model Jerry Hall away from fellow rock and roll gentleman Bryan Ferry of Roxy Music (more on that later as well). "You, Mick Jagger, don't keep regular hours!" This was the Studio 54 era, when danceable new wave and disco ruled and Mick's frequent late nights out made him a constant target for paparazzi like Ron Galella and gave him a permanent air of bleary-eyed decadence. And finally: "You, Mick Jagger, have the greatest rock and roll band in the history of rock and roll and you don't even play an instrument yourself!"

Here we go. This is where we find the disconnect; the point where the Mick Jagger Problem achieves liftoff. The joke goes over with the studio audience, of course, largely because of Gilda's charisma, genius, and conviction; but the accusation itself (affectionate as it clearly is) could not be more baseless. The joke works because it suits an *idea* of Mick Jagger that even thirty-two years ago was starting to metastasize. Inside of a half decade, it would almost completely take over the way we view Mick Jagger and obscure many of the facts. He *has* played instruments. He's been the Rolling Stones' harmonica player since vying for the position with the late Brian Jones in 1962. Listen to the malevolent solo at the end of the live version of "Midnight Rambler" (which you will find on *Get Your Ya Ya's Out*) if you want to hear the sound of an instrument being played by someone born to do it, a *musician*.

Even Keith Richards has praised Mick's natural ability to play the blues harp. "He's not thinking when he's playing harp," Keith famously said years later. "It comes from inside him; he always played like that, from the early days on." There's also the not so small matter of the riff to the Stones' 1971 No. 1 single "Brown Sugar." It's probably playing in your head right now. It started as soon as you read the song title on this page. I'd place it in the top, let's say, fifty, ever written, not just by the Stones but by anyone. And it's Mick's invention. Again, even Keith, who literally invents indelible riffs like "(I Can't Get No) Satisfaction" in his sleep, admits that this riff was the one that traveled across the rock and roll cosmos and took up residence in the head of the other guy. Not that it matters: Most people think Keith wrote it anyway. Mick's far too intellectual to create something so basic, primal, and gritty, after all.

When we consider the Rolling Stones, we think of the heart and we think of the groin. We don't dwell on the brain. "Keith is the heart," the veteran *New Musical Express* journalist turned music publicist Keith Altham remarked to me during an early morning telephone interview. "Mick is the brain." The heart and the brain. They must function together to survive, but in all matters of poetry and cool, we credit the heart. The heart pumps. The brain schemes. This idea of a manipulative Mick Jagger has caused us to put the finger on him for a laundry list of culture crimes regarding the Rolling Stones' long, dark past. Mick must have been the one who agreed to change the lyrics of "Let's Spend the Night Together," to "Let's Spend Some Time Together," at the behest of Ed Sullivan's frightened flunkies. He surely fired sickly, confused, bloated Brian Jones and left him to drown. He threw the Hells Angels he'd hired under the bus after Altamont. He forsook his rock and roll brothers and sisters for a retinue of Eurotrash counts and countesses . . . and Andy Warhol. He sullied the Stones' gravitas by hobnobbing with Paul Young and Duran Duran's Nick Rhodes in the early '80s as he wrestled with midlife and grasped for a solo pop career. He took our ticket money for the film *Freejack* and taxed the poor Verve for sampling a symphonic version of "The Last Time," on "Bittersweet Symphony." He's even to blame for a 2010 World Cup curse (all the teams he rooted for from the stands lost in upsets). Conversely, everything that Keith Richards has done (including nearly derailing the Rolling Stones for good and forever with his all-consuming decade-long heroin addiction) amounts to our greatest antihero at work. Keith cashes the same checks and has never really missed a business meeting where a major decision has been made. "Keith sat at the board tables in Geneva with a bowie knife, carving his initials into the table of this very conservative Swiss bank, while Mick and [former Stones business manager] Prince Rupert Lowenstein and myself sat around working out the tax plan," recalls former Stones staffer Peter Rudge. "But Keith never left the room." This perception of Mick as the band's lone miser and cynic has been encouraged at every opportunity by Keith. During their greatest period of estrangement in the mid-'80s, Keith happened to spy the jacket of a book by Yorkshire-born historical fiction writer Brenda Jagger, and from that moment, whenever his partner erred (in Keith's eyes), he was referred to (behind his back) as such.

Brenda. Her Majesty Brenda. Or sometimes simply "the bitch." This didn't stay an inside joke for long. "Keith has become a bit childish in some of his criticism of Mick," Altham says. Mick hasn't taken the bait. He's never really made an effort to reverse opinions, to undergo a Brenda-ectomy. His sit-down with close friend and *Rolling Stone* editor Jann Wenner in 1995 marked the last time to date that he has ever granted a lengthy question-and-answer session longer than the standard twenty minutes he usually allows. The cover story that British writer Zoë Heller wrote in the autumn of 2010 for the *New York Times Style* magazine was tellingly brief.

"Being interviewed is one of Jagger's least favorite pastimes," Wenner wrote in his opening paragraph, before getting into the relatively generous main course. Even during his brief chats with less prestigious inquisitors, Mick can be read as suspicious, truculent, and dismissive. In 1973, while interviewing then Stones guitarist Mick Taylor for the *New Musical Express* (which for the duration of this book will be referred to as *N.M.E.*), legendary British music journalist Nick Kent had the cheek to inquire of the singer about the possibility of a solo album in Mick's future. This was the response: [Busy eating sausage] " 'This isn't my interview.' "

Less sausages and more sugar might have endeared Mick to those who would have helped him build a sturdier myth and shield him from some of the potshots that would be fired in the years after "Rock Against Yeast." For example, in 2003, the late, very occasionally great *Blender* magazine (where I was a contributor), ranking the fifty worst rock stars of all time, listed Mick Jagger the solo artist at No. 13, immediately in front of hirsute new ager Yanni and the comically volatile Swedish guitar-shredder Yngwie Malmsteen. "Given the roll call of A-list rockers who have appeared on the Stones front man's four solo ventures, even a tone-deaf six year old could have produced something you'd want to hear twice," *Blender* observed. "Alas it seems there's never a tone-deaf six year old around when you need one." A cold shot from a music magazine that's had Tila Tequila on the cover. There is a temptation to defend Mick (as I just did) because of the silence from the Jagger camp. Keith and the like have turned some of us into playground refs. Two years earlier, the *New York Observer* published a column by Ron Rosenbaum entitled "Mick Jagger: Our Most Underrated Songwriter" in which the journalist keenly points out that Jagger's "jet-setting" lifestyle and "manic exhibitionist stage persona" too often overshadow "killer, slow aching ballads," like "Angie" and "Time Waits for No One," and the jangly, and perfectly glum "Blue Turns to Grey." Rosenbaum cites the "spare Beckett-like eloquence of 'No Expectations'" and compares his characterization in "Till the Next Good Bye" to that of Graham Greene. That year, 2001, Mick's fourth solo album, *Goddess in the Doorway*, sold about nine hundred copies in British shops its debut week. This despite a vast promotional campaign that included a feature-length prime-time BBC documentary (entitled *Being Mick* and featuring the catchphrase "You Would if You Could") and a rare series of interviews with the music press. Like the appearance of pop stars such as Wyclef Jean, Rob Thomas, and Mick-solo-project mainstay Lenny Kravitz, these efforts did little to better *Goddess's* commercial fate and may have actually worsened the Mick Jagger Problem. "Again it played into the image that people have always used to underrate him," Rosenbaum wrote of *Being Mick*, "to write him off as a jet-setting celeb, rather than the serious artist he was and still is." Keith could not resist the urge to pile on, publicly referring to *Goddess in the Doorway* as "Dogshit in the Doorway."

Shortly after the release of Keith's autobiography, *Life*, in the autumn of 2010, the webzine *Slate* ran a witty rebuttal from "Mick" as told to journalist "Bill Wyman." It's a response that actually might have addressed various Brenda issues; feisty, funny, clever, a little bitchy, but absolutely appropriate: "[Keith] has written a book that says, essentially, that I have a small dick. That I am a bad friend. That I am unknowable. The reviewers, who idolize Keith, don't ask why this is all in here. We have rarely spoken of such things publicly, and tangentially even then. We don't talk about it in private, either, and, no, he hasn't been in my dressing room in twenty years. I thought we both learned that there is no point in sharing anything at all with the press, save a few tidbits for the upbeat 'the Stones are back in top rocking form!' article that accompanies each of our tours."

It was, of course, entirely fictional; the punch Mick never threw. He simply seems to have no interest in improving his rep or letting us in beyond faux cinema verité promotional projects like *Being Mick*. He does not look back unless it's good business to do so. Mick doesn't require, like so many of the journalists who've written about him (myself included) context to appreciate or enjoy his own life. His skin is as resilient and dense as Keith's liver tissue. Kent, who has been chronicling the Stones with great insight since the early '70s, frames this injustice perfectly in his own 2010 memoir, *Apathy for the Devil*: "In the gooey showbiz sense of the word, he's always been smart enough to recognize that performers who actively look for love from their audiences often end up needy and burned-out, like Judy Garland. . . . and yet somehow he always ends up the villain whenever the Stones saga gets recounted— the control freak, the cold fish, the cunning, heartless greed head.

It's become one big fairy story—the Rolling Stones as perceived by the world's media—with Jagger as the resident evil goblin." During a telephone interview for *Vanity Fair*'s website (where I blog) in the late summer of 2010 while Kent was promoting *Apathy*, I queried him on this very subject after reading his memoir and asked him to explore the matter for me, and again it comes down to the relationship (or lack of relationship) with people who do what Kent and I do for a living.

> **MARC:** When did Mick cease to be a rebel hero? Keith still is. But Keith cashes the same checks that Mick does. And Keith almost torpedoed the band with his drug problem but he gets credit for being the real deal. The soul of the band. What's the story?
>
> **NICK:** Anyone who's read a Mick Jagger interview knows how evasive he is. He's not someone who is forthcoming.
>
> **MARC:** Does he not care?
>
> **NICK:** He likes to play games with journalists. He's been doing interviews for fifty years. He can't help being jaded about the process and at the same time he knows "I'm doing this because there's a record to promote or a tour to promote. I will give you three or four sentences but most of the time I will just give you one." But Keith Richards, if you sit down with him, he'll talk until you get a feeling of the man. He doesn't filter his opinions through this kind of "Should I say this to a journalist. How is this going to look. Will this look bad?"—he just lets loose. He doesn't really care. And deals with the consequence whether

it's running down Elton John or saying how he once snorted his father, which is outrageous and impossible to do, by the way. Anyway, Keith plays the media like a harp.

When I posed a similar question to Marianne Faithfull, Mick's iconic '60s lover and creative partner, also during an interview for *Vanity Fair's* site, she seemed somewhat amused by the notation. "I think people know he's pretty cool."

MARC: But they've turned against him over the years. His cool has waxed and waned, whereas nobody's ever turned against Keith, or you. Unlike Mick, you've always been cool. Why do you suppose that is?

MARIANNE: I don't know. I'm very lucky. I think they know my intentions are pure.

I'm not in it for crap reasons. I'm not in it to get laid. Not in it for them money. I'm in it for different reasons.

MARC: And a young generation can identify that. And respect it.

MARIANNE: They know I'm not taking. They can feel it. They know I'm giving.

I'm not sure generosity, of spirit or anything else, is what we think of when we think of Mick. Unlike Faithfull, or other permacool, aging musicians (Leonard Cohen, Lou Reed, Iggy Pop, David Bowie, Scott Walker, Lee "Scratch" Perry), he's no longer on the list of icons that each new generation feels compelled to explore and welcome as one of their own; one of the forever young.

We, the interested journalists, besotted, like Candy Slice, with that young Mick that we loved, the Mick who rocked us, want an hour. We get twenty minutes. What to do with the remaining forty? We indulge the idea of Brenda. Every vacuum must be filled and so we riff. Mick is an insecure Peter Pan figure. A rock and roll Bob Hope or Dick Clark, one who doesn't know when to call it a career and disappear with dignity and restraint. A miser, obsessed with the pecuniary details of every aspect of Rolling Stones Inc: the lapping Kali tongue logo on credit cards, power ties, coffee mugs, and key chains. We want Mick to be warm because the music of the Rolling Stones, especially on that perfect four-LP run, from 1968's *Beggars Banquet* through '69's *Let It Bleed*, '71's *Sticky Fingers*, and the 1972 double album *Exile on Main Street*, is so rootsy and loose, smoky and true. It makes us feel sweaty and sexy and . . . warm. How can that guy singing those tunes, every time we dial them up, how can he be such a cold fish? Did he get tired of our love? Our grandmothers and mothers and aunts screaming at him, throwing their panties, and fainting back in the early '60s? All those record company sleazes, the Jerry Aldinis, and the dealers and hangers on, the snitches in the late '60s, coming around and flattering, flattering, flattering? Did he close up then? "Everybody wanted a piece," Keith recalled in *Life*, harkening to the mid-'60s when Mick, and not Keith himself or the rapidly retreating Brian Jones, was the sole lightning rod. "You start to slowly treat everybody in that defensive way— not just strangers but friends. He used to be a lot warmer but not for many, many years. He put himself in the fridge." True enough there are people closely associated with the Stones, mostly during the '70s and '80s, who attest to this arch aloofness. "Twenty minutes in six years," one of them e-mailed me, explaining that the sum total of interaction that they shared with Mick.

Let's say that Jagger is indeed in cold storage. All brain, no heart. When exactly did this happen? When did Mick lose his connection to us? When did he stop being one of the people? Was it Altamont? Certainly when one watches *Gimme Shelter*, Albert Maysles, David Maysles, and Charlotte Zwerin's documentary on the band's North American tour of '69, there is indeed a moment where perhaps you can imagine Mick Jagger's very rebel soul leaving his body forever. One minute he's open; the next, closed for keeps. Mick sits in an editing room with Albert and David Maysles watching footage from the free concert. He is twenty-seven years old, the age that all great rock stars are supposed to check out. He is haggard. His fingernails are dirty. One year earlier, he almost believed in the revolution (more on that later as well). The violence of the concert is revisited; then the monitor that Mick is watching goes to white. He stands, utters a flat, faint, "Thank you," and the part of him that we still hunger for is, possibly, gone for all time, replaced by an aggressive privacy and the worst public image in rock history; replaced by Brenda.

Or was it? The only reason we even have this moment to cite is because Mick Jagger has permitted it. He's signed off, along with Keith, on releasing all the footage that would become *Gimme Shelter*—footage that captures him onstage at Altamont at his most powerless, frightened, and disillusioned. He could have burned it all. "I lost respect for Jagger in one instance," the musician, writer, and radical Mick Farren told me during another long distance phone conversation. Before we even began a formal interview, Farren warned me that he considers Mick Jagger "the

Fredo Corleone of the Stones." In *The Godfather*, Fredo was the one who wanted to be a great leader, but was tragically corruptible and ended up selling out the whole "family." Farren, too, believes you can see it all in *Gimme Shelter*. "When faced with some real Satanic majesty, Mick turned into basically a kind of a flapping old drag queen. 'Oh, people, why are we fighting. Oh. Brothers and sisters.' This is the moment when you assert your authority. To a degree, Keith did. 'Listen, you bastards, if it doesn't stop, we're out of here.' Cut-and-dried old rocker. Fuck this shit. That's what I expected from Jagger and that's what I didn't get. It was an emperor's-new-clothes kind of moment."

Still, we would not *have* that moment to form a solid opinion if Mick, the "brain" of the Stones, had decided to scheme.

Perhaps the very instant where some believe that Mick Jagger ceases to be of the people, ceases to give, and ceases to be warm is contained within perhaps his most unguarded and raw offering. When a rock and roll star gives up his cool, well, sometimes that's all he's got. We are dealing with a vast gray area when we deal with Mick: a complex, difficult, and troubling subject that has been, all too often, rendered in black-and-white. "When we finished the film and showed it to him, he couldn't at first bring himself to give us a release," codirector Albert Maysles tells me. "That took another six months. Fortunately, neither he nor the other Stones asked for any changes at all. So the film remained totally as we intended it to be. They asked that the scenes of violence never be shown apart from the film and we agreed wholly with that."

Without the release of *Gimme Shelter*, Meredith Hunter might have otherwise been completely forgotten by history. His remains currently reside in an unmarked grave in a Vallejo, California, cemetery. There's a sad, short 2006 documentary by Sam Green that concerns Hunter's death and very lonely, final resting place entitled simply *Lot 63, Grave C.*

"To me it importantly signaled Mick's caring and thoughtfulness with regard to what happened," Maysles says.

"People were just asking for it," Keith later said of Altamont. "They had those victim's faces." But Mick's face, frozen in time as he gets up from the edit bay and stares straight into the camera, is a victim's face as well. Keith, the ideologue who operates in black-and-white, is, crucially, never the victim. He's invested millions of dollars in medical-quality narcotics, lawyers, and handlers to create a certain impenetrable armor while holding on to some kind of warm energy; sometimes it's powered by a simple, boyish smile. This, as much as anything, is why young people still want to be like him. It just seems easier, cleaner, more fun, and, ultimately, although we never dwell on the millions required to insure it, safer. During the course of writing this book, the question became a kind of saloon Rorschach test; a parlor game for my rock-snob friends and peers. It's a simple question but the answer reveals everything (I believe; some might say nothing at all) about where you are at in your own life.

"Who would you rather be," the question goes, "Mick or Keith?"

Almost nobody wants to be Mick when this game is played (when was the last time you saw him smile?). When pop star Ke$ha sings about kicking dudes to the curb "unless they look like Mick Jagger" on her 2009 chart topping single "TiK ToK," we assume it's the Mick of old (whereas the "P. Diddy" that she references earlier in the song is age appropriate). And if Ghostface Killah didn't first deduce the rhyme and Kanye West didn't popularize it on the 2008 hit duet "Swagga Like Us" with Jay-Z and T.I., that blueprint wouldn't have even been consulted. In America, Mick is almost never name-checked outside of the British tabloids and the *New York Post's* Page Six (which inevitably marvels at his spry dancing at some fashion show after-party). Forget that Mick had a diamond-encrusted tooth before the term "bling" was invented. A few years ago, I too would have reflexively answered "Keith," no contest, but if you explore the facts and hear the stories beyond the public images, it's Mick in a blink. Mick Jagger is who you want to be when you're an adult. "I can't untie the threads of how much I played up to the part that was written for me," Keith bravely admits in his memoir. "I mean the skull ring and the broken tooth and the kohl, is it half and half? I think in a way your persona, your image as it used to be known, is like a ball and chain."

This isn't an anti-Keith book. I've stressed as much in the letters and requests I've sent to some of the subjects. I for one still love that Keith myth. I certainly respect the die-hard nature of the proudly dissipated dandy visage of his late twenties and even believe that Keith wears it with remarkable, improbable grace. I am fascinated by Keith's deformed fingers, the swollen joints and hardened tips, and that aforementioned skull ring, the constantly burning cigarette and vodka and orange drink consumption, which seems to mock death itself. I respect how he outlived Keith-acolytes like Johnny Thunders and laughed at every morbid "next to go," celebrity-death-list makers who'd placed him at the top. Have a listen to "Keith Don't Go" by E Street Band guitarist Nils

Lofgren and wonder if Nils feels like Chicken Little in a head-band today. With each year Keith survives, each fannish boy he buries, each gigantic check he cashes, it's more fanfare for the common man.

But Mick Jagger, for all his jet-setting, *is* that common man: vulnerable, searching, skeptical, never fully pledged to something as monolithic as rock and roll. The Rolling Stones are a covenant for Keith and they are a covenant for us. For Mick, they subsidize and sometimes impede a philosophical life-search. "Ian Stewart once said to me, 'If Mick ever finds his true identity, it'd be the end of the Rolling Stones,'" Keith Altham told me. Altham was referring to the band's founding pianist and de facto conscience, the Scottish "Stu" demoted to roadie by their then manager Andrew Loog Oldham and the second Stone to die (at forty-seven back in 1985). "The whole Rolling Stones thing in a way is a search by him for his own character." If Mick Jagger is playing, then he's still looking, and if he's still figuring out who he is, then it's up to us to avoid the temptation to come up with easy answers like "Brenda." There's a famous photo from the mid-'70s of Mick standing in front of a T-shirt that reads "Who the Fuck Is Mick Jagger?" His expression is inscrutable. If the Stones are indeed touring by the time you read this (and a fiftieth-anniversary outing is reportedly in the works), then the answer is still out there somewhere and will likely never truly be found. Hopefully this book will offer a few new possibilities: rebel, rocker, rambler, rogue. . . . Rethought.

Marc Spitz
NEW YORK CITY—MAY 2011

1

"I Dig to Sing"

Phil Spector, the deeply troubled but frequently sage-like producer and music industry pioneer, once said, "I believe that the English kids have soul . . . they say soul comes through suffering. Slavery for the blacks. And getting your ass bombed off is another way of getting some soul legitimately." If that's true, then Dartford, the area where both Mick and Keith came of age in the late '50s, bred the most soulful English kids going. About twenty minutes from London proper by rail, the suburb had been a constant target for Nazi bombs during World War II. By the time Michael Philip Jagger was born on July 26, 1943, the brutal raids were slowly becoming less frequent, the direction of the war effort moving in the Allied forces' favor. Benito Mussolini and his National Fascist Party were ousted from power the day before Mick came into the world. If you're looking for a good, early, Mick vs. Keith metaphor, the childhood home of Mick (then "Mike") managed to escape destruction, whereas the home of Bert and Doris Richards was nearly obliterated in the summer of '44, when Keith, an only child, was not quite two. From there, housing in Dartford was often makeshift. Many residents, like the Richards family, moved into hastily erected replacement homes among the broken bricks and twisted metal of the bomb sites. "Everyone was displaced," Keith said of his preteens. "They were still building it and already there were gangs everywhere." The sense of impermanence toughened Keith up and remains the source of his hard-edge image. Mick by contrast was raised in what Keith dismissed (perhaps a bit enviously) as "Posh Town," but the stalwart nature of the place informed both their personalities.

Mick and Keith were both middle-class kids with hardworking parents, but within the English middle class, as with the Americans, there were sublevels. If you were "posh," like Mick, it most likely meant that you were slightly upper-middle class with a house that was "semidetached" as opposed to virtually connected to your neighbors. You had the suggestion of a yard and a strand of individuality but were still looked down upon as provincial by Londoners proper (a prejudice that some insist Mick has overcompensated for). Dartford was divided by a railway. Keith literally lived on the other side of the tracks, a section on the border of a deep, wooded area marked by gothic factories, hospitals, and other industrial edifice. Mick lived on the slightly prettier side, but both were born at the right time in the wrong place. The advent of rock and roll would soon redirect them.

On paper, it would seem that Keith alone was built for rock. His war-veteran father was distant. "It wasn't possible to be that close to him," Keith said of Bert. "He didn't know how to open himself up." Mick and his father shared a strong bond. Basil Jagger, whom everyone called Joe, was a star athlete as a child and had carved out a respectable career for himself as a motivational purveyor of physical fitness. Father and son looked alike, with lean but extremely strong musculature, jutting ears, knowing brown eyes, and, most famously, pronounced, fleshy lips, thick and uncommonly rouged. He saw a lot of himself in Mick and processed the child accordingly with a caring but tough regimen of physical fitness and worked on sharpening the quick-witted boy's mental acuity. His creative side was encouraged by his mother. Eva Jagger, whose family immigrated from Australia, was determined to raise the perfect English family and embraced tradition. One particular interest was a love of in-home performing, resonating with her firstborn. "Performing . . . is something that children have or they haven't got," Mick told *Rolling Stone* in 1995. "In the slightly post-Edwardian, pre-television days, everybody had to do a turn at family gatherings. You might recite poetry, and Uncle Whatever would play the piano and sing, and you all had something to do. And I was just one of those kids [who loved it]." Mick's gift for song endeared him to his mother, and his skill and discipline as a young athlete filled his father with pride. When Mick was born, Joe Jagger was the physical education professor at a local college called Strawberry Hill but, thanks to an inborn determination, had already established a series of affiliations with national boards like the British Sports Council. He took his work home with him, creating a specific, regular physical regimen of calisthenics and weight training for Mick and his younger brother, Christopher. It was designed to build character and resolve: an aggressively healthy structure. No one would have expected, at that time, any backlash.

Whereas Mick could have been anything, and soon *chose* to be a rocker, Keith literally had no other option and very little to lose. He was, as a teen, beaten regularly by the local toughs who came to patrol the still-broken streets on his side of the tracks. Too young to become a loud, dandy Teddy Boy, Britain's pre-Elvis strain of juvenile delinquent culture, Keith rebelled quietly in his cowboy shirt and tight trousers, absorbing American rock and roll that was broadcast on Radio Luxembourg. Mick listened to the same station, fascinated by the sounds of Little Richard, Jerry Lee Lewis, the Everly Brothers, and Buddy Holly and the Crickets.

At Wentworth Primary School, Mick and Keith were acquaintances but not best friends as some have assumed. The different circumstances in their upbringing soon found them separated. Mick went on to Dartford Grammar School for Boys while Keith enrolled in Dartford Tech, where most students ended up learning skills designed to funnel them into the workforce. Mick drew high marks in grammar, English literature, French, and Latin. A natural leader, he was even made a student prefect, with charge over his classmates. It proved such a positive experience that decades later, a middle-aged Mick not only returned to his alma mater but funded a music education adjunct, The Mick Jagger Centre, to tutor local children.

Mick seemed destined for a full scholarship and easy entry into respectability and prosperity without detour or distraction. However, in March of 1958, when Mick was just fifteen, he and schoolmate Dick Taylor purchased tickets to a Buddy Holly concert in Manchester. "We were into Buddy Holly very early,"

Dick Taylor recalls. "After that we started playing." British teens of the late '50s looked to American rock stars (Elvis, Fats Domino, Little Richard) for inspiration, but they picked up their instruments and learned to play because of the local-born skiffle bands, who, in a proto-punk fashion, made that often intimidating leap from being a fan to being a player seem easy. "Homegrown music was quite the thing. 'If you can't play the guitar, play the washboard,'" Taylor says. "Learn three chords and that was it. We wanted to do it, and whether or not we thought we had the ability to do it was secondary. And so we soon started playing guitars and plastic ukuleles."

Technique, given Mick's natural sense of discipline, was easier to master than the spiritual overhaul that came with the advent of rock and roll. To his father's dismay, by the end of the '50s the boy had transformed into a precocious teenage philosopher-prince obsessed with rock and roll and girls, and, worse, became suspicious of uniforms and obedience. At the same time, London itself was changing. Mod culture was on the rise; teens who had buying power for the first time were now investing in sharp suits and dresses, scooters, and piles and piles of records. Mandatory military service would soon be phased out; birth control pills became readily available; and the austerity of the war years was replaced by a flaming desire for more: more experience, more life, louder, crazier sounds. Unspoken but unmistakable, this new wave of energy swept through England, alarming parents and inspiring kids. "We weren't rebelling in a vacuum," says Dick Taylor. "And it wasn't personal. It wasn't a rebellion against anyone specifically. It was a general rebellion against the stuffier aspects of English society at the time." Rock and roll, such a part of the establishment today, was viewed as impossibly crude fifty years ago, a kind of disease that somehow trickled into the local water supply and required immediate and aggressive filtration. "My parents were extremely disapproving of it all," Jagger has said. "This was for very low-class people, remember. Rock and roll singers weren't educated people."

Before long, rock and roll, as a sound, a rebel philosophy, had more sway over the pubescent Mick Jagger than his father's old-fashioned regimen could hope to. Again, there is photographic evidence of this available. During an episode of the BBC show *Seeing Sport* from the fall of 1957, Mick, then fourteen; Joe; and two others boys dutifully climbed a sandstone wall in suburban Royal Tunbridge Wells to demonstrate the proper footwear for such an exercise. "Here's Michael wearing a pair of ordinary gym shoes," Joe states, then picks up his boy's little foot and twists it toward the camera. The live audience laughs as Joe, the presenter, turned the boy into a sort of showroom mannequin. Mick, face full with baby fat, smirks and flashes the older man an amused but vaguely contemptuous sneer that would, a half decade or so onward, become an icon of unimpressed youth. Well into puberty, he was still abiding by his father's intellectual and spiritual model at an age when most boys had sex and only sex on their minds. "I never got to have a raving adolescence," Jagger recalled to the N.M.E. in 1973. He would, as the 1960s took off, truly begin to make up for lost time.

Joe Jagger was not relinquishing his hold on his eldest boy so easily and had what he thought was a secret weapon, another American import, equally fascinating as guitar, bass, and drums: basketball. Despite its relative lack of popularity in Britain, Joe had, by the decade's end, established and coached the basketball program at Dartford Grammar. He made Mick the team captain and even supplied his students with the proper sneakers, imported from America. It was around this time that Mick first heard the blues. He backtracked, by chance, from rock and roll to its older and purer foundation. "I worked on an American army base near Dartford, giving other kids physical instruction—because I was good at it," Mick said. "There was a black cat there named Jose, a cook who played R&B records for me. That was the first time I heard black music."

It's not difficult to deduce what the young Mick Jagger found appealing about the blues. In staid, leafy Dartford, listening to songs about gambling, running around with good-time women, and a cosmic, doomed sense of "my time here ain't long" fate were akin to a cowboy or gangster movie that one could play and replay, losing oneself in the lurid details. Blues was essentially storytelling, and it transported, working its magic on the listener in the same way that singing it transported the black sharecropper from his cruel and straining work under the sun. Whether swampy, acoustic Delta sounds or the spiffed-up electric R&B out of Chicago, the blues was a boredom-killer. Often lyrically hilarious and always hypnotic, it came with a beat one could play on a kitchen pan or the back of a schoolbook. "It was the *sound* that got us," Dick Taylor says. "When you first hear Howlin' Wolf or Chuck Berry—the sound is incredible. And for Mick it was the language. Chuck Berry was an incredible poet. The language was very rich. Mick got into his words. He would listen and write them down. We'd spend a lot of time spinning those records and trying to get the words exactly right. And I know we got a lot of them wrong."

R&B was essentially a new, fast, and smart slang, a mod way to communicate. For a few mostly white British kids of the early '60s raised in painfully quiet households and physically reprimanded for talking out of turn at school, it was finally (if oddly, given its African heritage) an idiom of their own. "It's a language that expresses the whole range of emotions, from sadness to blind hatred to sheer, crazed lust," wrote the late music writer Robert Palmer in his excellent study of the form, *Deep Blues*. "The slurs and rasps in the singing, the bending of the notes, the deliberate fluctuations in rhythm and tempo—all these blues techniques are designed to unlock and unleash emotions. The heavier the rasp, the more pronounced the bend, the deeper the feeling—a legacy of the music's roots in Africa, where spoken language is rich in tone, and the lower one pitches a phrase, the more feeling it conveys."

In the same bins where the American pop and rock imports were racked, Mick and Dick Taylor found blues LPs from independent R&B labels like Chess and Specialty. Fascinated by the covers, they'd pick up a Jimmy Reed or Howlin' Wolf record along with the new Chuck Berry, whom Mick had been fascinated by after seeing Bert Stern's 1958 documentary, *Jazz on a Summer's Day*, in which Berry sings "Sweet Little Sixteen," shot in profile like a president on a coin, or from the floorboards, giving him the appearance of a giant, which he may as well have been. "You could also get hold of records directly from Chess Records in Chicago," said Jagger. "I had come across a mailing address for them in some magazine or another. And when I had the money I would send off for records from them. They were really quite expensive for those days, because American record prices were higher than they were in England, and also to actually get them mailed out across the Atlantic cost a lot."

"He'd send money orders. I worked in the shipping room," says Marshall Chess, son of the label's cofounder Leonard Chess, today. "I remember sending boxes of records to England. Filling out the customs forms. That first wave of blues lovers wanted those Chess albums." Marshall Chess would meet Mick Jagger when the Rolling Stones passed through Chicago on their first U.S. tour in 1964, and at the dawn of the 1970s, after Chess was sold, he would formally join the fold and help launch Rolling Stones Records. At the time, however, he was just a kid, helping his father during summer break from school. And Mick was merely one of a few hundred misfit English kids going mad for this then esoteric noise, someone who today would be referred to affectionately as a "record geek." "It was rare. It wasn't an everyday thing, to get an order from England," Chess recalls.

The product would often take weeks to arrive, causing great anticipation and excitement, unimaginable by today's split-second downloaders. "You didn't even know if you were going to like the record when it arrived," Mick recalled. If you didn't you could always trade it. "We'd have a reel-to-reel recorder hooked up," Taylor said, "and we'd rig them up so we could tape the records and swap them. We'd also tape records off the radio. We were real fan boys. Pretty obsessed with the whole thing." Mick would remain a "record geek" even after he'd started making singles and albums himself. "I remember visiting his house on Cheyne Walk," Chess says, "And he had a long table in the living room. At the end of it, there was a turntable, with stacks and stacks of records. He had some Zydeco, blues. Some deep cool shit on that table. Not a lot of white people knew about Zydeco. He put on this Clifton Chenier song. 'Black Snake Blues.' It was a rare thing. I never saw a white guy other than maybe a Cajun who would have that side."

Blues music was also extremely sexy. It made the heart race; one jumped to it and surrendered composure to it. The lyrics, even to a student, were teaming with readily decipherable double entendre.

Mick's early sexual experimentations were likely in keeping with the gender segregation of the times. Boys at British public schools examined and explored their changing bodies together with a mixture of fascination and fear. "I think that's true of almost every boy," he has said. At age fourteen, he was still awkward and pimply, all ears and grin, his features yet to settle into the strange, somehow regal handsomeness of his early twenties, but R&B made him feel attractive inside, largely thanks to an uncanny ability to imitate the mostly black vocalists, sounding much like a man from the American South. "He had a gift for mimicry," Dick Taylor says. "He got really immersed in memorizing all the words and singing in all those accents." Even Joe was impressed by how he applied the same focus of sports and study to music: "I've never known a youngster with such an analytical approach to things," he said. "If he copied a song, he was able to capture the sound exactly." To the local teenage girls, Mick became newly fascinating, a sort of surrogate figure capable of conjuring the sounds and energy and sex of the new sounds on command. Black music gave him a kind of confidence that sports could not. "It attracted the girls," Taylor says. "If you could play and sing, you had a better chance. You could pull a tasty girl."

As the early '60s progressed, Mick went from collecting discs with haphazard fervor to slowly developing the refined taste of a collector to keeping a list of favorite tracks based on what he could sing well. When he and Taylor and another schoolmate, Bob Beckwith, finally decided to make the leap from fans to actual blues band, Mick was the natural choice to sing. By the time his first band, Little Boy Blue and the Blue Boys, made its public debut at Dartford's Church Hall in the summer of 1960, seventeen-year-old Mick was a long way from Clarksdale, Mississippi, but whether he knew it or not, his feet were firmly planted at the crossroads.

Mick had aced his A-levels, an advanced standardized test, and been accepted to the prestigious London School of Economics, which bred holders of high political office and wealthy bankers. This appealed to his parents. The philosophy of the L.S.E. suited the inquisitive, questioning teen perfectly. *"Rerum cognoscere causas"* was the school motto: "To know the cause of things." Everything was economics: social order, wealth, poverty. It wasn't pure math or tutelage in how to make the most money, as many disparagers of Jagger have cited: "He went to the London School of Economics, for God's sake!" The L.S.E. would become a hotbed for radicalism by the end of the '60s for a reason. That said, there was no reason to believe that anything would keep Mick from thriving in the City. There were certainly no high career aspirations when it came to Little Boy Blue, despite how great it felt to play the blues for people. "We were a teenage band," Taylor recalls. "We weren't thinking in terms of a career. We were thinking in terms of 'Let's just do it.' It wasn't about how or where it was all going." Mick lived at home at the time and dutifully took the train into London to study.

Ironically, it would be a trip home from the school's Houghton Street campus in the early fall of 1961 that would push Mick down the road to becoming a full-time musician. Mick was standing on the platform, as usual, carrying his beloved albums, including the Chess imports of Chuck Berry's *Rockin' at the Hops* and *The Best of Muddy Waters*, when a rough-looking kid in a purple Western-style shirt and cowboy boots approached him. Mick instinctively held his records close, sensing trouble. As the kid drew closer, he relaxed. It was his old friend Keith, now seventeen, expelled from Dartford Tech and attending Sidcup Art College, which he would also soon leave. Keith had come to the blues the same way Mick had—backward via rock and roll—and had a natural affinity for the sound as well. He'd already swapped his cowboy acoustic for a Hofner electric. As they rode the train together, Mick informed Keith that he'd been singing with Taylor. Keith admired the records and Mick allowed him to inspect them, fetish objects that they were; he felt proud that his harder-edged childhood friend was, as a young adult, now approaching him as an equal, if not the more culturally correct of the two. "I got a few more albums like these," Mick said. Keith asked Mick over to his house. "So I invited him up to my place for a cup of tea," he said. "He started playing me these records, and I really turned on to it." Keith told Mick about his guitar playing. Mick owned a guitar but couldn't really play. "What can you do?" Keith asked excitedly. Mick had an idea, one encouraged by his mother when he was a child; one that could never, ever be anything more than a trifle around the living room. "I dig to sing," he said.

"Preaching the Blues"

The Dartforders were becoming real Londoners. It started
gradually; Mick, trustworthy and cautious, had use of the family
automobile on occasion and had started taking Keith, Dick Taylor,
Bob Beckwith, and the occasional girlfriend on trips into the city
and as far as Manchester to see blues shows. Meeting Keith was an
electrifying accident, and both boys' ardor for R&B was now barely
containable. "It was great meeting someone else who was that enthusiastic," Dick Taylor says. "There's strength in numbers." They
didn't look sharp like the jazzers who'd monopolized the clubs of
London. They were scruffy students with bad skin and torn sweaters, but Mick and Keith afforded each other a confidence that neither boy owned only a few months earlier. They excited each other,
challenged each other, and that eventually produced an air of sophistication that emboldened both to soon leave Dartford for good.

Alexis Korner did look sharp. Korner was a trim, goateed, half-Greek, half-Austrian guitarist with a dandified wardrobe; a camp, antiquated manner of speech; and a tireless commitment to the blues. He had joined forces with a stocky, balding Londoner named Cyril Davies to infiltrate the city's jazz venues and turn as many people as possible onto the other great American form. Davies played his mouth harp until his round face flushed a deep and mad red. The strange duo had, by 1961, built their reputation as arbiters of the new music scene by actually backing Muddy Waters at their "blues night" at the Roundhouse Pub in the late '50s.

The Ealing Club was the main attraction for the young blues enthusiast. Little Boy Blue and the Blue Boys had visited during one of their blues-seeking sorties to London and up north. Now they were going every weekend without fail and slowly growing emboldened enough to imagine actually playing on the small stage. Each Saturday they'd hit the Ealing to study Korner and Davies' band, known as Blues Incorporated. Mick, who aspired to play the blues harp himself, often focused solely on Davies, watching from the wet floor as the elder blues enthusiast performed. "It was full of all these trainspotters who needed somewhere to go, just a bunch of anoraks," he recalled. "The audience was mainly guys—most of whom were pretty terrible—and the girls were very thin on the ground."

None of these Englishmen could hope to really be like Muddy Waters, but twenty-year-old Elmo Lewis, aka Brian Jones of Cheltenham, was certainly giving it a shot. Shortly after Mick and Keith had started frequenting the dilapidated Ealing, its poorly ventilated walls sweating, they met Jones and his friend, the conservatively dressed Ian Stewart, lantern jawed and only twenty-five, but boasting the air of a much older gentleman. Brian, like Mick and Keith, had become an evangelical blues fan in his teens, but while Mick was doing pull-ups in Dartford and Keith was floundering in art college, Brian Jones carried on like a moonshine-abetted hoochie-coochie man despite his flaxen hair, milky complexion, and generally angelic visage. Brian was already the father of two illegitimate children. He was such a character at the Ealing, exuding natural musical ability, that he'd been invited to sit in regularly with Blues Incorporated, something Mick and Keith, in their wool sweaters and corduroy blazers, could only fantasize about at the time. Occasionally, they would be asked up to fill in with a song or two while Korner and Davies took five, but Jones was a made guy. Both boys considered Brian a hero, his gift, attitude, and style something to envy and aspire to.

As he got more serious about this other area of nonformal study, Mick borrowed money from Joe and Eva to outfit Little Boy Blue with better equipment. Once inside, they wanted respect. They knew they had to bring a lot to get noticed among this crowd of serious fans. The whole scene was only about two hundred strong in 1962, but it was an intense two hundred, one that demanded Mick take Little Walter and Sonny Boy Williamson as seriously as Marx, Engels, and Keynes.

"Like the revivalists before them, the Stones and their peers felt themselves part of a crusade," George Melly writes in his pop treatise *Revolt into Style*. "They were going to preach the blues and they were going to live the blues too. But what were the blues about?" This was the subject of constant, lager-fueled, fish-and-chips-fortified, late-night discussions. These impressionable young Mods, armed with nothing but their instruments, a dozen import records, a few shillings, and an expanding array of emulated, mostly sexual experience, they analyzed the form, the clothes, the behavior, and even the politics of southern and urban blues, with no tutor or mentor—only their own rigid ethics to keep them going. "Serious, very serious," Jagger has said. "When we discussed it, we were like students. You know how students get serious about things?"

There were, even at this early stage, moments of great hybridization. Mick and Keith, despite their newfound confidence, didn't dare reveal, especially in the company of a purist like Ian Stewart or Brian Jones, that they had such catholic tastes. Rock and roll was not taken seriously. Pop was anathema. Mick and Keith loved them both. It would prove a secret advantage, one that would later help the Rolling Stones motor to the front of the pack once the scene began to take off.

Mick's voice isn't as naturally soulful or "black" as, say, that of Steve Winwood, who hailed from Birmingham, England. Winwood seemed a phenomenon or R&B prodigy, whereas, listening to Mick, you can hear the effort, and his phrasing is more interesting for it. Given his flair for mimicry, Mick could have handily employed the elastic, minstrel show baritone, suggestive of a southern sharecropper. There's an instance in *Gimme Shelter* where he proves just that, doing a verse of Mississippi Fred McDowell's "You Gotta Move" (covered by the Stones on *Sticky Fingers*): "Yo got tee-move." But on record it's pretty rare. The Stones' cover of Willie Dixon's "I Want to Be Loved," the B-side to their debut single, "Come On," finds Mick changing "want" to "wants," for example. More often than not, Mick instinctively sought a parallel instead between the original swampy archetype, the urban bluesman, the hipsters who worshipped them, and the British equivalent of down home: the Cockney. It's an amalgam. Like Frank Sinatra, or Billie Holiday, Mick has extra sensory power as a singer. He anticipates the band's direction and can ride along at his own pace without ever losing the groove. Lesser vocalists have to spit each word with rapidity in order to do the same. Instead, Mick enunciates every consonant. He can make a sibilant "Yes," sound like "Yeah." There's a calm to the delivery, a fast math that soothes and impresses even when the verses call for anger or frustration. There's irony in there too, but it's the remove of an intellectual and makes a pasty, bony kid in a sweater singing about chicken fried in bacon grease on "Down the Road a Piece" seem somehow less absurd. Who knows what else was tossed into the pot? Mick was always listening for inspiration. "He's a sponge," Keith would observe years later in his memoir. It was a backhanded compliment from an exasperated partner reflecting on all the times Mick came to him after a night at the disco. He'd absorbed some new style and had an idea for a Stones song. Middle-age Keith would recoil, but teenage Keith surely benefitted from Mick's knack for soaking up absolutely everything, then refining it into a personal style. Away from Dartford's yards and house rows, Mick could reinvent himself. He was meeting new kids every day—boys and girls, new students at the L.S.E.—and he could be anyone to them. He sometimes favored the voice of a Cockney tough. This was something he could parrot expertly, and some of it bled nicely into his singing. In "Little Red Rooster," "King Bee," and "Mona," he never sounds anything but English, though there's a real blues voice in the mix. Authenticity was, after all, about conviction—stepping on a stage and declaring, "This is me." And that "me" was in the early '60s a magpie, sometimes a mess, occasionally a boy genius.

Fashion-wise, Mick began cultivating a more lived-in look; a sort of urban student bohemian air, influenced, surely, by Keith and Dick's art school pose. He stopped bathing regularly, grew his hair out, began smoking, hoping perhaps to deepen his voice, and when not in class, slouched around Soho in threadbare sweaters, tight jeans, and boots. In order to be taken seriously, one had to appear as if one's mind was heavy, but in private, Mick was still a cutup, given to moments of gay mimicry.

When a tiny, coldwater bedroom apartment became available at 102 Edith Grove, Mick, and later Keith, moved in with Brian. It was walking distance to the L.S.E., where he was prepping for his first-year exams, and while the tiny adobe did not provide much quiet for study, it quickly became a think tank of a sort. Jones moved in his record player and radio. The three musicians and a fourth lodger, a skinny, unwashed blues fan named James Phelge, talked and drank until they collapsed on one of the mattresses spread on the floor. There was "no fixed rotation," according to Keith. They lived communally. The winter of 1962, when they moved in, was the coldest in two centuries and often the future Stones bound their bodies together for warmth. A boiled egg or a bottle of Coke was a rare treat. They lived mostly on potatoes. They even developed their own slang. If something was all right it was "Guvnor"; if it was square, it was "Ernie," as in "How fucking Ernie." It was ideal for a young, aspiring performer, but Mick frequently had to navigate both the world of the Guvnor and the world of the Ernie. Mick, of course, had an out. Keith and Brian never seemed to leave the building. Mick spent hours on the L.S.E. campus and often traveled to Dartford for hot meals and clean laundry.

While doomed to fall into a chemically fried and permanent state of apathy or entropy, Brian Jones was, at the time, the most ambitious of them all, determined to start his own band and lead the charge to turn every jazzer and pop fan into a blues devotee. Mick, Keith, Derek Taylor on bass, Ian Stewart on piano, and a rotating series of drummers including Tony Chapman and future Kink Mick Avory rehearsed at the nearby Bricklayers Pub whenever they could, with an eye toward getting their chance to apply the wisdom of two hundred hours shivering around a record player, hungry bellies pressed against their guitars. "Do we need a horn section? Do we need backup singers? Can they be black backup singers? How did he do this? Here, I'll show you. That's it, there." All the while, Mick hobnobbed with future Nobel Prize winners, published anarchists, and Parliament members.

On Mondays, after a weekend in the clubs, Mick spiffed himself up to attend classes, then returned to find Keith, Brian, and their new flatmate, Jimmy Phelge, in the same place where he'd left them, listening to blues and pop music and deconstructing it with the same fervor that Mick had just witnessed among the formally educated. "We would stick a pile of singles on the record player and lay there listening to them and making comments. It was always the same selection of records, including 'Donna' by Ritchie Valens, Jerry Lee's 'Ballad of Billy Joe,' Ketty Lester's 'Love Letters,' Arthur Alexander's 'You Better Move On,' and Jimmy Reed's 'Goin' by the River,' Phelge writes in his memoir *Nankering with the Stones*. "Some nights Mick would not arrive back at the flat until about midnight. He would come in and dive straight into bed, having maybe spent the evening somewhere else with other L.S.E. students. On other occasions he never came back at all and I presumed he had gone home to see his family in Dartford," Phelge recalled. Joe, Eva, and Chris were spared the seamier details of life in Edith Grove. In a way, the Ernie world was Mick's saving grace, providing a disconnect that would help him survive the tumult of the later decade. He was becoming adept at committing to a scene as necessary and removing himself as necessary, while others with less of a talent for such things, specifically Brian and Keith, were doomed to drown (literally and figuratively) in their affectations.

If the proto-Stones at World's End (the section of London where the Edith Grove flat was situated) were the *Young Ones*, that classic '80s British sitcom (this is how I imagine them when I read of this period), Keith, Brian, and Phelge would be Neil, Vivian, and Rick—antisocial, unfit for real employment, people who could only be what they were: outcasts, struggling, making a living on lentils and crockery—whereas Mick would be Mike, the one who could pass for straight and go out into the world, figuring out how to hustle a few bucks in his tie and dirty sport coat.

In addition to their Saturday nights at the Ealing, Korner and Davies began playing Thursday engagements at the Marquee, another Soho jazz hive, soon to be the premiere club of the '60s beat scene. An offer to perform on the BBC's *Jazz Club* left a spontaneous vacancy at the Marquee. Korner turned to Brian Jones to fill in and hold their residency for fear of alienating the club owner and losing it. This forced the still nascent band to commit to a name quickly. Brian suggested the Rollin' Stones after the Muddy Waters song "I'm a Man." The need for commitment came in a rush, as most things did at the time. This band would, after all, be very famous inside of eighteen months.

The Rollin' Stones—Mick, Keith, Brian, Ian Stewart, Dick Taylor, and Mick Avory—made their debut at the Marquee on the night of July 12, 1962, and never stopped playing, whether it was a lucrative gig, a free gig, an empty floor, or a full riot. It was easy for Mick to balance one Saturday night show with his studies and not find himself in the middle of a career quandary. The more they performed, however, the more crowds reacted to the energy of their communal, Edith Grove existence; the easy, male cama-raderie, which is always an appealing and salable force. It was there on the stages of small clubs like the Scene and the Ricky Tick and pubs like the Red Lion, as was the laissez-faire sexuality and, certainly, a growing comfort with the material: other people's songs played over and over again until they became their own. Word got around and a goateed blues fan from *Soviet* Georgia named Giorgio Gomelsky booked the band into his blues night at the Station Hotel in Richmond (which he'd christened the Craw-daddy Club). Here, the Stones, now known as "Rolling," not "Rol-lin'," became a draw for an ever-expanding wave of eager young Londoners. A residency was key; just like the hell-flat at Edith Grove, they could parse, and add and drop and perfect the idea of performance. "One night when the band was really giving out," Gomelsky recalled, "I signaled to my friend and assistant Hamish Grimes to get on a table so everyone would see him, and start wav-ing his arms over his head. Within seconds the whole crowd was undulating. This was perhaps the single most important event in the development of the Stones' ability to build a link between stage and floor, to connect and become joined to an audience, to bring about something resembling a tribal ritual, not unlike 'a revivalist meeting in the deep South,' as Patrick Doncaster described it a few weeks later in the *Daily Mirror.* No one had seen anything like this in the sedate and reticent London of 1963. It was exciting and foreboding. It heralded that a drastic social-cultural turn was on the books."

By the spring of '63, a few months shy of Mick's twentieth birthday, it was his band, the Rolling Stones, not their godfather's Blues Incorporated, who were the preeminent band on the London blues-rock scene. They'd even pinched their drummer from Korner's band in the winter of '62, convincing, at Ian Stewart's insistence, the imperious Mod Charlie Watts to join after months of campaigning for his talent and unflappable cool. Watts kept a jazz-style back beat and had the face of a stone-carved eagle. Around the same time that Watts gave them their first permanent drummer, Bill Wyman had replaced Taylor, who'd returned to school. Wyman, married and several years older than Keith, Brian, Mick, and Charlie, was more of an Ernie. He'd done his mandatory military service before it was repealed. "The only one of them who was truly working class," according to Keith Altham. Bill knew and loved his blues and, famously, owned a powerful Watkins amplifier that the Stones coveted, and quickly demonstrated an interlocking chemistry with Watts. Improbably, the Rolling Stones soon had the entire scene's most solid rhythm section; one that could stir up a real riot.

"Once you saw them in Richmond, you realized they were really cool," Peter Asher, then one half of pop duo Peter and Gordon and the brother of Paul McCartney's girlfriend Jane Asher, says today. "There were more and more people every week. You got a feeling of something building. And you really noticed Brian and Mick. They were very competitive. Brian was fabulous. He had a big green Gretsch and would put all this vibrato on it." Brian still took most of the harmonica solos on their short set of blues covers (mostly from Bo Diddley and Chuck Berry), but Mick had a trump card that would help him garner the majority of attention, perhaps more than he could handle then. It was at this time that Mick entered into a three-year relationship with eighteen-year-old Chrissie Shrimpton, who approached him after a show and boldly asked for a kiss.

Such instances were becoming more and more commonplace, but Shrimpton had something that other Rolling Stones fans did not. She was from a well-to-do family, with a very famous sister.

Shrimpton's older sister Jean, "The Shrimp," was already world famous as the face of the new mod London fashion scene. She'd dated movie star Terence Stamp and was engaged to famed photographer David Bailey. Jean was Bailey's muse, and her broad nose, bow lips, gigantic eyes, and handsome chin would peer out from fashion magazines and print ads throughout the world. Chrissie was not blessed with a similar symmetry. Her lips, like Mick's, were full. She wore her hair in bangs that were too long, or with austere headbands. Her eyes seemed permanently unimpressed. Of the dozens, perhaps a hundred photos I've seen of Chrissie Shrimpton, I've only seen one of her smiling. She had a chip on her shoulder and enjoyed picking fights with Mick and anyone else who made the mistake of crossing her, but she was a Shrimpton, and in late 1963, this was akin to marrying into pop culture royalty. Word traveled fast about the Shrimpton girl's new favorite band.

"He's great," David Bailey recalled Chrissie Shrimpton telling him of Mick. "He's going to be bigger than the Beatles." Both Mick and Chrissie were so young that it's hard to single out this love affair as one of mutual opportunism, but Mick, not Brian, was quickly emerging as the star of the band. He was becoming famous and Chrissie Shrimpton enjoyed that fame. Being associated with an up-and-coming rock and roll sensation certainly made Chrissie feel special, something rare when you consider a life of constant comparison with a beautiful, famous older sister. They didn't seem to like each other very much. Witnesses recount dozens of fights, both in public and in private; Chrissie is the implicit "girl" in many of the Stones early "put-down" singles like "Out of Time" and "Stupid Girl." But it was a crucial relationship at a crucial time.

The Beatles themselves showed up one April night at the Crawdaddy Club, unannounced, as a nervous Stones ripped through Bo Diddley's "Roadrunner" at top speed. Not yet the global superpower they would soon become, the Beatles were still the biggest new pop group in England, whereas the Stones were barely making enough to meet their rent of sixteen pounds per week at Edith Grove (where Chrissie seldom ventured). They could see what life as a pop icon looked and sounded like, but they were still scruffy students (or former students) sleeping in a pack like foxes.

It was the arrival of Beatles affiliate and self-styled pop hustler Andrew Loog Oldham, a flamboyant young industry vet at just nineteen years old, that would eventually convince Mick to pick a road and travel it. Oldham was a persuader. "He was his own freelance hustler—very young, very cool, looked great," says Peter Asher. "He was a mover and shaker. Absolutely I was impressed by him. Watching him in action [one could see he was a guy] going somewhere." He caught their show on April 28, 1963, and inside of a month, the Rolling Stones were recording their debut single, a nimble cover of Chuck Berry's little-heard "Come On" and a strolling take on the aforementioned "I Want to Be Loved," at Olympic Studios, the grand London recording factory where they would create their most iconic late '60s music. "Everything happened quickly," Mick has recalled. "But you had to be quick in those days because there was so much going on and you could get lost in the rush."

Oldham's youthful confidence bolstered the new group, and yet there was no guarantee they'd enjoy any success at all outside of the London club scene. Brian was near megalomaniacal in his drive to succeed. Keith needed the band to work. He was in no hurry to join the workforce at some office, applying what little art and design skills he'd learned at Sidcup Art College when he wasn't playing guitar in the cloak room. He'd done a few pallid runs through the ad agencies of London but returned to Edith Grove and the comfort of his records and guitar without any takers. But Mick took all of the attention and whispers that he was a star in the making with trepidation. To drop out of the London School of Economics on a full scholarship and counter so aggressively the plans and wishes of his family was a huge conflict. There were two influences that may have made his choice a bit easier and less painful. First, it helps to realize that this was not an age when pop groups enjoyed decades-long careers like actors, authors, or painters (or pop groups today). Rock and roll was still young and there was an implicit ephemeral quality to it. Second, if there was any group that seemed like they were changing such rules, it was the Beatles, and Oldham's connection to them was impressive and already yielding some results. Short on potential singles, Oldham and the Stones asked John Lennon and Paul Mc-Cartney if they had anything useful. McCartney had been developing a chugging, bluesy number called "I Wanna Be Your Man" that seemed perfect. According to legend, he and Lennon retired to a corner of a nightclub to finish it together before playing the complete version to the band and their manager. The popular take on this event (recounted by Mick himself in the 1978 Beatles parody *The Rutles: All You Need Is Cash*, which we will soon visit) hints that this was a throwaway (Ringo, after all, sings on the version the Beatles themselves would record) as far as Beatles standards went, but it was more than good enough for the Stones, who were, like many of their peer bands at this point, a covers act. There's a bit of truth to this, but the Stones inject "I Wanna Be Your Man" with the kind of masculinity and menace that made the Beatles look good. It's a middling composition, and their furious take on it made it a hit that November, their first Top 10. And so, in the fall of 1963, with a three-year contract with Decca Records orchestrated by Oldham and their first successful single in stores, Mick and Keith finally moved on. They moved from the dangerously squalid flat on Edith Grove and into a more appealing home in West Hampstead (while Jones moved in with his then girlfriend Linda Lawrence's family), and on October 22, 1963, after nearly two years of study, Mick informed his teachers and parents that he intended to leave L.S.E., citing a rare opportunity to become a performer. His L.S.E. professors offered him the chance to re-enroll the following year, which Mick found a great relief. For all he knew, he would be back should this rock and roll experiment ultimately prove short-lived.

Joe and Eva Jagger were considerably less comforting. "It was very, very difficult," Mick said years later, "because my parents obviously didn't want me to do it. My father was furious with me; absolutely furious." His parents feared for him, even as they raged at him, but clearly the days of straddling the world of the Guvnor and the world of the Ernie were over. Mick had to commit to one or the other and opted to take a huge risk on his own talents, as well as those of his fellow blues zealots.

"Suppose we failed," Brian Jones recalled. "We'd have tried to the best of our ability and we would have had nothing to regret in later life—when possibly we'd all be working in offices and married and settled in some suburban house. But if we didn't give it a proper fling, we would probably end up kicking ourselves—like never knowing how good we could have been. And we figured that a lifetime of regret, of thinking back, just wouldn't work out."

One month later, while the Rolling Stones were backstage during a taping of the British pop dance show *Ready Steady Go!*, another former L.S.E. student, John Fitzgerald Kennedy, was assassinated in Dallas. President Kennedy's death would bring about a mourning, heaving desire for both escapism and an edgy awareness of the kind of constantly looming darkness that the headier days of Camelot tended to mask. The Rolling Stones, now with the power of a fully committed lead singer, would provide both.

"Stone of Hope"

"It's about time we had Howlin' Wolf onstage!" a beaming Brian Jones announces, then quickly gets out of the way. There's footage from a 1964 episode of the American teen music program *Shindig* in which Howlin' Wolf, the towering blues man with the uniquely gruff voice, appears. He's fifty-four years old, not exactly the type of attraction *Shindig* was used to featuring, but the Rolling Stones, having popularized the songs of older black American blues artists, were now acting as their de facto chaperones, taking every available opportunity to turn the kids on to the original artists who inspired their sound. This was likely more a by-product of their still flush enthusiasm for the form than any concentrated effort to pay it back. They were gushers, not activists, but when the band visited America they were soon exposed to the myriad injustices, not just musical or professional, but social, that their great heroes had been reckoning with for decades. The Stones insisted on the Howlin' Wolf booking and sat not just respectfully but reverentially at the old man's feet as he wailed for the cameras, reversing, for one small moment, a lengthy and institutional order.

Before ever leaving Europe, the Stones had already met and played with some of their greatest African-American influences. They toured with Chess Records star Bo Diddley, striking about a half dozen Diddley covers from their set, out of respect. The tribal "shave and a haircut" Diddley beat was a band favorite, a cornerstone to their early sound. The Stones also toured with Little Richard and the white Everly Brothers. These were stars of the '50s and very early '60s, no longer inciting teenage fervor wherever they went. The Stones of '64 were faced with a strange dilemma: how to process the surprise success of this heavily influenced music without offending their heroes. "This was our first contact with the cats whose music we've been playing," Keith has said. The possibility for awkward moments was unending. The America that the Stones first visited in the spring of '64 seemed, in the words of Dr. Martin Luther King Jr., "a mountain of despair." The Civil Rights Act guaranteeing voting rights and outlawing discrimination on the basis of race and sex would not be passed until July, and in many pockets of the country, things proceeded as usual even after that; WHITES ONLY signs still hung in front of diners, water fountains, and public bathrooms. There were still lynchings and cross burnings. A black man risked his life by looking a white man dead in the eye, or talking back. Protests were mounting: marches and walkouts. African-Americans, many of them the same age as the Stones' white teenage fans, bravely clashed with police dogs and took the brunt of fire hoses. How could the Stones find success in America without becoming part of the problem, and profiting from the injustices? How could they sell the black man's music to white America with respect and grace? They would have to tread carefully.

Like the Beatles that February, the Stones landed at John F. Kennedy Airport in June of 1964 and were met by about five hundred screaming fans. Like the Beatles, they proceeded to host a press conference where they fielded questions about their long hair ("Are you guys wearing wigs?"), their influence on the nation's teens, and the Beatles, Beatles, Beatles ("Do you play the same music?"). As with the Beatles, local DJ Murray the K, the self-described "Fifth Beatle," inserted himself into the group's inner circle. Once in Manhattan, they discovered their hotel, the Astor in Times Square, was surrounded by about two hundred screaming female fans. At night, the Stones were feted by New York society. They went twisting at the Peppermint Lounge and attended a party for socialite and Warhol star "Baby" Jane Holzer. The Holzer affair is famously chronicled by new journalism pioneer Tom Wolfe in his "Girl of the Year" essay, which provides a good window into how Mick Jagger was already becoming the face not just of the Rolling Stones, but of the faster, smarter, and harder new '60s itself. "Wait until you see the Stones," Holzer is quoted as saying. "They're so sexy! They're pure sex. They're divine! The Beatles, well you know, Paul McCartney—sweet Paul McCartney. You know what I mean. He's such a sweet person. I mean, the Stones are bitter. They're all from the working class you know? The East End. Mick Jagger—well, it's all Mick. You know what they say about his lips? They say his lips are diabolical. That was in one of the magazines."

Mick's "diabolical" lips made their American television debut on the local talk show *The Les Crane Show*, but it aired very late and was hardly a splash to rival the Beatles' debut on *Ed Sullivan*. Over the next week, they would find that America was vast and far more difficult to conquer. Things went from exhilarating to humbling quickly. They flew to Los Angeles, another soft landing, culturally. These were show business cities, hardly the Deep South, but the idea of a bunch of white kids attempting to "play black," was not an easy one to sell to the old showbiz guard. On the *Hollywood Palace* show, a variety hour featuring a revolving series of guest hosts, the Stones had the bad fortune to get booked when Dean Martin was presiding. Martin, like his pal Frank Sinatra, was at first highly suspicious of the British Invasion bands, with their scruffy demeanor and long hair. Rather than welcoming them as an ambassador of American entertainment, the aging and clearly threatened superstar gleefully (some say drunkenly) subjected them to a mean-spirited Rat Pack treatment: "Their hair isn't long," he joked before introducing them. "Now something for the youngsters," Martin read off cue cards. "Five singin' boys from England who sold a lot of al-bee-yums." The audience laughs nervously. Backstage, the Stones are laughing as well, at Martin's Brylcreemed hair and tuxedo. It seems surreal to them. "They're called the Rolling Stones. I been rolled while I was stoned myself. Here they are at ya." Mick sang a jumping "I Just Wanna Make Love to You," while Brian played harmonica and Keith stalked around looking dour and furiously pounded the strings of his guitar like they were piano keys.

"Rolling Stones, aren't they great?" Martin cheered as the number ended. He rolled his eyes and signaled his exasperation to the studio audience. The sixty seconds were clearly painful for him. The Stones did a half bow, then decided against it. "Fuck Dean Martin," their tired eyes seemed to say. "You know something about the groups today; of course they have long hair. It's not true at all. It's an optical illusion. They just have low foreheads and high eyebrows." It would get worse. Shows in San Antonio, Detroit, Minneapolis, Omaha, and West Virginia would be half full, with hostile law enforcement ribbing them about their hair and their loud, sexed-up "black" music.

Only the two-day recording session at Chess in Chicago returned the band to the realm of fantasy fulfillment, but for all their agog joy, they would have to face some potential cringe-worthy moments as well. Even though Chess was run by the Jewish brothers Leonard and Phillip Chess, the Rolling Stones would be among the very first white artists to record there. "We never had outside people," recalls Marshall Chess. "That was a very major rarity. You had to be on Chess to record there. We were always recording our own artists. We had our own engineers." The Stones got to stand in the very studio where their heroes recorded and lay down what they assumed would be considered genuine Chicago rhythm and blues tracks, including the jaunty instrumental "2120 South Michigan Avenue," the late-night, boogie-woogie piano blues "Stewed and Keef" (featuring Ian Stewart and Keith Richards), an echo-drenched "Reelin' and Rockin'," a country blues version of Muddy Waters' "I Can't Be Satisfied," and their soon-to-be-a-hit cover of Irma Thomas' "Time Is on My Side." All the while, they drew a fascinated crowd of label staff, artists, and spectators. "They were white guys, they were young, they looked strange," said Marshall Chess. "They drank whiskey out of the bottle. We never had that in the studio. Blues guys drank out of a glass." On that visit, the Stones met heroes Buddy Guy, Willie Dixon, and Chuck Berry, who penned their debut single "Come On." Berry was supportive but brief and slightly aloof, encouraging them to "swing on."

Waters, Keith famously insists (although some claim this is apocryphal), was supposedly whitewashing the Chess ceiling. The implication was that these giants had to do menial chores in order to subsidize their income, as the opportunities that the Rolling Stones enjoyed as white rock and roll stars was not available to them. Being a hero to a young fan was one thing, but the reality of their struggle, both financially and in order to receive the kind of dignity they enjoyed when touring Europe, was another. Thanks to their "undergrad" study at the Ealing Club and in Edith Grove, the Stones themselves could imagine what it was like to be hungry, to make sacrifices for the sake of their music, and to be judged for their love of the lowbrow rock and roll (as opposed to traditional jazz). They were judged by the way they looked and dressed as they traveled the Windy City. "No one at Chess and very few people in Chicago had seen anyone with long hair," Chess says. "That night after the session, I drove Brian Jones back to the hotel and they were yelling, 'Homo!' at us from the streets. With his hair, they thought he was my boyfriend." Still, this was a trifle compared with the only slowly vanishing inequalities of 1964 America.

It would be the finale of the Stones' second tour of America in the autumn when the band would be faced with possibly their greatest moral dilemma of this kind: what to do when one of their heroes makes an issue of a perceived inequality.

The place, again Southern California: the Santa Monica Civic Center, a three-thousand-seat arena by the ocean. The occasion: the taping of the *T.A.M.I. Show*—short for Teen Awards Music International, a pop film with multiple acts like their beloved *Jazz on a Summer's Day*. The hero was, of course, James Brown, not yet the Godfather of Soul or the Hardest Working Man in Show Business, but already as much a star in the black community as the Stones were to white teenagers. Both bands were candidates to top a bill featuring a dozen stars, both black and white, performing rock, pop, and soul. This would not be the last time Mick Jagger would have to deal with issues of race over the music that he loved to play. He'd still find himself in the middle of a storm twenty-five years on, in 1989, but this was the first time it compelled the twenty-one-year-old to really address whether or not he and a black counterpart were truly equal, and to take a stand. If the Stones believed that James Brown should not be treated any different from themselves or any other band no matter what his race, then they had to commit 100 percent to blowing Mr. "Star Time" off the stage . . . for the good of humankind.

There were no formal dressing rooms in the bowels of the Civic, just a large, communal backstage area where Mick sat on a folding chair and stared at his shoes. The muffled sound of a production crew member shouting at a coworker and the bleats and half notes of an orchestra tuning up worked his already jumping nerves. There was a knock on the wall. Mick was jolted. He opened it and was shocked to see Marvin Gaye standing there. Gaye was handsome and wearing a dark suit. About five years Mick's senior, he, like the other Motown artists, the Supremes and Smokey Robinson, greeted the group warmly, making it clear that they dug the group's look and sound. The Stones returned the compliments, making it known that while traveling through America on two full tours, they listened almost exclusively to Motown, whose hit factory pretty much owned the airwaves at the time. "Don't worry about James Brown," Gaye said, crouching to comfort Mick. "People love you because of what you do onstage." Gaye had yet to become a titan of American soul. Like Diana Ross, Smokey Robinson, and the Stones themselves, he was just a star on the rise, with a few hits to his credit; but the words meant a lot. The Stones had covered his hit songs as well, including "Hitch Hike" and "Can I Get a Witness." To most white listeners, James Brown was an unknown, too, but the Stones knew what it meant to follow him. At the start of the tour, they'd seen the act live. Ronnie Bennett, later Ronnie Spector of the Ronettes, with whom they'd also toured England, had played host to the visiting Englishmen. Keith and Ronnie were having a secret affair and Mick was enjoying the company of her cousin and fellow Ronette Estelle. "They were so far away from home, I guess they just needed to be around a family sometimes," Spector explained in her memoir, *Be My Baby*. Mick and Keith would eat home-cooked breakfasts, play records, watch TV. One night, during their short stay in the city, Ronnie brought Mick and Keith over to Harlem's legendary Apollo Theater, where James Brown was scheduled to headline. "Mick Jagger was the biggest James Brown nut ever," Spector recalled. "When we were on tour in England, he kept us up half the night asking questions about James Brown. What was he like offstage? Where he'd learned to dance. How much did he rehearse? I finally had to tell Mick, 'Enough already. I don't even know James Brown. I'm a Ronette, remember?' "

Mick and Keith were taken backstage after Brown brought down the house and were briefly introduced by Spector. "I don't think James Brown even knew who these weird English guys were, but Mick and Keith were practically shaking."

Now, as the hour drew closer, it was a becoming a true challenge not to obsess about James Brown once again. With the exception of Berry, who would be the first act to perform, the *T.A.M.I. Show* was all about showcasing the new. The technology (a camera system called "Electrono-vision") was new. The sounds were new. Surf rock (the Beach Boys), girl groups (the aforementioned Supremes), pop soul (Gaye, Robinson and the Miracles), teen pop (Leslie Gore), British Invasion (Billy J. Kramer and the Dakotas, Gerry and the Pacemakers), and the American garage rock it inspired (The Barbarians): black, white, American, and English, all playing on the same stage to the same crowd. And if the world was really new, then Mick had to prove it. It was not an unimportant showcase for the Stones, career-wise. They had a few American hits but they weren't in the Beatles' league yet. The *T.A.M.I. Show* film would be distributed to more than a thousand theaters throughout the country—a serious boost in exposure.

Brown arrived at the Civic Center and was promptly informed of what the Stones already knew. "I remember James coming up and saying 'Of course I'm the last act on the bill, right?'" says Steve Binder, director of the *T.A.M.I. Show*. "I told him, 'No, actually you're going to be followed by the Rolling Stones.' James looked at me and smiled and said, 'Nobody follows James Brown.'"

Visually, the Stones had what it took to anchor the show. Like very few of their fellow British invaders, they were uncommonly fascinating on camera; better even than the Beatles; sinister and wry, more like Elvis. The lens seemed to pick up their raunchy inner monologues and transmit each suggestive expression straight into the viewer id. At that point, they were TV veterans, starting with appearances on *Ready, Steady Go!* in '63 and finally following the Beatles to the Ed Sullivan Theater in New York on this last tour. If nerves didn't get the better of them, they stood a fighting chance of justifying the hype that went along with newsreel footage of fainting girls and hastily boarded limousines.

With no separate quarters for the bands backstage, behind the wall of the proscenium it was a sprawl where shop was talked, friendships made, admiration expressed, cigarettes bummed. When one band would rehearse, others would gather in the wings to watch. But James Brown was nowhere to be seen. His absence was conspicuous.

"The Rolling Stones from Liverpool are gonna be there—the fab-looking guys with the moppy long hair," went the lyrics to the "*T.A.M.I. Show* Theme," sung by hosts Jan and Dean. If nothing else, this underscores just how difficult it was to delineate yourself from the Beatles in '64. Every band with a British accent might as well have been from Liverpool. Jan and Dean opened the show and introduced Berry, who duckwalked through "Maybelline" before ceding the stage to Gerry and the Pacemakers, who played along to a meandering blues segue before performing their own ballad "Don't Let the Sun Catch You Crying." Smokey Robinson and the Miracles, their leader somewhat hoarse but still at turns smoldering and kinetic, followed ("You Really Got a Hold on Me," "Mickey's Monkey"). A dapper Gaye played the aforementioned "Hitch Hike." Leslie Gore brought undiluted teenage gothic drama with "You Don't Own Me." Jan and Dean returned to perform their skateboard ode, "Sidewalk Surfin'."

The Beach Boys, one of the biggest acts on the bill, delivered their standard set, highlighted by their new single, "I Get Around." It's hard to imagine today, what with the endless tours and lawsuits, but the Beach Boys were once every inch the teen idols the Beatles and the Stones were. In the *T.A.M.I.* footage, Mike Love proved to be a confident if uninviting front man, and a smiling Brian Wilson was a year and change shy of his mental breakdown. Billy J. Kramer and the Dakotas followed, then the Supremes, and finally the Barbarians, a negligible but fun garage-rock blues band (who would have their only major hit with a British Invasion novelty track, "Are You a Boy or Are You a Girl," which would appear on the monumental *Nuggets* compilation). Shortly after that . . . history.

"Ladies and gentleman, James Brown," Dean announced. Backstage the five Rolling Stones, weary from endless touring and miles from home, looked like criminals about to face a firing squad. They exchanged a few wordless glances, a second language at this point, then decided to boldly face it, to walk as a group to the wings and face their fate.

"We went on, a little nervous because we didn't think this audience really knew us, but when we went into 'Out of Sight,' they went straight up out of their seats," Brown writes in his memoir, *James Brown, The Godfather of Soul.* "We did a bunch of songs, nonstop, like always. . . . I don't think I never danced so hard in my life, and I don't think they'd ever seen a man move that fast." Brown knew the Stones were watching from the wings. Everyone was watching; all eyes were on him. Sliding in his patent leather shoes, putting his pinkie-ringed hand on his hip, he dropped to his knees in his checked jacket and vest, then jerked up again like a piston. With all the super-physicality, there did not seem to be one grunt or huff emanating from his throat. He seemed to be burning oxygen, breathing through hidden gills. Next Brown emoted wildly through "Prisoner of Love," grimacing, and walking to the mic like it was a flotation device in a roiling Pacific Ocean. Next, he led the band through an impossibly fast, almost proto-punk version of "Night Train," shouting out destinations "Miami, Florida! Raleigh, North Carolina!" the way Dee Dee Ramone would later count out the next Ramones song with a swift "1-2-3-4!" He finally exhaled at the end of that one, then sat on the drum riser and caught his breath theatrically as if to say, "Man, how about that?"

But he wasn't finished. He got up and did his "good foot" dance back to the mic, then dramatically collapsed to the floor again, a signal for his band to pick him up and try to help him off-stage. It was all a ruse, of course. Defiantly, he ran back to the mic, milking the crowd, which screamed even louder. The band picked him up again. And again he ran back to the mic. "When I was through, the audience kept calling me back for encores. It was one of those performances when you don't even know how you're doing it," Brown writes. "At one point during the encores I sat down underneath a monitor and just kind of hung my head, then looked up and smiled. For a second I didn't really know where I was."

A mere fifteen feet away, Mick Jagger was as covered in sweat as Brown was, and he hadn't even begun to sing. He felt light in his shoes; dizzy. "The Stones [were] standing between all those guards," Brown remembered. "Every time they got ready to start out on the stage, the audience called us back. They couldn't get on—it was too hot out there."

"After James there was just enough time for the technical crew to get a smoke or a breather and to reconfigure the stage with the microphone setup or if they had their own drummer like the Stones did, bring their instruments on, twenty minutes," Binder says. Twenty minutes . . . to follow that.

Jagger lit a final cigarette and warmed his voice with a little Jack Daniels as the crew prepped the stage for the Stones. The sound of the fans clamoring for the band only made him worry about the challenge ahead: How does one justify following what just happened out there?

Jan and Dean returned to the stage to welcome "those fine fellows from England, the Rolling Stones." Looking nervous but resigned, the brave young men from South London assumed their headlining position. And they pulled it off. The Rolling Stones did the impossible and made the viewer forget Brown's epochal spot. They were something so different, ironically derived from the same beat, but after a half dozen TV appearances they were adept at presenting a new breed of energy—and of making a viewer believe that they were watching some sexed-up space invasion. That's how they matched James Brown. Surprise and sex. This isn't to say that the future Mr. Sex Machine wasn't carnally explosive. But there was a context for his performance, superhuman as it was, whereas the Stones, clunky and frightened, were like nothing anybody had ever seen before: male and female, familiar and strange, coming right at the viewer, leaving them no time to think, only to surrender themselves. Patti Smith, in the pages of *Creem* magazine (where she was a contributor), recalled the sensation years later:

"The singer was showing his second layer of skin and more than a little milk," she wrote. "I felt thru his pants with optic x-ray. His was some hard meat. This was a bitch. Five white boys sexy as any spade. Their nerves were wired and their third leg was rising. In six minutes five lusty images gave me my first glob of gooie in my virgin panties . . . blind love for my father was the first thing I sacrificed to Mick Jagger . . . masculinity was no longer measured on the football field." At the time, Smith was a closet rebel teen from Jersey, a good Catholic girl. The *T.A.M.I. Show* performance presented options.

Again, technically, it's far less accomplished than Brown's acrobatic marvel. They started right into "Around and Around" with skinny Mick dressed in a sweater and clapping along to the beat at the mic. He looked much amused at all the sexed-up chaos; soon that old smirk returned to his lips as if to say, "This wasn't so bad after all." Brian burned with hard charisma. Keith looked geeky. Charlie and Bill looked like gargoyles in training. The Stones slowed it down for "Time Is on My Side," recorded on the previous tour and now a hit single. Next they played "It's All Over Now." Mick, finally having fun, changed a lyric from "She hurt my eyes open" to "She hurt my nose open." Sprung from his dread and fear, he found his body behaving oddly. He repeatedly jumped into the air as if trying to use the stand as a pole-vaulting stick. He danced a bit more than usual; you can see him experimenting with his own body. Here, perhaps, the Mick Jagger of '69 was truly born—out of necessity and, in a way, an innate sense of morality. He kept up with James Brown by becoming . . . James Brown. It wasn't perfect. "Mick cloned himself into James—with all the dancing and jumping," Binder agrees. For the finale, the Stones launched into "It's Alright," an under-rehearsed Bo Diddley beat, with Mick shaking a pair of maracas as the rest of the cast of the *T.A.M.I. Show* and the dancers joined them onstage for a sing-along, everyone together, black, white, young, slightly less young, a symbol for the times. James Brown was again conspicuously absent, but later in his memoir, the Godfather of Soul would be magnanimous, offering words of brotherhood to the Stones and confessing that when he saw them, he "saw the future."

Ironically, it would be Mike Love who never got over having to play before the Rolling Stones that day. Twenty-five years later, during both bands' induction into the Rock and Roll Hall of Fame, an apparently drunken Love raged from the podium, "I'd like to see Mick Jagger get out on this stage and do 'I Get Around' versus 'Jumpin' Jack Flash' any day now. I know Mick Jagger won't be here tonight, he's gonna have to stay in England. But I'd like to see us in the Coliseum and he at Wembley Stadium because he's always been chicken shit to get onstage with the Beach Boys."

They'd already proved otherwise, by the beach in '64. "If they preceded James Brown, we wouldn't have had half of the performance that the Stones gave. It inspired them." Of course, once "It's Alright" ended and the bands went to their respective corners, tour buses, recording studios, and homes, integration resumed its maddeningly slow pace. Even the *T.A.M.I. Show* itself met with a divided audience. In the black neighborhoods, they thrilled to James Brown; he was the headliner no matter who played after him. In the white areas, it was the Stones. But by 1965, Brown would have his first Top 10 pop hit, "Papa's Got a Brand New Bag." He'd notch

another by year's end, "I Got You (I Feel Good)," which he'd perform alongside super-vanilla teen idol Frankie Avalon in the film
Ski Party. Even the Stones would be on their way toward gaining
hard-won credibility in the black community, all without a drop of
red blood being shed.

"As Tears Go By"

"We're gonna do a real old song," Mick Jagger, sixty-five years of age, dressed in very tight black T-shirt and trousers, informed the crowd at New York City's art deco Beacon Theater, "one of the first we've ever written. In fact we gave it to someone else—because we felt slightly embarrassed by it." Watching Mick sing "As Tears Go By" in Martin Scorsese's 2006 documentary *Shine a Light* some forty-two years after it was written is one of the few instances of subtlety and reflection the modern Rolling Stones show offers. It's a nostalgic moment, sure, like a lot of such concert experiences, but it accomplishes the very same thing it did in '64 when he and Keith awkwardly composed it (Mick writing much of the words and vocal melody, Keith its melancholy chords). It slows the pageant down and presents a less widely considered Rolling Stones to their larger live audience: the brooding folkies.

The stadium shows tend to ignore the moody, downbeat poetic numbers. The players who in the mid-'60s crucially wrote "Heart of Stone" and "Play with Fire," in addition to "Get Off of My Cloud," are all but absent. At theater shows like the one at the Beacon, they unpack this incarnation and we remember how emotionally complex this band is.

It's been said that if Brian Jones had had his way, the Stones would have continued to play nothing but the dirty Delta and Chicago blues. This is likely why Andrew Oldham paired Mick and Keith and not, say, Keith and Brian, or Mick and Brian. Once Mick and Keith began writing original material, Jones certainly emerged as their greatest instrumentalist and arranger, adding an almost second vocal via the gorgeous, plaintive recorder of "Ruby Tuesday," the jazzy marimba of "Under My Thumb," the elegant dulcimer on "Lady Jane," or the buzzing, gloomy sitar on "Paint It, Black," and even imprinted would-be standard blues or acoustic tracks with avant-garde touches ("Stray Cat Blues" and "Street Fighting Man" both on *Beggars Banquet*, his final curtain as a vital Jagger-Richards contributor). There was a one-song creative hurdle all three had to clear first.

"As Tears Go By" is the moment when it all begins; a point of serendipity, the instant the Stones delineated themselves as not just songwriters, not merely rebels, but romantic figures, never again to be easily dismissed as thugs. Here, Mick Jagger, already a sex object, became a poet. It's an amazing feat for something basically written on demand for Oldham. Oldham, who saw how much money the Beatles were making off sheet music and other publishing revenue streams, had money on his mind, and Mick and Keith gave him art.

"As Tears Go By" was a song for a woman; a "girl's" song; one that Mick and Keith didn't dare present to the band as a possible number for them to record (the first one that was deemed Stones-worthy would be "The Last Time," written in early '65). If the Stones had been writing something for themselves, they surely would not have come up with something so delicate and sophisticated. Sometimes the best art comes from the need to impress girls. This particular exercise was written for Marianne Faithfull, then a buxom, sweet-faced former convent student, or "angel with big tits," as Oldham succinctly described her. Faithfull intrigued the young Stones and their manager in other ways too. She was the daughter of Eva von Sacher-Masoch, a Viennese baroness. Her father, Major Robert Glynn Faithfull, was a respected military officer and intellectual. Faithfull's great uncle was notorious Leopold von Sacher-Masoch, whose erotic writing (most famously the nineteenth-century novella *Venus in Furs*) inspired the term "masochism." In person, the teenager was well spoken but erotically primal, an ideal daughter of the new age. She was also (and this would be proven over and over again to Mick, who found her irresistible) perfectly unavailable. Faithfull would soon marry London art and social scene-maker John Dunbar, three years her senior.

"John called me and said he'd met this extraordinary girl and was desperately in love. She was so beautiful and amazing and I had to meet her," says Peter Asher. "So I did and everything he said was true. I thought, 'Boy, John's really scored. She's totally gorgeous. Intelligent. Perfect in every way.'"

Asher accompanied Dunbar and Faithfull to the record release party that would change the alluring teenager's life forever. It was a fete celebrating a record release by Italian chanteuse Adrienne Posta in March of '64, and both Andrew Loog Oldham and the Stones would be in attendance. "Marianne hadn't met them. It was Andrew who spotted Marianne first, but I'm sure she caught Mick's eye. She was spectacular. Lit up a room. Andrew walked over to her and asked, 'Can you sing? We will make a record with you. You're going to be a star.' Then [he asked] the Stones, 'Will you write a song for this girl?'"

The Stones, already inspiring hundreds of teenage girls to urinate on themselves whenever they played, did not make much of an impression on Marianne. "At this point the Stones were not much more than yobby school boys," Faithfull recalled in her memoir, *Faithfull*. "They had none of the polish of John Lennon or Paul McCartney and compared to my John they seemed very crass and boorish indeed."

Mick, Keith, and Brian, as well as Oldham, were smitten by this "poised, well-brought-up, upper-class English girl," according to Asher. But Faithfull did not want to be a pop singer, and despite her beauty, Mick and Keith didn't particularly want to spend their rare bits of free time working. And yet Oldham, in a constant state of device, had a synergistic and potentially very lucrative vision for all four of them. "I had this thing that whatever I decided people could be, they became. I got nothing but moans and groans from Mick and Keith. They were too tired from the gigs to write songs." Oldham, with his camp "Darlings," intrigued Faithfull. She didn't think much of his promises and plans, but sensed that there was a person who was a total original, a rarity, and someone she should explore. She left the party with a vague idea that she might see Oldham again. Numbers were exchanged but no hard commitments made.

Mick was also unavailable, not that this really mattered to

Faithfull at the time. He was nearly two years into his relationship with Chrissie Shrimpton, such a catch when the Stones were just on the bubble of fame. Some have suggested that Mick, already establishing his social-climbing tendencies, was looking to trade up (and Faithfull seemed certainly to be a trade-up). Most likely, the Jagger-Shrimpton affair, begun when both were so inexperienced, had now run its course. Shrimpton, who was for a time employed by Oldham and the band's label Decca, could not help but feel estranged from her ceaselessly busy paramour. The constant touring and its temptations created a divide that they couldn't bridge. From the moment that Mick met Faithfull, he began to fantasize about having a girlfriend who didn't seem to need constant reassuring. She seemed, especially for a teenager, perfectly independent. Surely someone like that would be able to understand and keep pace with his own life and maybe even help him evolve out of a sweaty, down-and-dirty blues scene into a different London: one of wealth and culture. If he wasn't pursuing this, he knew instinctively that it had become necessary. And so in his fantasy, she'd give him books to read, tell him what paintings to ponder and what films to take in. She'd help him grow up some but wouldn't require that he dispense with the low culture he so sincerely adored. His time at the L.S.E. and recent sortie through New York City's society gave him a window into such a world, and he'd liked what he saw. With Faithfull on his arm, Mick could evolve into a mod Lord Byron figure; romantic and searching, but also able to talk trash with the boys, shoot pool, and drink in pubs. Now that would be something. It was an ideal, and from the moment he met her, he pursued it aggressively. Mick wanted her not just as a sexual partner but as a key to his new self. The poetic romance of the imagery in "As Tears Go By" was perhaps uncon-sciously designed to release this figure from the cocoon.

When Oldham demanded that Mick and Keith come up with a song for her, there was no real precedent, only projection ("I want a song with brick walls all around it, and high windows, and no sex" were the only instructions Oldham offered). "As Tears Go By" was projected, out of Mick's frustration, fantasy, and natural intelligence. It was nothing he felt yet, but like all great artists, he could convincingly present something that he knew someone would feel because it was true. Not his truth, per se, but a univer-sal truth. Mick and Keith worked on the song, smoking cigarettes, locked in the kitchen of the flat they all shared, with nothing but a guitar.

Shrimpton was kept away as they wrote, Keith strumming, Mick humming the vocals and scribbling lyrics with a pencil. Keith's chord changes were magisterial and Mick's lyrics were sur-prisingly gentle and reflective. They called it "As Time Goes By," showing little concern about the association with the world-famous ballad from *Casablanca*. "What have you got?" Oldham asked upon returning to the kitchen after having left them all night. "Mick, who was pissed off and hungry, told me they'd 'writ-ten this fucking song and you'd better fucking like it,'" Oldham wrote in his memoir.

Oldham was already moving and shaking: He booked studio time, sent word to Faithfull in the country, and signed up Lionel Bart, the hottest songwriter in Tin Pan Alley and composer of the smash musical *Oliver!*, adapted from Dickens' *Oliver Twist*, to for-tify Faithfull's debut single with an original composition called "I Don't Know How to Tell You." It had only been a week since the party, but there was already a master plan in place. Marianne Faithfull, Andrew Oldham, Mick, and Keith convened in Olympic Studios, where the Stones would later record several of their peerless full-length albums, to lay down the tracks. Faithfull noticed Jagger and Richards in the control room intriguingly sullen, and certainly nervous. They seemed new to her. They played her a recording of the song with Mick on vocals and a studio musician on acoustic guitar. The tune immediately afforded the pair a depth she didn't really expect. Tears don't "fall" they "go by." They pass into memory. The narrator watches children from a distance as the sun begins to set. They are "doing things I used to do, they think are new" Mick sang, delivering the amazing line with sincerity on the demo, sounding nothing like his "bay bay," bluesman self but more like a gentle folk singer or even a female chanteuse.

As recording commenced, Oldham's master plan was slightly altered. The A-side would become the B-side and Faithfull's debut single would now be "As Time Goes By" (now altered by Oldham, who staked a cowriting credit for the song, to "As Tears Go By"). Oldham knew it was the better song, but also sensed that the move would bolster Mick and Keith's confidence and there'd be more like it in the future. "It was like a Francoise Hardy song, really," Faithfull recalled. "Maybe that's what Mick had picked up from me when we met. Slightly existential but with a dash of San Remo song festival. The Euro pop you might hear on a French jukebox, or rather it's what Andrew saw in me at the party and told Mick to write—Andrew's always been into that." Oldham gave Faithfull the lyrics scrawled in Mick's handwriting, which she studied without ample time to find the emotion. Like Mick, she was operating on instinct, following some mysterious and prescient voice. Songs were cut quickly then, not lived with. As a result, Faithfull's version is a bit prim, as her nervous voice too carefully enunciates each line ("Rain fowl-ing on the ground").

Mick and Keith watched in the booth as she sang it. Something came together on the track, the song that awoke something in Mick awoke something in Marianne Faithfull, too. It was a quick session, only two or three takes. They all left the studio and crowded into a car to take Faithfull back to the station. Released in June of 1964 on the Stones' label, Decca, "As Tears Go By" was, as Oldham predicted, a big hit, but not only that. It gave Faithfull the first part of a great pop myth and began her association with the Stones, though not immediately her romance with Mick. "As Tears Go By" really is the beginning of that romance, as it binds them forever in time.

While he publicly dismissed it as "girly," Mick Jagger knew this was a gateway song, one that would allow them to experiment with ballads. Shortly after its completion they would work slow songs like Arthur Alexander's melodramatic "You Better Move On" and their own "Tell Me" convincingly into their repertoire. The Stones themselves recorded "As Tears Go By" after all. It was released in December of '65, closing the year of the Beatles' "Yesterday" and "You've Got to Hide Your Love Away," Dylan's "Desolation Row," and the Moody Blues' "Go Now." All those songs, along with Jagger's version of "As Tears Go By," truly marked a new era for elegantly melancholy pop that would influence goosepimple masterpieces like the Kinks' "Waterloo Sunset" and the Left Banke's "Walk Away Renee." "It's the mystery of songwriting," Asher says. "Where they come from. When I first heard it I thought, Oh wow, Mick and Keith can write songs like that.

They're not just trying to copy their R&B heroes anymore. It's clearly why they're still here."

Faithfull concurs. "It's an absolutely astonishing thing for a boy of twenty to have written," she recalled. "A song about a woman looking back nostalgically on her life. The uncanny thing is that Mick should have written those words so long before everything happened (between us). It's almost as if our whole relationship was prefigured in that song. A lot of people felt that way."

By 1966, Mick Jagger had finally won the love of Faithfull, freeing himself from Chrissie Shrimpton for good and stealing Marianne from John Dunbar—and waiting out Faithfull's initial fixation with Keith. Inside of a year, they'd become the prince and princess of the Chelsea scene that Mick coveted. And as time went by, of course, they'd find themselves torn apart, but they remain connected in myth. When Martin Scorsese filmed "As Tears Go By" for *Shine a Light*, he shot Mick in majestic profile; his voice low with age, he enunciates every word, like a Shakespearean actor playing Lear or Prospero—slow, careful, and true. Faithfull rerecorded it as well in middle age. "I rerecorded it at age forty and at that moment I was exactly the right age and in the right frame of mind to sing it. It was then that I truly experienced the lyrical melancholy of the song for the first time," she said.

"You know, it's like a metaphor for being old: You're watching children playing and realizing you're not a child," Mick reflected in 1995. "It's a relatively mature song considering the rest of the output at the time. And we didn't think of doing it [initially], because the Rolling Stones were a butch blues group." After "As Tears Go By," they were so much more.

When I interviewed Faithfull for the *Vanity Fair* site, I asked her if her relationship to the song has changed over the years. "Yes, it does," she said. "But I still really like it. You know, I was very lucky with the Stones song I got. Because it's really good. A lot of people didn't get such a good Stones song when they recorded a Rolling Stones cover. I got the best." When I reminded her that she gave them something in return as well, a big pop hit that afforded them some confidence to kick with the new, sensitive, feminine-side tapping pop fray, she agreed. "Yeah, of course I did." Thinking of Mick's rendition in the Scorsese film (which she apparently has not seen), I ask her what it feels like to sing "As Tears Go By" now, in her sixties. "I feel like it's a very old friend."

"We Piss Anywhere, Man"

The Rolling Stones of 1965 had hits, they had sex appeal, they even had sensitivity after "As Tears Go By." They had everything but that one crucial ingredient that would make them more than the pop sensations of the previous ages: a philosophy. By '65 this was now expected of rock and rollers. "Pop stars of the late '50s and early '60s were working-class kids who jumped on the Elvis bandwagon," says Keith Altham. "They were sixteen, seventeen. Most had very little formal education. With the Beatles and the Stones, they came from a slightly better-educated background. You found yourself talking to young guys who'd taken their A-levels. Jagger was a part of that. A pop star had opinions—and consequently there became a slightly more serious approach in interviews. Bob Dylan was probably a catalyst in this respect." In '65, twenty-four-year-old Bob Dylan had hit singles and teenage fans but was also queried by the media as they might a middle-aged or elderly politician; he was obliged to explain his lyrics, what he was protesting, what he believed in and stood for. Mick, Keith, and Brian Jones, like the Beatles, found Dylan both inspiring and intimidating, especially when the implication was often that beat combos like the Stones didn't have the sophistication of a poet and a leader like Dylan. Even Dylan himself famously quipped, "I could have written 'Satisfaction' but you couldn't have written 'Blowing in the Wind.'"

By the winter of '65, the Stones, active for three years, with Mick and Keith only just moving into their own domiciles after bunking together first with Brian and later with Andrew Loog Oldham and Mick's soon-to-be ex-girlfriend Chrissie Shrimpton, were marketed as gang-like, a posse of Droogs marauding; primal where Dylan was cerebral.

Oldham played down Mick and Keith's middle-class origins whenever possible. "He always made sure we were as violent and nasty as possible," Mick has said. Oldham had even looked into optioning the Anthony Burgess novel A *Clockwork Orange* as the band's own noir version of A *Hard Day's Night* and *Help* (but ultimately failed to secure the rights). Whereas Dylan's manager Albert Grossman was ursine and imperious, protecting his boy from the world, Oldham saw his charges as five shaggy hand grenades and gleefully threw them at the established guard. "We realized right from the beginning that we were making our appeal to young people," he told *N.M.E.* at the time, "and by making a concentrated effort towards freedom on their behalf we would upset those we neglected. We chose the young instead of the old, that's all. The old resented it. The Stones are still the social outcasts, the rebels. We worked on the principle that if you are going to kick conformity in

the teeth, you may as well use both feet." It was Oldham who composed the neo-beat poetry printed on their album sleeves, and Oldham who employed the group's natural insolence and pouting faces
to draw stark lines between the old world and the new. The Stones'
give-and-take with the British media was as intricate and masterful
as any Tin Pan Alley craftsman could ever hope to be. In fact, it can
be argued that Mick Jagger's greatest philosophical statement of
that crucial year of 1965 is not "I can't get no satisfaction," but rather
"We piss anywhere, man," uttered on a cold night in front of a petrol station that refused them use of a toilet. This is in no way meant
to minimize the seismic "(I Can't Get No) Satisfaction," which is
now so overplayed that it's *underplayed*; have a listen today and you
will be reminded of what a truly thrilling single it is. People write
this about "(I Can't Get No) Satisfaction," of course. It routinely
tops lists of Greatest Ever This or Best That of All Time to the point
that we feel we perhaps don't need to listen to it anymore, but it's appearance in a Summer 2010 episode of *Mad Men* (taking us back to
the summer of '65 and perfectly articulating chain-smoking Don
Draper's own frustration with useless information) was like ice
water to a booze-flushed cheek. "Oh yeah! *That* song." And still
"(I Can't Get No) Satisfaction," alpha song that it is, work of art that
it is, is still just a song. "We piss anywhere" is an ideology.

The whole incident lasted only about two minutes, the length
of a great vintage pop song, but in its own way, it was more powerful, and far more political, than many of the Stones hits that came
afterward. "We piss anywhere" was "released" on March 18, 1965,
and took only a day or two to climb the "charts" and stir up the
kind of attention that would help the Stones' crossover, like Dylan's,
from pop concern to political football. They were now "spokesmen,"

for the "do what I like set," as Altham would write in *N.M.E.* the following year.

In the John Ford–ian sense, the legend has already been printed and the actual details are less important, but here's how it *probably* went down. The Stones, a new UK No. 1 to their credit after "Little Red Rooster," their sultry Willie Dixon–penned sex bomb, topped the charts shortly before the winter holidays, were returning from another sold-out and riotous gig in a movie theater in Romford. It was just after midnight and bitter cold. All five were piled into their black Daimler touring car.

Feeling nature's call, the group stopped at a Francis Petrol station in Stratford outside of London. At first, they were polite. Bill Wyman asked the attendant, a clean-cut gent named Charles Keeley, if he could please be directed to the bathroom as the others got out and stretched. Keeley, like much of his generation, knew who the Stones were but had yet to come around to them. He'd been working all night in the cold, and at this hour, he didn't care for the looks of them. He ordered the group to get back in and keep driving. When they complained, Mick Jagger took command of the situation, nudged Keeley back, and announced, "We'll piss anywhere, man."

In his testimony, Keeley described being surrounded in the dark by "shaggy haired monsters" who all began chanting in unison: "We'll piss anywhere! We'll piss anywhere!" "One danced to the phrase," Keeley recalled. As if to prove this, Wyman proceeded to unzip his fly and urinate on the garage wall. The Stones then piled back into the Daimler and they sped off, giving the reverse victory salute through the window.

Again, the actual details of this event are somewhat fuzzy

("We'll piss" got shortened to the more universal "We piss" over time). It's been reported that it was Brian Jones and not Mick Jagger who said it, and that both Brian and Mick, not just Bill Wyman, did the peeing anywhere.

When Keeley telephoned the authorities, the Stones were charged days later with disturbing the peace and given an appearance date before the local magistrate, who called them "morons" and berated them for the length of their hair, their "filthy" clothes, and "clown[ish] behavior."

Mick's response was atypical of his good, middle-class manners, but he likely could not control himself. He was still pumping adrenaline from the concert. And he truly did have enough, after yet another stress-inducing gig in the midst of another long, promotional tour. Characteristic or not, the outburst was seized on by both the press and teenagers all over the Western world who had been looked at sideways because they traveled in gangs and looked like trouble when they only wanted to get out of the cold, get some food, and have a pee. It became an exemplary and heroic moment; the logical next step after asserting the power of the teenage dollar: demanding teenage respect. It all made great copy. "Andrew saw how the Stones rebelled against conformity, in contrast to how the Beatles were controlled by Epstein," Altham has said, "and he saw the value in letting them have their heads. Then— and this was both his genius and his Achilles' heel—he saw it could be exaggerated, taken a step further and made to look as though they were working-class heroes. They weren't—yet. They were middle-class kids rebelling against a middle-class background."

The notion that the Stones should act in a way that would firmly establish them as volatile Cains to the Beatles' true blue

Abels was already planted in the band members' heads, and so here was the water-passing, watershed moment. The Beatles pissed where pissing was designated. The Stones did what they liked. The Beatles played the palace at the Queen's request. The Stones would just as soon storm the place.

"We piss anywhere" made it OK for boys to swoon over the Stones as well. Like the Beatles, they drew both men and women to their shows, but the young men must have felt less conflicted screaming along to the Stones. Losing their composure at a Rolling Stones show was merely an initiation rite, kind of like the pledge of fidelity to a gang.

"As manager, what Oldham did was to take everything implicit in the Stones and blow it up one hundred times. Long-haired and ugly and anarchic as they were, Oldham made them more so and he turned them into everything that parents would most hate, be most frightened by. All the time, he goaded them to be wilder, nastier, fouler in every way, and they were—they swore, sneered, snarled, and, deliberately, they came [off as] cretinous," British journalist Nik Cohn writes in his collection *Awopbopaloobop Alopbamboom*. "It was good basic psychology: Kids might see them the first time and not be sure about them, but then they'd hear their parents whining about those animals, those filthy long-haired morons, and suddenly they'd be converted, they'd identify like mad."

Oldham next came up with a slogan: "Would you let your sister go with a Rolling Stone?" It ran atop a feature in an issue of another extremely important (and now sadly defunct) British music weekly, *Melody Maker*. "The headline was a great example of everlasting meaning via product placement," Oldham writes. "I had dreamt up the line 'Would you let your daughter go with a Rolling

Stone?' which would be translated into 'Would You Let Your Daughter Marry a Rolling Stone?' by the high priests of Fleet Street, who wished to avoid the ramifications of the word 'go' . . . it got the headline and became one of the many slogans wrapped around the Rolling Stones for life." The notion of a good, virginal English lass bringing a surly, chain smoking, black man–worshipping, and now wealthy and insouciant sex lout home for tea drew a panic tantamount to a mini Red Menace. It was a hit single without music.

Of all the British Invasion bands, the still feral Stones on the surface had actually seemed to change the least from the street-level club act they'd been. They only flirted with wearing identical uniforms once, before dropping the idea forever. It was their first-ever TV appearance, playing their debut Decca single on *Thank Your Lucky Stars*, a British version of *American Bandstand*, on July 7, 1963. The Stones appeared in matching black trousers, checked sport coats with velvet collars, blue shirts, leather vests, and black knit wool ties. "Originally Andrew put them in the houndstooth jackets and leather gear so that they had some uniform presence," *N.M.E.* writer Keith Altham says in Oldham's memoir, "contemporary to the Beatles. Gradually he realized that it wasn't gonna work and they weren't gonna wear them." The show was flooded with letters protesting their long hair and general scruffy demeanor despite the attempt at being presentable. The band soon realized that they couldn't win and might as well go full tilt in the other direction. Letters of protest, after all, amounted to good press. This would come to be a freedom that the Beatles would envy. "Paul was jealous," Peter Asher recalls. "They got to wear whatever they wanted, whereas Brian Epstein made them wear these fucking suits."

John Lennon felt jealous that they were permitted to exult in bad-boy reverie while the Beatles were bound to a lovable "mop top" image. This isn't to say the Stones were immune to packaging. Oldham had successfully lobbied to remove Stewart from the Stones-proper lineup. Stu's Jay Leno jaw and lack of androgyny was deemed a marketing liability, and so he was relegated to erstwhile pianist and roadie. "Look, from the first time I saw you, I've felt I can only see . . . five Rolling Stones," Oldham informed them. "People worked nine to five, and they couldn't be expected to remember more than four faces. 'This is entertainment, not a memory test.'" The way they looked, their image, as much if not more than how they sounded, or what, if any, philosophy they actually had, was the most important concern, but by 1965, their actions began to take on greater cultural significance.

"There were three things that one would have known about the Rolling Stones at the time (if you were not a fan)," filmmaker Peter Whitehead tells me. Whitehead, who would later film the seminal documentary of the '60s London scene, *Tonight Let's All Make Love in London* (featuring Syd Barrett-era Pink Floyd, John Lennon, Julie Christie, Michael Caine, and the Stones). Whitehead continues, "One, they were a bit like the Beatles. Two, they pissed on a garage, and three, that famous saying which was going around: 'Would you let your daughter marry a Rolling Stone?' I never listened to the Rolling Stones. I listened to Bartok's House of the Dead and Beethoven quartets. It was possible to know who they were without knowing who they were."

And yet "We piss anywhere, man," a spontaneous outburst, whether subconsciously encouraged by Oldham or not, was more honest and subsequently more perfect agitprop. This was, after all, four young men urinating on perhaps the ultimate symbol of modern, American, imperialist power: the gas station. The very fuel that was helping the war in Vietnam escalate. "It is an act of rebellion," Whitehead says. "The idea of the thing. The petrol station. It's about cars. About oil. About big business. It's about this and that but frankly, everybody's got the completely wrong take on it. We're not discussing the Rolling Stones here; we're discussing the fucking idiocy of the British media. The guys were drunk. A bit stoned. They had a lot to drink; they stopped to get a couple of Kit Kats and a sandwich and wanted to have a pee. There's no loo in the English garage so they went around the back. We've all done it. But they happened to be the Rolling Stones. The establishment wanted anything they could use to develop an anti-PR campaign to this successful youth culture embodied in the Beatles and the Stones, who were effectively changing the consciousness of the British establishment and attacking American imperialism and the dumbing-down process of English culture by kitsch American culture."

It was uncanny how well the undiluted notion of "We piss anywhere" matched the image of a sneering Mick Jagger. Even the music on their next album, *Out of Our Heads*, released in July, seemed to play into the "We piss anywhere" ethos. "I'm Free," one of the album's singles, contained the chorus "I'm free to do what I want any old time" and demanded "love me," if only because he was so free, and while Oldham played this up, the media were playing upon him. It was a fragile, combustible symbiosis, one that would nearly ruin the band in the next two years, but not before making them huge. The Stones were now selling millions of records, just like the Beatles, but it would be another year before the Fab Four would have their own potential "We piss any-where" moment, the following March, when John Lennon was quoted (out of context) telling the *Evening Standard*'s Maureen Cleave: "Christianity will go. It will vanish and shrink. I needn't argue with that; I'm right and I will be proved right. We're more popular than Jesus now." From 1965 on, whenever a pop artist, talking politics or philosophy, and in Lennon's case, the most vol-atile subject of them all, religion, sparks a furor among the old guard, there's a little bit of Mick's original utterance on that cold, dark night. Lennon ultimately apologized. Most do. The Stones never did. "We piss anywhere" helped take them upward, but it would soon blow back in the wind. The mark of Cain was on them now.

6

"Under the Influence of Bail"

It started with a case of mistaken identity in early 1967, the "Winter of Love." Brian Jones leaned against the bar at Blaise's, a hip London nightclub. Blaise's hosted light show–enhanced concerts by Pink Floyd and the Jimi Hendrix Experience and quickly became a hub of the city's new psychedelic rock scene. Once the band's handsome and talented leader, Jones was now tottering, full of scotch and downers. His chiseled jaw was distorted with bloat and seemed to melt into his thick neck. His brain was addled with pathological insecurity and jealousy. Brian was furious at Mick and Keith for usurping his position in the Stones. They'd emerged, in the last two years, as a formidable songwriting partnership. This, coupled with the media's fascination with Mick, the face of not just the Stones but the London scene itself, bruised Jones' Napoleonic ego. Mick and Keith didn't take care to assuage him, either, but rather delighted in this new power they wielded over him. Jones turned his anger inward, ingesting heroic quantities of pills, pot, hash, and booze. He was also one of the first pop stars, along with Lennon and Pink Floyd's Syd Barrett, to embrace LSD full on. Acid did not have a good effect on Jones' already fraying psyche. It was, after all, designed to destroy the ego, and Mick and Keith had already done that, so the chemical seemed to burn away everything else, leaving a shell of a pop star. Jones was mistrusting and violently abusive of his soon-to-be ex-girlfriend Anita Pallenberg; convinced that Mick or Keith or both would steal her away, just like they stole his post in the band that he founded with Ian Stewart. Stewart had been demoted. Brian figured that he would be next. By early '67, he'd changed the world but couldn't live with himself, or mix with anybody else. He couldn't enter a place as bustling and happening as Blaise's without asking for trouble, and it would soon come his way.

London nightclubs were no longer places to dance, preen, and drink Cokes. Time was, stars could come with an entourage and relax, their particular excesses so far ahead of the public that the cops and dirt-digging tabloid reporters didn't even know what to look for. They were now unsafe. Swinging London, as seen by the straight world, was either an abstraction, akin to a rumor of bad behavior one merely shrugs off, or a cheeky, kitschy world of Beatle haircuts and clean fun. Then came pot. As '66 turned to '67, acid followed, and as it altered the perception of those who took it, it changed the way the public viewed the scene. The world of London youth was now a place where good English girls and boys lost themselves to wild ideas, strange music, and morally vacant sex. And worse, while pot wore off eventually, LSD could destroy your mind forever.

But in the late '60s LSD had already been used by both the American and British governments as a potential mind-control agent, a weapon in the Cold War. Previously, the powers that be only feared the Russians and the Chinese when they indulged their nightmares about the chemical settling into the wrong hands and polluting the minds of good, God-fearing capitalist men, women, and children. Timothy Leary was already under fire for proselytizing about this new poison. Now parents and politicians had a new bogeyman, and media emperors like Rupert Murdoch (who owned the British tabloid *News of the World*) had a new haymaker: the intellectual, opinionated post-Dylan rock star, luring the kids toward their doom by example.

"The psychedelic underground and the pop scene were starting to overlap," Pink Floyd producer Joe Boyd writes in his '60s memoir, *White Bicycles*, "and it was getting hard to maintain the original atmosphere. It was also difficult to ignore the increased attention of the police; the longer the queues, the more customers were getting frisked and busted . . . The media stopped winking and grinning about 'swinging London' and started wallowing in horror stories about teenagers being led astray." It felt like the old foundation was slowly being chipped away, and a wave of fear and resentment spread over those in power.

"We were shocked by resistance to our progressive ideas," recalls writer, artist, and activist Caroline Coon today. "The establishment set itself implacably against us. And arresting us for drug offenses was a lawful way to attack us. New drugs, as they became popular, were made illegal in order to legitimize the harassment of this political and cultural rebellion. It really was acutely Them vs. Us. And once we realized that the police were involved in monitoring and stopping our socio-political movement, we realized that we were under surveillance, that we were not paranoid, that there actually were such things as undercover cops and snitches." Folk artist turned pop star Donovan's No. 2 UK hit, "Sunshine Superman," prompted some to call for a ban simply because they suspected its dippy lyrics *may* be filled with drugged-up slang. The previous year, Donovan became the first major pop star to be arrested on drug charges. The BBC broadcast of a documentary entitled *A Boy Called Donovan* that showed him smoking pot at a party might have doomed him.

By 1967, the Rolling Stones were more influential than ever, and it's easy to see how they might have felt invulnerable and a bit too messianic. After three years of constant touring and recording, they would finally start to see some real money, swapping conceptualist Andrew Loog Oldham for stocky, hard-boiled American business manager Allen Klein. Klein's upbringing in a New Jersey orphanage almost surely contributed to his notoriously gruff and aggressive manner. In his thirties, he'd guided the financial dealings of superstar soul singer Sam Cooke, one of the first black artists to own his own publishing. After Cooke was murdered in December of 1964, Klein diversified and began "auditing" record companies on behalf of a slew of British Invasion bands like the Animals and Herman's Hermits in effort to make sure they received every penny of royalties owed. He took 20 percent, but the missing money he found usually more than made it worthwhile ("Remember, no one has to sign with me if they don't want to," he'd tell a *Playboy* interviewer in 1971). Klein (who clearly enjoyed his reputation as "the biggest prick in the music business") had his sights on both the Beatles and the Stones from the start. Already in the Stones' camp when he'd heard the news that the Beatles' manager, Brian Epstein, had committed suicide in August, he'd allegedly pulled over to the side of the road and shouted, "I got 'em!" Oldham, who was, like Jones, increasingly losing himself to drugs, brought Klein into the fold as a business advisor.

Within the year Klein would control both bands. With regard to the Stones, this fortuitously dovetailed with the Stones enjoying self-penned (and therefore highly lucrative) hits that topped the charts on both sides of the Atlantic and finally vied with the best of the Beatles' oeuvre. "Paint It, Black," "19th Nervous Breakdown," "Mother's Little Helper," and "Ruby Tuesday" were perfectly constructed sonic art pieces with smart lyrics that frankly observed darkness and nudged hypocrisy, sadness, and decay with precocious humor and existential depth that heretofore seemed impossible for a three-minute pop song. The Stones did so without compromising a shred of toughness. They could be blunt when necessary. Take the "Stupid Girl" (possibly Chrissie Shrimpton) who brags about things that she's never seen, bitching all the while. Or "Don'tcha Bother Me," on which Jagger warned all the other Stones-y groups suddenly gone dark, as well as the lounge lizards dropping names and dressing like elegantly wasted hippies, "Don't'cha copy me no more. The lines on my eyes are protected by copyright law." Both tracks appear on *Aftermath*, the Stones' 1966 release, the first album to avoid reliance on cover tunes. Recorded at RCA Studios in Los Angeles in the year of *Revolver, Pet Sounds*, and *Blonde on Blonde*, it showcased the Rolling Stones like nothing before it. One could hardly imagine this band jumping on a bandwagon themselves anytime soon, but like Icarus, or the hero of *Aftermath*'s "Flight 505," they went searching for a "new life," soared too high, and just as they were "feeling like a king" with the "world at their feet," they crapped out and ended up in the "sea." What brought the plane down? Ego, bad luck, and lots of good, clean LSD.

Mick later confided to Cecil Beaton (according to his diary) that he took acid about once a month, and only in a "congenial setting." "They can't stamp it out," he confided. "It's like the atom bomb. Once it's been discovered it can never be forgotten, and it's too easy to make LSD." As ever, it would be the Beatles who broke ground as far as public admission of LSD experimentation was concerned. Paul McCartney, who turned twenty-five at the cusp of the "Summer of Love," was breaking away from his mop-top image just as much as Lennon, and increasingly they could not be spun. McCartney admitted to a reporter that he himself had taken LSD. In a series of well-meaning if naïve follow-ups, he made matters much worse by stammering, "They're talking about things that are a bit new they're talking about things that people don't really know too much about yet people tend to put them down a bit and say weirdo psychedelic—it's really just what's going on around and they're just trying to look into it a bit so the next time you see the word any new strange word like psychedelic, drugs the whole bit, freak out music don't immediately take it at that. Your first reactions gonna be one of fear."

"Do you think it'll encourage your fans to take drugs," yet another reporter asks him, barely containing his glee.

"I don't think it'll make any difference. I don't think my fans are gonna take drugs just because I did." That thousands of his fans dressed and styled their hair like the Beatles, built shrines from merchandise bearing their images, and listened to Lennon sing "Tomorrow Never Knows" in their college dorm rooms as pot smoke filled the air didn't compute with the Cute Beatle. Or, more likely, he didn't care anymore. He was bigger than Jesus, too, after all.

The Stones were, like much of their decadent scene, acquainted with acid, but unlike Lennon had, by '67, only written obliquely about it: on "19th Nervous Breakdown," Mick recalls, "On our first trip I tried so hard to rearrange your mind." *Aftermath*'s "Going Home" is a long, weary, proto-psychedelic account of wanting to return home after a long trip. According to Faithfull, now living with Jagger in a posh town house in Cheyne Walk, his natural leadership qualities emerged while under the influence. He used acid to develop the mind in the same way he used exercise to develop the body. Mick was "calm and cool," according to Faithfull. Within the Stones and their endlessly shifting power struggles, acid was used as a bonding tool. Initially Keith and Brian took trips together, but Keith's barely concealed that his feelings for Anita had created a rift. Mick and Keith on acid was a cascade of warm, supportive, brotherly energy that seemed to validate and reward all the amazing work they'd done together. Keith had used the Klein-maneuvered influx of cash to purchase Redlands, a thatched-roofed country mansion in Surrey (Mick would buy his own estate in Newbury a few years later). With its green hills, flower beds, and ancient stones, it was the perfect locale for a psychedelic idyll. Far from the city, under the stars, with a skull full of frizzled matter, it was easy to believe the world was changing for the better, and the Stones, truly pampered now, let their guard down fatally. They behaved like new royalty, not fully realizing the extent to which London law enforcement was gunning for them, along with an even more sinister and effective ally: the panic-fomenting tabloid media.

A buzz spread through Blaise's that January night. "There's a Rolling Stone here." The clueless *News of the World* reporter was convinced that he had cornered Mick Jagger himself at the bar. Jones, mistaken for Mick, saw this as a real opportunity to exact revenge on his former ally by confessing that he enjoyed hash to calm down and speed when he needed an energy boost, and that he felt no guilt whatsoever about utilizing these chemicals. When asked whether he, like McCartney, was given to acid trips, Jones, as "Mick," hinted that he was already beyond acid and on the prowl for the next super-high: "I don't go much on LSD now that the cats have taken it up. It'll just get a dirty name." He downed his drink, looked around, and declared that the party had become boring. He invited the reporter to accompany him elsewhere to partake in smoking a lump of Moroccan hash. The reporter left the club convinced he'd been invited by Mick Jagger to go get very stoned. He had a hot story.

When the second of a planned multipart article entitled "Pop Stars and Drugs: The Facts Will Shock You" was published in *News of the World* on February 5, 1967, private, middle-class Mick was aghast to read quotes attributed him, openly confessing to drug use, along with lurid tales about the exploits of peers like the Who, the Moody Blues, Cream, and the already persecuted Donovan. He vowed to sue. With social ties to both the Beatles and the Stones, Robert Fraser, a well-connected gallery owner warned Mick that if he did he would be making "the Oscar Wilde mistake." As any fan of Stephen Fry knows, Wilde, at the height of his own popularity with the production of *The Importance of Being Earnest,* was accused by the Marquis of Queensbury of being a sodomite after his relationship with the Marquis' son, Lord Alfred Douglas (known affectionately as Bosie), was discovered. Wilde sued for libel, thereby exposing himself to a slew of personal attacks and countercharges that later found him incarcerated in Reading Gaol; his plays closed, his books were banned, and he became estranged from his family. Paul McCartney, for one, revered Fraser as "one of the most influential people on the London '60s scene." His old-style salons fostered a really intellectual bond between the smart, young pop stars and the slightly older Pop artists and designers of the day like Peter Blake, the photographer Michael Cooper, and film director Christian Marquand. Socialites, those who purchased rather than produced art, were a glamorous component as well. Guinness heir Tara Browne and John Paul Getty Jr. gave the Stones even more of a powerful and decadent air as they all passed through Fraser's apartment and gallery, smoking, blasting R&B records, and discussing matters both lofty and trashy.

Fraser was gay and on his way to developing a serious drug problem, but like Mick, he came from an upstanding family and could thrive in both the straight and the hip worlds. He felt himself strongly drawn to the latter, whether it was showcasing pop artists like Warhol and Jim Dine or mixing with the increasingly hard and occasionally seedy retinue around the Stones. "He wants to be on the outside edge where there's criminal activity," Mick noted in the foreword to the Fraser biography, *Groovy Bob.* The cautious Fraser kept his head while Mick just burned.

Mick, in a rare moment of naïveté and lack of foresight, surely brought on by an inflated sense of power and his new wealth, did not learn from Wilde's mistakes. He wouldn't back off, and filed suit, forcing the *News of the World* to essentially find a way, any way, to prove that he was indeed a drug user. He was now a target for amoral police sergeants like the infamous Sgt. Pilcher, looking to drum up publicity and appease outraged taxpayers by knocking these pious, candy-colored pop stars down a peg, and a sitting duck when it came to frame jobs and setups, the truth easily reached retroactively. He placed himself unwittingly in the position of not being able to sin at all, in any way. Every aspirin tablet had to be accounted for, an impossibility given the Stones travel schedule, business pressures, and the increasingly shady retinue that surrounded their larger and larger estates. Those close to them were not safe either. "If [LSD] wasn't meant to happen, it wouldn't have been invented," Faithfull blithely observed, not realizing she was sealing her fate. "I think I'm really powerful . . . they'll smash me," she prophesized.

It would seem at first irresistibly easy. "The police did not have to do any detective work and, encouraged by the tabloid press, the police thought busting pop stars would be very popular and win them promotion," says Coon.

Mick didn't seem to have his guard up when he turned up to sing along with the Beatles five days after the publication of the *News of the World* article, during the live recording of "All You Need Is Love," part of England's contribution to a global satellite broadcast. His thoughts were on the imminent release of the Stones' follow-up to *Aftermath*, *Between the Buttons*, on the extensive European tour planned to promote it, and on making a home with Faithfull, and the rugs and tapestries and antiques they would furnish it with. On business affairs, family. On February 13, just over a week after the *News of the World* article hit the kiosks, Mick and Faithfull took a drive out to Redlands to blow off some steam during a weekend getaway. Accompanied by Chelsea scene-maker Christopher Gibbs, a close friend, as well as Fraser, his employee Mohammed Jujuj, and two hippie hangers-on, Nicky Kramer and David Schneiderman, the latter of whom referred to himself as "The Acid King," they spent the weekend hiking, eating good food, and tripping on White Lightning acid, while playing Bob Dylan's *Blonde on Blonde*. Over the course of the weekend, people came and went, including Tony Sanchez, another London nightlife figure, drug connection, and author of the future classic of Stones literature *Up and Down with the Rolling Stones*, artist Michael Cooper, Charlie Watts, and George Harrison and Patti Boyd (who left before the cops closed in, fueling the rumor that they were staking the place out and waiting to move in so they wouldn't have to bust a beloved Beatle).

The party was still going strong when nearly two dozen officers, mostly men, but three women in tow, bundled in dark coats and hats, moved in. Chief Inspector Gordon Dineley produced a search warrant and began rifling through clothes, cushions, and cupboards in search of drugs. The whole event was perversely mannered, with the cops asking politely if they might turn the music off (and Richards, not quite sure who these alike-dressed dwarves were, offering to turn it "down" instead). In Fraser's possession they found some heroin, and in a coat that Mick claimed belonged to him, but was actually Faithfull's, they found some pep pills, purchased legally in Italy. Schneiderman refused to allow the police to open the film canisters where he kept his drugs, claiming they contained exposable film. It was all over in about an hour, but not before Marianne Faithfull emerged, clad in a fur rug, having just enjoyed a hot bath, and agitated some of the officers. Zooming on acid, Faithfull saw this as a way to exercise some form of power over them. She found it amusing and was too high to realize that she was planting lurid images in the minds of these agitated cops, ones that would soon be run through the cognitive dissonance of the police-media information pipeline. Faithfull was inadvertently creating a surprisingly durable tabloid invention: Miss X.

As Miss X, Faithfull was stripped of her clothes, her dignity, her name, and her identity as Mick's partner. Under a cloud of "strong smelling incense," as it was recounted, this Miss X did things a Miss X would do. The account of her behavior when presented to the public was fair game for further distortion and soon an urban legend was born. According to this legend, when the cops entered, she was naked, covered in fur, with a Mars candy bar inserted in her vagina (implicitly to be eaten by Mick).

Paranoia set in as the high wore off. Lawyers were called and questions asked. Someone set them up, but who? The least-known characters, the two hippie hangers-on, Schneiderman and Kramer, were the obvious suspects. They weren't part of the scene; they'd merely weeded in. Kramer was allegedly roughed up by nightclub muscle man David Litvinoff, a cohort of the notorious London gangsters, the Kray brothers (and later a consultant on Mick's film debut *Performance*). Kramer was deemed clean after allegedly being pummeled to the point where any sane man would spill. Schneiderman vanished into the ether. He must have fingered them to the *News*. Within a week, it went from all you need is love to all you need is a good lawyer. "When we got busted at Redlands, it suddenly made us realize that this was a whole different ball game and that was when the fun stopped," Faithfull recalled. "Up until then it had been as though London existed in a beautiful space where you could do anything you wanted." Exhausted and newly paranoid, the Stones left London that winter while awaiting trial.

Brian Jones correctly assumed he'd be the next to be busted, and Mick and Marianne traveled to Spain and Morocco as their barristers made a case and the tabloids went mad with daily reports of all the lurid Redlands details. These red-top reports also motivated the youth to organize in outrage like they'd never done before and made folk heroes of Mick and Keith. "Clive Goodwin, the editor of the leftist Marxist antigovernment newspaper *Black Dwarf*, got word that the *News of the World* was publishing (another) lurid character assassination of Jagger," Coon recalls. "He rang me—he knew I was involved with a drugs case myself—and he asked me to help him organize a demonstration. We started ringing everyone we knew, telling them to be outside the *News of the World* the next evening, a Saturday night. Our aim was to stop the *News of the World*'s Sunday morning paper distribution. About two or three hundred people turned up. We all lay down in Fleet Street blocking the way of the huge distribution lorries. Of course, we were eventually moved on by the police. So we marched past 10 Downing Street and up Whitehall and, at four o'clock in the morning, there we were holding a peaceful vigil on the steps of Eros in Piccadilly Circus. The busting of Mick Jagger and Keith Richards was one of the key, politically galvanizing moments for the emerging hippie youth movement in Britain. People rallied around, not only to stars like Mick, Keith, and Robert Fraser, but to all of us, the common people, who suddenly, being easy targets because of the gloriously different way we dressed, were being busted too."

The Rolling Stones drug trial at the courthouse in Chichester in June of 1967 was one of the first modern legal circuses, a precursor to the court appearances of Charles Manson, O.J. Simpson, Michael Jackson, Phil Spector, and Lindsay Lohan. There were so many news clippings (mostly thanks to Miss X) that pop artist Richard Hamilton, a friend of Fraser's, would later create a protest piece for a 1968 exhibit entitled Swingeing London. One piece depicted a grimacing Mick, dressed in a pale, velvety green dandy's coat, handcuffed to a smiling, darkly handsome Fraser. These were nonviolent offenders, handcuffed together like hardened criminals and paraded for the cameras. The establishment's message was unmistakable: "Toe the line or this will happen to you." And now, thanks to artists like Hamilton, the Stones and their followers had their response: "This is absurd and unjust." A Hamilton collage of the tabloid headlines further framed the proceedings as a show trial. And yet it didn't only profit the tabloids. For all their suffering, the madness turned the two besieged Rolling Stones (and later Brian Jones) into rock and roll's folk heroes: more polarizing, newsworthy, and intensely interesting than the Beatles could ever hope to be. The atmosphere of Us vs. Them had never been stronger, and the Stones, facing real jail time in the violation of the Dangerous Drugs Act, were now much more than pop stars; they were potential martyrs/heroes.

Mick and Keith rose to the occasion, wearing long hair and a new outfit every day for the bank of photographers. The defendants dressed like the louche, decadent rock stars they were and made no effort to employ a blue pinstriped suit to endear themselves to the judge. "This is who we are," they seemed to say. They dressed like rich hippies, but hippies nonetheless. "This is us, and you are putting all of us on trial." Fans carrying signs held vigil outside the courthouse. The event actually consolidated the London club scene, forcing them to mobilize and organize. Release, a group that provided legal relief funds for those railroaded on drug charges, drummed up funds for the Stones and others. The Who, mentioned in the infamous *News of the World* piece, rush-recorded versions of the Stones' "The Last Time" and "Under My Thumb" (the former is excellent and the latter, less so). Who drummer Keith Moon joined the fray, in mod gear and shades, holding up a sign reading STOP POP PERSECUTION. The Stones were privately shaken but publicly they turned Us vs. Them into great courtroom theater.

When the prosecutor asked Richards, "Would you agree in the ordinary course of events, you would expect a young woman to be embarrassed if she had nothing on but a rug in the presence of eight men, two of whom were hangers-on and the third a Moroccan servant?" Richards replied, "Not at all," adding, when pushed, "We are not old men. We are not worried about petty morals."

It was obvious to all that they were doomed. The world was watching (the press covered the meals being delivered to the courthouse as if they were arrivals of heads of state: "Mick's having smoked salmon today"). They were going to be made examples of and they were going to get stiff sentences well beyond what the charges merited. Mick prepared himself for it. He set his business affairs in order; he made peace with Faithfull and with his family, who were supportive through it all. But when he stood up before the judge, on the morning of June 29, 1967, the sentence shocked him to the core. "Michael Philip Jagger, you will go to prison for three months." He tried not to crumple as it sank in and a cry of disbelief was heard in the pew, but he felt himself go blank. He summoned all the discipline he could to keep standing. Something told him, "Don't let them break you; stand up." Richards was sentenced to six months. Fraser, getting a larger sampling of the dark side than he'd bargained for, got a year. That night, the news of the gruesome death of sex bomb Jayne Mansfield on a rainy New Orleans highway provided some distraction from the almost surreal proceedings. Would the Stones really have to spend the next ninety days in prison; dressed in heavy denim and eating and sleeping with murderers and rapists?

Between the bust and the trial, the Stones shot a promotional film for "We Love You," a rush-recorded single that would function as both a thank-you to supportive fans and a stopgap should incarceration prevent the band from recording and releasing new material. "We Love You," which sounds as hastily made as it actually was, begins with a jail door slamming. John Lennon and Paul McCartney showed solidarity by adding backing vocals to the track, but neither can be heard distinctly. The lyrics are pretty basic: "We don't care if you hound we. And love is all around we . . ." The piano hook gets into your head and stays (whether you wish it to or not) but it's not Mick and Keith's best moment on record, and coming on the heels of the brilliant *Aftermath* it's even more of a shrug. Peter Whitehead, approached to shoot a promotional film, thought about the trial and the verdict and devised a theme. "I saw it as a typical crime of the establishment against artists as was the case with Oscar Wilde." Whitehead's take was communicated to Mick, who immediately embraced it.

A church was found to double as a courtroom, Faithfull's hair was cut short to call to mind "Bosie," and Keith, as the Marquis, stood before Mick, passing judgment. At one point, a fur rug was introduced into evidence, calling to mind Miss X and the Mars bar. It's a better promo than it is a song, and Mick (at one point naked and wrapped in the rug) seems to find catharsis acting out the "murder" of Wilde (who never recovered personally or professionally). "I don't think they were afraid," Whitehead says. "They were just desperately and profoundly sad, having seen, yet again, just how the British right-wing conservative government could behave. They were absolutely convinced they were going to go to jail. Which means living in a cell."

After a meal and tearful good-byes, they were separated, Richards sent to Wormwood Scrubs in London and Mick and Robert Fraser to the hospital wing of the Lewes prison, a gothic, Victorian-era prison house, forty miles or so out of the city. While Mick Jagger and Keith Richards would only spend about a day behind bars, when they were first separated from society, there was nothing to indicate that they would not be there for the duration of their respective sentences.

This actually must have been the first moment of true quiet Mick had known in three and a half years. How to pass the time when minutes felt like days? He had access to all the stimulation in the world, and then nothing. He could still recognize himself, his inner thoughts and outer appearance. He wasn't malnourished; nobody had beaten him; they didn't even cut his hair or strip-search him; He was just captive. But what about the acid philosophy? Isn't the mind infinite? If he was going to be a martyr for the new consciousness, surely he needed to test its mettle?

Faithfull came to visit, bringing with her cigarettes, paper, and pen. When he saw her he lost his cool and burst into tears. He'd kept a good face; he was a good leader. Not every pop star was cut out for it. Lennon was. McCartney fumbled with it. Bob Dylan fled. The Moody Blues were never candidates anyway. Neither was Donovan. Most of us can't truly appreciate the rough juxtaposition of being pampered one day and banged up in cement the next; idolized by one half of the nation and fingered as a villain by the other (the half with the power to destroy you). He was only a half decade removed from Dartford. "The point of arresting rock stars like Mick and Keith was basically political intimidation," Coon says. "And I will guess that Mick and Keith, like anyone else subject to the epitome of state authority, did feel intimidated. Police harassment exerts a very private and personal cost."

Keith has related tales of the other prisoners, the hard men and outcasts treating him like one of their own, hooting cries of support as he was led down the row. They threw cigarettes into his cell. Mick tells no such tales. What we have from Mick's experiences is more concrete, and possibly more evidence of the stronger character. While in prison, Mick wrote some lyrics for "2,000 Light Years from Home," their greatest psychedelic rock song. It's a song about abject loneliness, reflecting a surreal remove from proper society that was, as per the zeitgeist, equated with deep space travel. Mick's body was in a small cell, but he was imagining himself a hundred, two hundred, six hundred, then a thousand, and, finally, two thousand light-years away from the gray bars, staring back at earth from the conflagrations of Aldebaran in the Taurus constellation, the muse star that captivated Thomas Hardy and Tolkien. Invoking Aldebaran was utopian, as the distant star is, in many science fiction yarns, habitable. Like De Sade, Wilde and Genet, and Orton, Mick Jagger turned a cell into a study. Others were writing as well, moved to their core by the questionable justice. Some editorials approved of it (this was the same contingent that advocated for the mandatory drug testing of pop stars, after all). It served them right, the arrogance! Most found it to be a travesty, the product of LSD panic, tantamount to a witch trial.

The most famous and influential of these came from an unlikely source in conservative editor William Reece Mogg of the *Times of London.* In a July 1, 1967, editorial entitled "Who Breaks a Butterfly on a Wheel," Mogg laid the evidence out flatly: "Mr. Jagger was charged with being in possession of four tablets containing amphetamine sulfate and methyl amphetamine hydrochloride; these tablets had been bought perfectly legally in Italy," before putting the purported crime in context. "If after his visit to the Pope the Archbishop of Canterbury had bought proprietary airsickness pills at Rome airport, and imported the unused tablets into Britain on his return, he would have risked committing precisely the same offence. No one who has ever traveled and bought proprietary drugs abroad can be sure that he has not broken the law." Mogg singled out Judge Block for inflating the "normal penalty" which is "probation" while taking pains not to "speculate on the judge's reasons, which we do not know." He simply asked: "Has Mr. Jagger received the same treatment as he would have received if he had not been a famous figure, with all the criticism and resentment his celebrity has aroused?" He also challenged the considerable portion of the populace who were not young and outraged, but older and satisfied. "They consider

that Mr. Jagger 'got what was coming to him.' They resent the anarchic quality of the Rolling Stones' performances, dislike their
songs, dislike their influence on teenagers, and broadly suspect
them of decadence . . . As a sociological concern, this may be rea-
sonable enough, and at an emotional level it is very understand-
able but it has nothing at all to do with this case." Mogg closed his
editorial by drawing comparison to Stephen Ward, who was impli-
cated in the last great British morality play, the Profumo scandal.
Ward introduced showgirls Mandy Rice Davies and Christine
Keeler to John Profumo, the acting secretary of state for war. It
was later discovered that Keeler was also sleeping with a Soviet at-
taché. After a prolonged attack on his character, Ward took an
overdose. "There are cases in which a single figure becomes the
focus for public concern about some aspect of public morality.
That case killed Stephen Ward." If the Mick Jagger conviction
was allowed to stand, the public would essentially have blood on
its hands. Richards, by the way, is not mentioned in the editorial;
only Mick.

"I was sittin' in jail and some one threw it [*The Times*] through
the window, which is illegal in jail," Mick recalled. When he read
the editorial, he wondered just how persuasive it would be. By
right, it would at least make people realize that he was a human
being as well, not just a symbol. "It was against the normal press
conduct and shows a strong sense of purpose. That was something
I'll always remember and be grateful for." Richards, in Wormwood Scrubs, was informed of the Mogg essay as well. Over the
course of the day, the outrage grew louder until it was apparent
that the court had to backpedal. Mick and Keith were ordered released on bail pending appeal and were immediately granted their

freedom, at least temporarily (charges were later overturned on appeal; Fraser served out his sentence).

"If William Rees Mogg had not written his 'Butterfly on the Wheel' *Times* editorial, which, I'm sure, was instrumental in getting Mick and Keith released, then the plan would have been to mount an appeal of arrest and sentence in the usual way, just like the legal action that became necessary to help young people who were not famous and who did not have 'great and the good' *Times* editorials protesting on their behalf! Without the *Times* editorial Mick and Keith would have spent much longer in jail, as long as 'ordinary' people who were being busted every day and night," says Coon.

It was clearly explained to both Mick and Keith upon release that July that although they walked the streets again, they were most certainly not off the hook; in fact, they'd be scrutinized even more closely than before. They were reminded that they had the rare power (or were perceived to have such) to lead others to harm. Abuse of this, they were warned, would figure into any further sentencing. "Whether you like it or not, you are the idol of a large number of the young in this country," the judge scolded before releasing Mick. "Being in that position, you have very grave responsibilities. If you do come to be punished, it is only natural that those responsibilities should carry higher penalties." Mick protested weakly, claiming, "This was all pushed on me by the prosecution." He repeated this same statement to reporters at a brief and tense press conference shortly thereafter. Looking sedated and drawn, Mick spoke slowly and wearily. "People have been talking about responsibility for a long time," he rambled. "I'm not sure if this responsibility is quite as great as they may count because I believe that individuals make their own minds up more than people think." Mick never apologized. The seeds of a different Mick, satanic, not messianic, can be detected here, and it would certainly be something he would explore intellectually and express lyrically in the coming year. "Many of us realized we had to roll up our political sleeves for the long haul," Coon says of the cultural shift in '68 and '69 from delighted and hopeful to hard and reactionary. "As with any socio-political movement, we had to learn how to deal with violent people who attach themselves to what was going on. It didn't help that, very naïvely, the Rolling Stones thought it would be 'cool' to get outlaws such as the Hells Angels involved, not to mention their interest in Satanism and the occult, which became the dark, reactionary side of psychedelia."

Next, the Stones entered the studio to record the follow-up to *Between the Buttons*: an acid lark called *Their Satanic Majesties Request*. Although boasting few moments as magnificent as "2,000 Light Years from Home" (easily the highlight), it has its charm now, and is no more or less a hodgepodge mess than more celebrated masterpieces where great songs are outnumbered by bursts of quickly discarded ideas (please see all of Radiohead's post "Kid A" albums). Blessed with the Wildean ability to reduce complicated matters to their most trenchant points with a perfect quip, Mick later dismissed the album as made "under the influence of bail." At the time, the band was giving it all they had, trying to make their own *Sgt. Pepper*. But what they had was severely compromised. Years later, he elaborated to Jann Wenner: "I think we were just taking too much acid. We were just getting carried away, just thinking anything you did was fun and everyone should listen to it. Also we did it to piss Andrew off, because he was such a pain in the neck. Because he didn't understand it. The more we wanted to unload him, we decided to go on this path to alienate him." Unsurprisingly, this concoction of discarded blues riff, John Barry Bond theme horns, jug-band blues, Tabla rhythms, snoring sound effects, and Bill Wyman vocals was not a major commercial hit either. Happily things were about to come into fierce focus.

The Stones' next offering would truly be the first song to snugly fit their new, politicized, rebel folk hero garb. Built around a Bill Wyman bass riff and a turn of phrase inspired by Jack, Keith's Redland's groundskeeper, "Jumpin' Jack Flash" marked the Stones' association with their most important producer and collaborator, Jimmy Miller, and the next, arguably most powerful phase of their career. "It's about having a hard time and getting out," Mick has said. "Just a metaphor for getting out of all the acid things." Richards, as is his wont, puts it much more succinctly: "I'd grown sick to death of the whole Maharishi guru shit and the beads and bells. Who knows where these things come from, but I guess it was a reaction to what we'd done in our time off and also that severe dose of reality. A spell in prison at Wormwood Scrubs would certainly give you room for thought!"

"No man dies for what he knows to be true," Oscar Wilde said. "Men die for what they want to be true, for what some terror in their hearts tells them is not true." "Jumpin' Jack Flash" is about staring down that terror, seeing it for what it is, and moving on. That's its power (that and the riff). The band shot a video for it with filmmaker Michael Lindsay Hogg. They seemed like a new machine, like someone gave them a shot of B-12. Even Brian looks reinvigorated. They have never looked cooler before or since: Keith in his fly glasses, Mick smeared with war paint. He knew there was a war going on. And he knew fighting had to be done, but was he willing to die for what he "wanted to be true"? By the middle of 1968, Mick would still be contemplating what to do with the power that he'd finally come to accept as a reality, wanted or not. Would he keep out of trouble or seek it? The world was bending in the Stones' favor. Young people were rising up all over the world and they were looking to their rock heroes for direction more than ever before.

"I Went Down to the Demonstration"

It's hard to imagine today, but there was a time when a major rock star not only *could* but *was obliged to* walk among the people; to pledge his or her power directly to an important cause and not just via a donation or a photo op or a red-carpet crawl. How legitimate they were, and even record sales depended on this level of credibility. Between 1968 and 1979, when the Clash was on the verge of playing large venues and selling millions of records, this was not only obligatory; it was fashionable, part of the package. In the '70s, certain rockers like David Bowie and Alice Cooper, whose very images were dependent on being different from the people, got a pass, but especially during times of great change, the young uprisers depend on their musical heroes to literally be there for them.

As the Great Society of Lyndon Johnson was tarnished and

the Vietnam War escalated, as the fight for civil rights met with violent resistance by those fearful of progress, as the feminist movement grew, and as workers all over the globe went on strike and marched for fair treatment and wages, those rock heroes, considered generals and majors of the mobilized counterculture, were expected to weigh in with support and guidance. Some, like Marlon Brando and Jane Fonda, rose to this with a fervor that bordered on hubris. Singer-songwriters Phil Ochs and Joan Baez were on the ground in a more sober and pragmatic fashion, but they lacked the cultural power of a Dylan or a Brando or a John Lennon or a Mick Jagger. Mick was first approached by the Left when Labour Party and Parliament member Tom Driberg, a gay, progressive politico with ties to the new youth culture (Allen Ginsberg was one of his close friends), suggested that Mick consider running for Parliament to capitalize on the new power of millions of young British baby boomers who'd reached voting age in 1966. Mick was flattered but declined. Still, as the Left gained power, they kept their eye on this new kind of leader.

"We were certainly watching them in the sense that we were dancing to their tunes—the Stones and the Beatles were the most popular groups at the time. We weren't particularly thinking of the Beatles at that period as radical in any way; they just made pleasing music. But Jagger we felt—there was more of an edge to him and his music at that period and he didn't like what was going on—sexually and politically—and that became very obvious," says the writer and activist Tariq Ali today. "If you were even slightly radical you had to be at the demonstration and you had to be prepared to be abused by the government and its supporters."

The year 1968 marked the apex of problem vs. solution culture.

People truly wanted to know whether their heroes could walk the walk; were they tourists, visiting the revolution, then retreating to their mansions, or were they going to lead? "There was a real sense of commitment—the feeling that if we all got off our ass we could actually bring about some change—a big sense of 'We can do it! We can do it.' People got caught up in that, rightly so," Ali recalls.

The Stones' expanding retinue included drug dealers, radical activists like Michael X, and leg-breakers affiliated with London gangsters Reggie and Ronnie Kray, but it somehow didn't seem out of step with the new thrust. The youth movement of the late '60s was not entirely pure. It was a social movement as much as a political one, and the war in certain circles was nothing more than a metaphor for a general sense of anger and unrest. "It was about the war but it wasn't about the war—it was about everything," writer and activist Mick Farren says. "It had become a much more dangerous brew."

Demonstrations were theater constructs and media events, drawing horny students and story-hungry journalists as much as true believers on both the Left and the Right. In 1968, there were those cynical or jaded souls who "attended" gatherings, even riots, as if they were social events. In this way, the interest of John Lennon and Mick Jagger, both of whom watched the antiwar and oppression movements closely, could be viewed as even more sincere. These informed "cats" didn't, after all, need to carry pictures of Chairman Mao to make it with anyone. When Mick spouted Marxist and sometimes anarchist theory in the pages of the recently launched *Rolling Stone* and *N.M.E*, it was tantamount to sending up a test balloon, designed to gauge just how much the political discourse of the L.S.E. classrooms was becoming reality. "I see a great deal of danger in the air," he said at the time. "This is a protest against the system. And I see a lot of trouble coming in the dawn. We have got them on the run now and we have to finish what we started. The way things are run in Britain and the States is rotten and it is up to the young to change everything. The time is right now. Revolution is valid. The kids are ready to burn down the high-rise blocks and those stinking factories where they are forced to sweat their lives away. I'm going to do anything that has to be done to be a part of what is about to go down."

Unfortunately palace revolution requires lots of planning and one cannot really imagine a Lennon or a Jagger attending regular meetings. Still, both men sensed and publicly acknowledged that there was possibly a role they could play, a pivotal one, that would not only enhance the perception of their bands as not just pop groups but real forces, but might also amount to some good. Lennon had given an interview in *Rolling Stone* in which he was more outspoken than the Beatles had been (or were ever allowed to be) before "Destruction." Quoting his own "Revolution," Lennon said, "Well, you know, you can count me out, and in, like yin and yang. I prefer 'out.' But we've got the other bit in us."

The rate at which the world seemed to be changing was dizzying. Every month seemed to bring new reports of student and worker protests all over the world, so much so that it seemed beyond coincidence, but rather some kind of cosmic synergy, an unmistakable signal to all still on the fence that they needed to pledge themselves or get out of the way: hunger strikes among college students in New England, resistance gatherings in Spain, West Berlin, Poland, and Brazil. The rise of the I.R.A. and the P.L.O., the radical feminists and Black Panther Party; the canonization of Che Guevara, and in March, a demonstration in London. On March 17, twenty-five thousand marchers convened in Grosvenor Square to protest the Vietnam War in front of the American embassy, the largest anti–Vietnam War rally in England. Tipped off that this was happening, the police were out in full riot force on horseback and brandishing collapsible truncheons to cow the angry and potentially violent mobs, stop oncoming cars, and search them for weapons or contraband. "It was just building and building," Farren recalls. "It was very peaceful but then rumors started going around that people had been massacred. There was a rush forward and suddenly the cavalry charged. Mounted policemen. The charge of the light brigade! Guys swinging very long nightsticks and cracking heads."

Mick was living at Cheyne Walk, walking distance from the square, nesting with Marianne Faithfull, in a beautiful apartment house draped with tapestries and covered with rugs. Their pal Christopher Gibbs designed it, and Faithfull furnished it on various shopping excursions though the city's boutiques. It was more like a café back room in Morocco or a den in Bombay, and might have been the perfect place to withdraw from chaos, amid antiques and incense smoke. It was clear that he again had a real choice to make too. He could literally watch from his window, or he could put on his boots and hit the street, where kids were carrying signs and chanting "Ho Ho Ho Chi Minh," and others simply screaming "Anarchy!" The protesters enthralled him. Some of this enthusiasm was fostered in the classrooms of the London School of Economics. Surely Faithfull had an influence as well. "I come from a very left wing socialist family," she told me, adding that as a musician, she's "always been attracted to revolutionary material."

Tariq Ali knew that Mick would be at the demonstration. He'd called and informed Ali that he was going to march. "He said, 'I'm coming on.'" But he did not want to speak. He was there as an observer, a sort of artist-journalist, traveling on the periphery, although rumors began to spread that he was dancing in front of police horses and chucking bricks at shop windows (most of which were boarded up). In truth, he and Faithfull kept near the bank of cameras and didn't charge into the fray. It was a personal risk, nonetheless. With the mounted police, caught up in an anarchic clash, however, he certainly ran the risk of being just another long-haired agitator. He certainly wasn't dressed in stage wear, but rather a simple polo shirt and overcoat—student garb. "They certainly could have smashed his head," Ali agrees. "They smashed a lot of heads that day. He wanted to be among the crowd. He didn't care what the consequences of going out would be; that's absolutely true—obviously had he been beaten up by the cops that day there would have been one hell of a storm in the country as a whole; it was a risk and he took the risk."

Once people did start recognizing him, Mick felt something strange and unexpected. He witnessed the focus of the movement actually weakening. Those fixated on the embassy and the unjust war were now contemplating "Mick Jagger." It was a sinking feeling. There was no way, beyond continuing to write and record music, that he could make a difference. An immediate, direct participation, no matter how expected of him, was ultimately impossible. He'd discovered this in an honest and commendable way, by actually trying and failing to fight. After about a half an hour, he fled back to the safety of Cheyne Walk to watch the protest on television like every other outsider.

Lennon was going through the same thing, wondering how much he would add to or distract from the cause. There were rumors going around the crowd that Lennon would pay the legal bills for anyone arrested, but he did not show his face.

Later in the month, Mick convened with Keith, Brian Jones, and the rest of the Stones, who were recording the follow-up to the ill-fated *Satanic Majesties* with "Jumpin' Jack Flash" producer Jimmy Miller at Olympic Studios. Mick had a new track with the working title "Has Everybody Paid Their Dues" written. The lyrics reflected images of Grosvenor Square and Paris reset for a hot, volatile June, sensing that the heat of summer would only inflame an already agitated movement and allowing Mick to reference Martha and the Vandellas' 1964 No. 1 hit "Dancing in the Streets" with typically barbed wit that at once validated and took the piss out of the revolution as social opportunity. Keith strummed, like a folk singer, running his acoustic guitar through an analog tape recorder to create distortion. Brian Jones, in one of his final bursts of creativity, added a tamboura to the acoustic strumming track, and Charlie Watts produced a marching snare drum beat on an old toy kit from the '30s. With Nicky Hopkins on piano, "Street Fighting Man" is a folk song slightly psychedelized with the Indian drones and run through the zeitgeist. Miller recorded it on an old-style tape machine that caused the noises to bleed into a drone that approximated the surge and white noise of the crowds at Grosvenor. Mick sang in a slow drawl like a man dizzy with heat and fear and the rush of "we just might succeed," before ultimately determining, "So what can a poor boy do except to sing for a rock and roll band?" It's interesting to note that Lennon too sang "Revolution" in a slow, deliberate and pondering fashion with the same sense of curiosity as to what his role should be: "out/in."

"It was a great song," Farren says. "But it was kind of like Mick hedging his bets. I didn't hedge my bets. Jim Morrison didn't hedge his bets. Mick Jagger and the Beatles did. You can count me out/in."

The chaos and bloodshed of '68 didn't stop just because the Stones decided to seal themselves off in the studio. In April, as the Stones were still working on the track, Martin Luther King Jr. was killed in Memphis. Later that spring racial tension flared in London when Enoch Powell delivered his "River of Blood" speech, fomenting anti-immigration sentiment. In South Africa, uprisings against the system of apartheid produced casualties, and in May, students in Paris organized a strike to protest the De Gaulle administration.

Director Jean-Luc Godard was in Paris during the riots, monitoring them but, like Jagger, unsure whether he could be of any greater use to the movement. Godard, along with other leaders of the nouvelle vague like Françoise Truffaut, Louis Malle, and Eastern European filmmakers like Milos Forman and Roman Polanski, lobbied to cancel the Cannes Film Festival that spring. He knew that his true power, however, was as a provocateur. In interviews, Godard, a former film critic, ten years into his career as a director, following the groundbreaking *Breathless* (based on a script he'd written with Truffaut), compared the revolutionary artist, filmmakers in his case, to the Vietcong.

As the Stones were recording what would become their follow-up to *Their Satanic Majesties Request*, later titled *Beggars Banquet*, at Olympic Studios in London, Godard approached them to ask if he might film their progress. The Stones' new status as outsider folk heroes post-Redlands appealed to the Frenchman, a decade their senior, and fit nicely with a vision he had for a new piece of cinematic agitprop. Godard headed to London in June of '68 to set up cameras and lights in the sparse studio while the Stones recorded a new song. It was called, originally, "The Devil Is My Name," written by Jagger after reading Russian novelist Mikhail Bulgakov's book *The Master and Margarita*. The book, released in 1967 and considered vogue by the politicized, young intellectuals, chronicles the devil and his entourage spanning time from the days of Christ and Pilate through Soviet Russia of the '30s. As Godard and his crew observed, the track metamorphosed from a dirge, vaguely Dylanesque, and mostly acoustic guitar driven to the epic with the unique samba beat that we know today. Its title changed as well to the superior "Sympathy for the Devil." Mick had dabbled in the occult, briefly fraternizing with the author and filmmaker Kenneth Anger and composing, on a new Moog synthesizer, the droning soundtrack to his singularly creepy short film *The Invocation of My Demon Brother* (homoerotic albinos, soldiers disembarking a helicopter, Charles Manson associate and convicted murderer Bobby Beausoleil, Church of Satan founder Anton LaVey, and lots of fire). While Anger took his fascination with the Stones (whom he considered powerful witches) seriously, Mick's fascination was fleeting. It wasn't a song for the devil; it was a song *about* him. Mick knew what it was like, now, to be demonized.

Godard, with his dark glasses, ever-present cigarette, and imperious, intellectual cool, seemed at first like a perfect collaborator. Like the Stones, the nouvelle vague auteurs took American iconography (gangster pulp, Hitchcock studio films, and cool jazz, rather than the blues) and made something new. Godard envisioned a juxtaposition of the Stones at work on a song that doesn't quite come together right away with a series of vignettes, both witty and perverse, that would cumulatively address the idea of struggle; creative with regard to the Stones and, as far as the planned vignettes went, the politics of the American minorities and the Vietcong. Footage, mostly silent, of the Stones—Bill, sullen as usual in his bright pink boots, Keith stoned and aloof in shades, Brian bloated with drink and isolated, strumming an acoustic guitar in a cubicle, and Mick impatiently instructing his band mates as they try to get the vibe right ("Three verses, straight through, then a solo . . . it should start off very cool.")—segues into a contingent of Black Panthers, heavily armed, reciting agit-prop like *Mein Kampf* and Le Roi Jones' *The Dutchman* and actually engaging in revolutionary (if highly, even mawkishly, symbolic) acts. A car arrives and virginal, white-clad, barefoot women are led out to be fondled then executed (throwing the white male establishment's basest fear in their face). When we come back to the Stones, we see progression: "progress" being a key word. Keith is now on bass, searching for some kind of groove, and "Sympathy" is a bit livelier. Mick is still trying to get it, "I been round for many a long—aw shit!"

Watching today, those of us who know the song well will find its rough assemblage compelling. Knowing what the final result will be, there's a sustained tension as we wait for the Stones to nail it and give us our familiarity. "I shouted out, who killed Kennedy," Mick sings. This is on June 4, 1968, and we know what's coming. Mick, of course, does not. It's a creepy feeling. Four days later,

Bobby Kennedy was shot in the kitchen of the Ambassador Hotel in Los Angeles and "Who killed Kennedy" becomes "Who killed the Kennedys," and the Stones, once again sealed in their bunker while blood is shed, use the violence to sharpen their commentary and power. Godard next deconstructs the notion of celebrity leader by pestering an ingénue (Anne Wiazemsky, the costar of his similarly politicized *La Chinoise,* of the previous year) with highly philosophical questions ("Do you believe drugs are a spiritual form of gambling?"), all of which are responded to with a simple, "Yes." When we next see the Stones there are congas and "Sympathy" has a groove. As Mick records his vocal, Keith, Brian, Anita, and Marianne gather around doing the famous "woo woos" (supposedly this was staged by Godard, as the backing vocals were already recorded), as if to say, there can be no spontaneous acts. Everything, even rock and roll, even revolution, is contrived. Excited by the prestige of presenting Godard's first English-language film, and the commercial potential of a Rolling Stones concert film (which is how it was sold and later, how it would be marketed), the studio hated the film (which Godard had entitled *One Plus One*) and forced an edit in which the Stones played all of "Sympathy for the Devil." When the Stones saw the final result, they weren't quite sure what to make of it. Godard and Jagger clashed in the press after the film was screened. As for the meaning of the film, Mick admitted, "I have no idea," somewhat irritated at having to explain the project to the British and American media. "The lead chick [Anne Wiazemsky] comes to London and gets totally destroyed with some spade cat, gets involved with drugs or something." When Godard groused that the band had abandoned him once the studio began meddling, Mick responded by dismissing the director as "a twat."

"These radical images married to the Stones didn't quite have the fucking impact that obviously was the intention," Farren says. "You had a very interesting film of the *Beggars Banquet* sessions— intercut with a lot of girls standing on used cars talking about the Vietcong. If it hadn't been Godard and the Stones, it would have been an amateurish student movie. It meant well but it didn't tell me anything I didn't know."

"Street Fighting Man" was released as the first single off the Stones' promised new album, *Beggars Banquet*, hitting the radio in August just days before the Democratic National Convention was set to kick off in Chicago. There, fifteen thousand antiwar protesters convened in Lincoln Park and clashed with the police after refusing to obey curfew. The single was timed perfectly, and validated Mick's decision that, ultimately, he had much more power as a singer than he could ever have as another marcher. Haskell Wexler's *Medium Cool*, a drama built around actual footage of the Chicago riots, opens with a similar realization: at a cocktail party where journalists are talking about just how much to get involved when they see people bloodied and injustices. "All good people deplore problems at a distance," one reporter laments.

"Street Fighting Man" hardly seems hopelessly dated like other songs of the "come on people now, smile on your brother" variety, largely due to the fact that the twenty-four-hour news media has frequently turned to it for soundtrack coverage for every subsequent revolution, most recently those in Tunisia and Egypt. Although it does stand as a reminder to Mick of the moment he truly pondered storming the palace and then came to realize the limits of his power. "Poets don't sign petitions," the poet-father of a restless '68 French radical says during a pivotal dinner scene in

Bernardo Bertolucci's *The Dreamers*. "They sign poems." Jagger the rocker was more valuable to the revolution than Jagger the brick thrower. "You always got to have good tunes if you're marching," he later said, "but the tunes *don't make the march*."

In the ensuing decades, Mick would distance himself from political causes to the point of disengagement. There's a hilarious exchange between Mick and yippie icon Abbie Hoffman in Stanley Booth's *True Adventures of the Rolling Stones*. "Why don't you give us some bread?" Hoffman asks the band. "For what?" Mick inquires. "The trial," Hoffman answers, "the Chicago Eight." "I've got to pay for my own trials," he quips.

In his middle age, Mick collected relationships with wealthy and powerful figures like Bill and Hillary Clinton and Tony Blair (neither of which provoked much controversy but certainly left some of the die-hard '60s radicals a bit crestfallen). There was a time in the mid-'60s when liberal Chelsea dwellers and the hipper echelon of Parliament, smitten by Mick's surprising intellect, encouraged him to run for office. Ultimately, he wasn't willing to bleed for any movement. He'd decided politics was a bit flakey. "They're the same fucking things," he observed of the street-warring factions of '68. "They'll degenerate to putting helmets on and fighting each other. When they come out they won't know who the fuck they are." There were fissures even between the party-loving hippie contingent and the full-stop Trotskyites. "They didn't trust us dope fiends and we didn't trust them," Farren says. "I wasn't going to be in no fucking Red Guard, thank you. Like Mick and like Lennon, I like good whiskey. I like twelve-year-old scotch. I don't want to be in 1984 drinking victory gin." By the time Margaret Thatcher was elected, and England's Welfare State began to be dismantled, Jagger had fully gravitated to the other end of the socioeconomic spectrum. "It was a decisive time for a lot of people, especially people who'd made a lot of money," Ali says. "They felt taxes were too high and trade unions were on the verge of taking Britain. They got nervous and I was very surprised to find that Jagger had become a Thatcherite. It's ironic that in the '60s the Stones and Jagger had been far more radical than the Beatles; once John Lennon broke with the Beatles he became free and Jagger went in the other direction. All that [high society]. I know Marianne Faithfull, I used to see her off and on; she was quite upset he'd gone that way. She didn't know that he was that political, but she stayed. Mick was an intellectual and like other radical intellectuals during the Reagan-Thatcher years, he said 'Oh, it's not going to work. We've lost. Better make your peace with the system.'"

And yet, at a time when few people were openly critical of the Bush-Blair union, Mick penned the song "Sweet Neo Con," a scalding attack on the Bush administration, Halliburton and big-oil profiteers, and hypocrite Christians. A genuine protest song, it's a highlight of the Stones' creative comeback, A *Bigger Bang*, and seemed to come out of nowhere, evidence perhaps that Mick has never really stopped thinking about the divide and which side to choose. "He got his conscience working again and I was pleased," Ali says.

While nothing as jarring as "there should be no such thing as private property" has left his famous lips since the late '60s, you can't ever fully count him out—or in. "He was never an anarchist," Ali says. "If anything he was more socialist. Can you be a multimillionaire and be a socialist?" Ali laughs. "Intellectually you can."

The popular kid. A natural athlete, Mick (fourth from left/back row) in his early teens at Dartford Grammar School for Boys. (1960)

Mick and Keith open their very first fan mail. (1963)

Shakin' at the Crawdaddy Club— the Rolling Stones' first residency. (1963)

"The anti-Beatles" outside the pub. (1963)

Mick with his rival . . . and idol James Brown backstage at the filming of the T.A.M.I. Show. (1964)

Sucking on the blues harp in RCA Studios, Los Angeles. (1965)

The Romantic figure in fur. (1965)

Mick with his first serious girlfriend, Chrissie Shrimpton. (1966)

With Ed Sullivan in New York City. (1966)

In cuffs after the Redlands bust and on the way to rock's first circus-trial. Pop artist Richard Hamilton used this shot for his collage "Swingeing London." (1967)

Mick and Keith with Brian Jones in Morocco. (1967)

The dark prince of the new youth culture. (1967)

With partner and muse Marianne Faithfull. (1968)

Recording Beggar's Banquet at Olympic Studios while Jean-Luc Godard films Sympathy for the Devil. (1968)

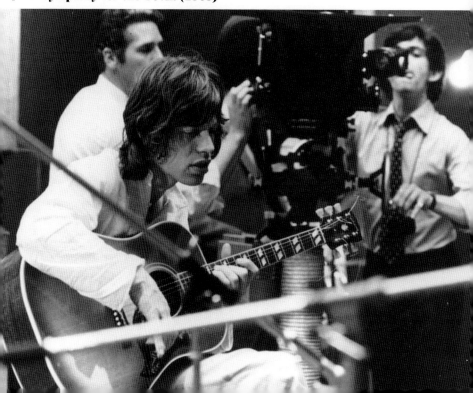

On the set of
Performance
with costar
and Stones
power broker
Anita
Pallenberg.
(1968)

A return to
the live
stage and a
wake for
the recently
deceased
Brian Jones
at Hyde
Park.
(1969)

"So, Remember
Who You Say You Are . . ."

When did Us vs. Them become Us vs. Us? When did the impenetrable foundation of the Rolling Stones first begin to show signs of fissuring, and who do we blame for the divide that has never been fully repaired (or credit, as it sure made for a more interesting and combustible band)? Anita Pallenberg. This isn't to say when in doubt, blame (or credit) the woman. *Cherchez la femme* as Mick himself might say. It's merely a testament to the power of this particular femme fatale.

Time has not been on Anita's side. There's a prescient moment in the fourth season of the great British sitcom *Absolutely Fabulous* in which Edina Monsoon (Jennifer Saunders) is lost in a dreamy haze following a crash diet. In her head, she is visited by God (as played by Marianne Faithfull) and the Devil (as portrayed by Pallenberg), who discuss the nature of humankind in the modern world. "They won't have any use for you and me soon," Faithfull warns. "I'm bored anyway." Pallenberg shrugs. "What's the point of me if I'm acceptable?"

Pallenberg has never been acceptable, and likely never will. If there's anyone who suffers from schadenfreude more than Mick Jagger when it comes to getting old, it's Anita. She was also such a revolutionary beauty in her time. In January of 2010, the actress, artist, and Stones muse, now in her mid-sixties, was snapped by a *Daily Mail* photographer while attempting to light a cigarette outside a Waitrose grocery. In the photo, Pallenberg's blonde hair is stringy, her face wrinkled, and she wears a turtleneck and baggy coat. She's unrecognizable as the lush-lipped, blonde gamine with the just-been-fucked gaze, lounging naked, wrapped in a sheet in *Dillinger Is Dead*, Italian director Marco Ferreri's 1969 art-noir film. As if the "What a Drag" headline (a nod to the Stones' "Mother's Little Helper") weren't cruel enough, the paper also ran a series of photos of Pallenberg in her youth (as well as Keith and Brian in their youths. Mick, of course, is represented by a recent photo).

And yet there remains a dignity to Pallenberg that can't be taken away; certainly because, like Keith, given her drug nightmares she should not be alive. But she not only lives on, she's now a dark rock legend. The few films she made in the '60s have now become cult classics: *Barbarella*, the aforementioned *Dillinger Is Dead*, the madcap adaptation of the erotic novel *Candy*, and, of course, *Performance*, perhaps the ultimate '60s cult film. Writer-director Harmony Korine, who cast her as Queen Elizabeth in his deeply strange, 2007 satire, *Mister Lonely*, once called Anita Pallenberg, "The female Chuck Berry," and she was probably as important to the classic-era Rolling Stones as we understand them as Berry was.

In her twenties Pallenberg spoke in the broken English of a Federico Fellini starlet or a fey male duke turned vampire. She was fearless in her exploration of drugs, bondage, and the occult. The Stones wore her clothes; not the clothes she designed, mind you. Built like skinny girls themselves, they borrowed her garments and made every other male rock band and rock fan want to dress that way as well; that highly creative, elegant, trashy aesthetic that has also been copied by every *female* rock and roller for the past forty years. Pallenberg, according to an oft-repeated observation by Keith Richards, "knew everything and she could say it in five languages." She was one of just a few, alongside Marianne Faithfull and Andrew Oldham, who contributed musically through philosophy, inspiration, and the way they spoke, dressed, and generally comported themselves. "Anita was like a life force, a woman so powerful, so full of strength and determination that men came to lean on her, to become as dangerously dependent on her as a heroin addict is on his drug supplier," Stones insider and drug connection Tony Sanchez, a.k.a. "Spanish Tony," writes in his memoir from this period, the notorious *Up and Down with the Rolling Stones.*

"Anita was a big force in the Stones," journalist Nick Kent told me in our interview for *Vanity Fair*'s website. "She didn't have any skill to bring to the Stones, but what she had was image and attitude. She couldn't play guitar or drums or bass. It's questionable whether the Rolling Stones would have had a woman playing in their group, but if they had, then Anita would have been that woman."

Pallenberg's conceptual vision for the Stones was nearly as complete as Oldham's. "I feel as though I'm rather like the sixth Rolling Stone. Mick and Keith and Brian need me to guide them, to criticize them, and to give them ideas," Pallenberg told Sanchez in *Up and Down*, adding, "I'm certain that any one of them would break up the band for me. It's a strange feeling."

This seemed to be the rule in the Stones during the mid- and late '60s, the period when the band was at its surging best: Whoever had Anita Pallenberg's affections somehow had most of the power. Whoever didn't have her wanted her with a highly distracting fascination at best, a corrosive jealousy at worst. Those who had her and lost her, lost their "demon." Anita knew all about demons.

Pallenberg was like the conch shell in William Golding's 1954 allegorical novel, *Lord of the Flies*. If the Stones were the marooned British schoolboys, trying to establish some kind of order in their strange world of drugs, celebrity, and oppression, she provided some kind of system to combat "the Beast" in the forest. To hold her was to have the floor. If you couldn't keep the floor, then mutiny was inevitable.

Pallenberg was raised on the kind of old European culture that doesn't really exist anymore. Born in January of 1944 in Rome, she was shipped off to a prestigious German boarding school after the war by her father, a prosperous travel agent. She was thrown out of school for truancy but remained in Munich and studied art. As a teen, she returned to Rome in the late '50s at the height of *La Dolce Vita* decadence, and in her early twenties began befriending many in the Federico Fellini circle of actors, models, and artists, and auditioning for parts. Decadent, bisexual, blonde, and intellectually hungry, she was already adept at bewitching both men and women. There are some people who have a preternatural knack for being in the right cultural place at the right time. It may very well be a sixth sense: a gift. Pallenberg next found herself in Greenwich Village modeling and hobnobbing with Allen Ginsberg and the nascent Warhol Factory stars and the radically experimental Living Theatre troupe before returning to Europe. It was there that she attended her first Rolling Stones concert in Munich on September 14, 1965. Backstage she met Brian Jones, who was already beginning to get jittery at the prospect of losing his hand in the Stones. He famously told her, "I don't know who you are, but I need you," and from that point on they were inseparable.

They looked perfect together, with their shiny, blond hair cut identically and mingling. In photos, Jones truly seems to meld with her; you can almost see the possession of his soul go down. As the Stones continued their mad tour through Europe, Pallenberg would travel with them or meet them at shows still marked by screaming girls. For a time, she restored his power to the group. She fed him ideas, which would help him distinguish himself as the bolder, more perverse and brave Stone. He donned a Nazi officer's uniform for a photo shoot. He indulged in orgies, S&M, all of which seemed designed to make Mick and Keith seem provincial. As he had when he first met them, already the father of three children, Brian had once again impressed and worried them with his intense lifestyle, this time one of moneyed and theatrical depravity.

But like Ralph in *Lord of the Flies*, Brian Jones couldn't hold the conch for long. The pressure to top himself creatively, the aforementioned acid frizzle that had melted away a good portion of his sanity by the end of 1967, and the ceaseless paranoia that replaced it, made self-control, much less control of the Rolling Stones, impossible.

When Pallenberg began auditioning for film roles, using her new notoriety as a Stones girlfriend to gain the attention of directors like Volker Schlöndorff (who directed her alongside British actor David Warner in *Michael Kohlhaas—Der Rebell*), Jones' paranoia increased considerably. Film was an alternate reality, an imaginary world where fidelity, emotionally and sexually, could be suspended.

Jones knew he could lose Anita to any number of handsome actors. He also knew that Mick and Keith were attracted to her, only fueling the jealous delusions. Already half crazy, he was steaming toward utter devastation. His physical abuse of Pallenberg was becoming increasingly apparent to the other Stones. Keith Richards was aghast and decided Pallenberg needed rescuing.

When Keith finally made his play for Anita, shortly after the Redland bust, while on a getaway to Morocco, he was not the "Keith" we now know. In footage of him pre-Anita, strumming his guitar with awkward and unbounded glee, he frequently seems almost nerdy, and toothy, a Buddy Holly type, not the fearless rock and roll pirate he'd become after donning her clothes, digging her drugs, and absorbing her "demon." Mick was still living in Chelsea with Marianne. They were talking about starting a family. He'd achieved the goal he set for himself back when he swapped Chrissie Shrimpton for Faithfull. He was now a powerful, well-connected member of London society, able to fraternize with poets, painters, art and antiques dealers, and hipper Parliament members. But now Keith had the conch.

"I found there was an enormous talent in Keith, and Keith was really a shy little guy in those days, couldn't come out of himself. And I had all this kind of Italian energy and outgoing personality, so it was really easy for me," Anita has said. "And somehow it finally came out. Then he started to write songs and he started to sing them himself. I thought it was wonderful." Keith's previous lead vocal contribution to the band had been the wry and winking drug ditty "Something Happened to Me Yesterday," which closes the American and British versions of *Between the Buttons*, the band's follow-up to *Aftermath*. Now Keith began working on a new blues song, "You Got the Silver," inspired by Anita, and perfect for him, not Mick, to sing. Was Mick worried that Keith would start vying with him for lead vocals on various Stones tracks? Probably not, but the mere consideration announced a shift in Stones power. Keith had been fully drawn out. He was now bigger than life, just like Jones had been, and just like Mick was. But now it was up to him to reckon with all the jealousy and superstitious paranoia that came with possession of the conch.

Anita, an underrated actress with perfect comic timing, would not give up her aspiration to movie stardom. She was too independent to merely be a Stones aide-de-camp and rock wife. She accepted the role of the Black Queen in Roger Vadim's futuristic sex farce, *Barbarella*, opposite Vadim's wife, Jane Fonda. "How much are they going to pay you?" a worried Keith asked her when she told him she was off to France to shoot the film. "I'll just give you the money." She refused this offer, and after proving the highlight of *Barbarella* (uttering lines like "To the Matmos with this winged fruitcake" with camp glee), she next shot the adaptation of *Candy* (penned by Keith's future drinking buddy Terry Southern and directed by Stones' Chelsea social scene cohort Christian Marquand) in Rome. Richards again offered her money to not do the film. He was especially jealous of a scene she had to do with Marlon Brando (who, in the days before political correctness, was cast as a randy Indian guru). "Keith heard that Marlon Brando and I had a scene, so he took the first plane and he was out there. It was the same story, so eventually I tried to time it out to work where Keith was working."

Ironically it would be a film shot much closer to home that would justify both Brian Jones' and Keith's paranoia.

Mick had been looking for a film to mark his coming out as a movie star ever since Andrew Loog Oldham's planned adaptation of *A Clockwork Orange* fell through.

John Lennon had recently broke from the Beatles to play "Gripweed" a wisecracking musketeer for Richard Lester, director of the band's *A Hard Days Night* and *Help!*. *How I Won the War* was a darker film, along the lines of Kubrick's *Dr. Strangelove* or the future war-set dark comedies like *Catch-22* or Robert Altman's *M.A.S.H.* Lennon, covered in blood, has a battlefield monologue about why he enlisted that, in a few frames, sets him apart from every other pop star turned actor with the possible exception of Elvis in *King Creole* and Frank Sinatra in *The Man with the Golden Arm*. Faithfull and others around Mick who also sensed the way cinema was bending into dark realism encouraged him to choose something dark and daring. When his friend Donald Cammell, a painter and yet another habitué of the Chelsea art and society scene, told him about a script he'd cowritten entitled

The Performers, Mick promised to read it. Cammell, also looking to get into film, shared an agent with Mick. Brando, a close friend of the artist as well, had shown interest in playing the lead role of Chas, an East End syndicate's hard man (or leg-breaking "performer") on the run after a job goes haywire. The gangster finally hides out in the bohemian den of Turner, an emotionally disturbed rock star, struggling to recapture his mojo, and Pherber, his decadent, darkly brilliant girlfriend (as well as various hangers-on). It was a perfect part for Mick; close enough to home, but daring and attention-grabbing in its subject matter.

Financing the film debut of Mick Jagger would be an easy sell, and nobody, at the time, anyway, seemed to trouble themselves with the actual details of Cammell's script: gender identity confusion, orgies, intravenous drug consumption, and bloody violence.

Cammell cannily approached Pallenberg with the role of Pherber, knowing very well the fragile dynamic in the Stones camp following her break with Brian and current cohabitation with Keith. Cammell knew Pallenberg from the European art and social scene and he correctly assumed that the extreme nature of the script would appeal to her. Pherber would be the showiest role of her career, her first real lead. She is in nearly every scene of acts two and three, the sort of narrator, ribbing Chas and speaking for the increasingly inarticulate, vain, and numb Turner, whose most consequential utterances amount to "Do you think I should wash my hair?"

Although Brando dropped out, to be replaced by another close friend of Mick and Cammell's, matinee idol James Fox, his method approach seemed to infect the production from the start.

Fox quickly subsumed himself into the city's gangster culture, studying with associates of the notorious Kray brothers, hanging around the nightclubs and boxing matches where the hard men gathered, and slowly turning himself into a hair-trigger thug.

The film, now titled *Performance*, like Michelangelo Antonioni's *Blow-Up* before it, would expose the dark side of swinging London, with "acid, booze, and ass" being replaced by "needles, guns, and grass," as Joni Mitchell would observe on the title track of her 1971 classic *Blue*. Pherber was a junkie, and by '68, heroin was epidemic among the hip London art scene. Eric Clapton was strung out. So were John and Yoko. The drug carries a decadent air perfectly suited to both Pallenberg's rapidly expanding cult of personality and her personal proclivity, having bonded with Keith inside the opium dens of Morocco.

Mick, observing that Fox was becoming Chas, and Pallenberg was already Pherber, deduced that he too had to become Turner, but in many ways, he was still the son of a suburban P.E. instructor. A toot of cocaine at a party was fine. Some pills, or perhaps a joint, but hard drugs were anathema. At heart, Jagger was much more together than Turner, and a movie, after all, was just a movie, wasn't it? "Whatever you do, don't try to play yourself," Faithfull recalled telling him as he prepped for his debut. "You're much too together, too straight, too strong. You've got to imagine you're Brian: poor, freaked-out, deluded, androgynous, druggie Brian. But you also need a bit of Keith in it: his tough, self-destructive, beautiful lawlessness. You must become a mixture of the way Keith and Brian will be when the Stones are over and they are alone in their fabulous houses with all the money in the world and nothing to spend it on." And so it was decided that he would channel those who did, first Brian, then Keith, and, in the same way Fox embedded with the gangsters, he would embed with Anita—well, really just bed her, his one concession to the method. Mick even dyed his hair an inky "Chinese black," according to Faithfull. Ironically, this immersion into utter darkness came at a time when the couple's life together was at its most idyllic. They were living in Cheyne Walk, a few houses down from Keith and Anita. Mick could walk over and work on songs at Keith's yellow, psychedelic grand piano. He and Marianne were planning a family; she'd gotten pregnant at the beginning of '68 and they'd named the child, a girl, Corinna. Keith and Anita were talking about starting a family as well. It seemed to be a new era of maturity and functionality for the two main Stones and the women that they loved. And then filming began.

When Keith first read Cammell's script and realized that his best friend and his girlfriend would share a bath and a bed, he was, like Brian Jones before him, furious and threatened. No social climber or sucker for Chelsea culture, Keith didn't like or trust Cammell. Worse, not content with merely pairing Pallenberg with Mick, Cammell threw "Lucy" into the mix. A near mute, played by the boyish Michèle Breton (another Cammell conquest), Lucy's raison d'être seems to be to shock and confound. Keith faced a dilemma. To ask her not to start up with Mick would be tantamount to inviting her to do so. Monogamy, after all, was provincial. The Stones, as Keith famously scolded Judge Block when bravely facing his Redlands bust sentence, were not old men. "Petty morals" didn't make it. And yet, to play it cool could mean losing her forever. It was one of only a handful of moments in his young life when he was completely powerless and he reacted by simply shutting down and waiting it out. This proved an excruciating tactic. Before filming wrapped, he, too, was a junkie.

"I never imaged Mick would be fucking Anita," Faithfull writes in her memoir. At the time, she was living in Ireland with her mother and her young son Nicholas, expecting the birth of her daughter. Why would Mick do such a hurtful thing to his best friend and creative partner? you might ask. There were elements of philosophical hedonism at work: an existential "if it feels good, do it," as Faithfull recalled. Most likely, however, Cammell is the villain here, and if Mick is guilty of anything, it's of valuing his potential as a movie star over loyalty to his mate.

Under the circumstances, with Cammell egging them on, it was tempting to rationalize, this was Turner and Pherber, not Mick and Anita. But then, Mick's spirit was stronger than Cammell's. He could never fully submerge in any method or bow to any direction. "The only person who might have showed some restraint was Mick," Faithfull writes. She adds, "It was only natural that [Anita] would find Mick's incarnation of Turner irresistible. Their characters were propelled toward each other and she already had a hard time distinguishing what was real and what was imaginary."

Filming began in a funky two-story house in Lowndes Square near Knightsbridge (substituting for the Powis Square exterior) and from the start, all involved surrendered to the inspired material. *Performance* truly is powerful, from the curated bits of art, iconography (Martin Luther King Jr.'s photo tacked to a wall here, a strummed bit of Robert Johnson there), to the downright strangeness (and Englishness) of the accouterments (the tank of squirming, phallic eels, a box garden of mushrooms). It's also a great British gangster caper like *Brighton Rock* before it or *Get Carter, The Long Good Friday, Lock, Stock and Two Smoking Barrels,* or *Sexy Beast* after it—full of ultraviolence, pinstripes, and dark humor. "I had a dog as a kid," one of the gangsters who would later come to snuff the gone-rogue Chas mutters. "It was a wire-haired terrier."

On a steady diet of good wine and sweet-smelling hash, rehearsals began in the spring of 1968. Richards was not invited to the set and too proud to protest; instead, he sat in the Blue Lena outside the Lowndes Square house, seething, as his best friend and girlfriend discussed their roles in the upstairs bedroom. In his memoir, Keith talks about composing the singularly dread-filled guitar parts for "Gimme Shelter" during this exact period.

The very first actual scene shot for *Performance* was a love scene between Mick, Pallenberg, and the tomboyish Michèle Breton. For the next seven days, Cammell and his associate director Nicolas Roeg treated the three-way scene like a separate film, shooting Mick, Pallenberg, and Breton in various states of actual intercourse with handheld sixteen-millimeter Bolex cameras. As with the love scene in Roeg's subsequent *Don't Look Now* with Julie Christie and Donald Sutherland, it has since passed into urban legend that Mick and Anita are really doing it. One thinks he can see the very moment of penetration; a certain giggle on Pallenberg's part; an exhale from Mick. More likely, however, the true carrying on went down in "rehearsal." Cammell directs like the painter he was: The light had to be perfect, a warm, lemony, sunlight, filtered through the wool blankets.

Up the street in a pub, Richards downed ale and smoked cigarettes and tried to forget what was going on, cursing Cammell's perverse manipulation. "He got a hard-on about intimate betrayal," he would later write in his memoir. Faithfull bravely visited the set and tried to take it in stride. She too was sexually drawn to Anita and had attempted to make love to her one night, after all. "I didn't say anything about Mick fucking Anita at the time of the film because I knew the only way for it to work was for him to really appeal to her," she has said. To combat his pain, Richards increased his heroin consumption at pal Robert Fraser's nearby flat, strumming his acoustic guitar, and singing his new tune "You Got the Silver" with melancholy and longing (it would ironically be one of the last Stones tunes that Brian Jones would add his fading magic to). Keith was furious with Mick, who never acknowledged that anything untoward had happened. He was deeply wounded by Pallenberg, who would also return from the set strangely quiet. When she discovered that she was pregnant, Keith had to entertain, even fleetingly, the devastating possibility that the father might be Mick. This was, of course, not the case, but even a few seconds of such pondering would easily devastate even a hard man like Keith. "Even the customarily fearless Keith couldn't handle this one," Faithfull writes.

There have been told accounts of Mick falling in love with Anita, which certainly explains his silence. More likely, he was in love with the idea of making a smashing debut as a film star and committed to follow Cammell deep into whatever gorge he was headed down. He had left himself a rope to climb back out of the imaginary reality. Falling in love with her would trap him in Powis Square forever. "So remember who you say you are, and keep your noses clean," Mick sings on "Memo from Turner," his contribution to Jack Nitzsche's unnerving soundtrack to the film.

Nitzsche was a cohort of Phil Spector and part of the *T.A.M.I. Show* orchestra. He'd become a key contributor to some of the Stones great singles, most famously the man arranging the famous children's choir on "You Can't Always Get What You Want." "Memo from Turner," finished after filming wrapped, is collected on the Rolling Stones' epic box set *The London Years*, along with other hard-to-find singles and B-sides, but it's the first real Stones song that's not a Stones song. Ry Cooder, not Keith, who refused to contribute, plays the malevolent slide guitar, and Mick, as Turner, sings disjointed lyrics courtesy of the cut-and-paste technique of William S. Burroughs (an influence of all three key Stones at the time).

James Fox, who could not shake Chas long after the principle filming ended, forgot who he said he was. He joined a religious cult called the Navigators and gave up acting for more than a decade. "He had a very hard time," Mick said later. "It sometimes happens and he decided the stage was a sort of place for sinners and left it." As with watching the love scene today with some hindsight and knowledge about what happens next, it's unsettling to see Fox's Chas shout, "I'm normal! There's nothing wrong with me!"

Breton lost herself in the drug culture for a time and never made another film. Pallenberg and Richards, as well as Marianne Faithfull, were sucked into a whirlpool of drugs, illness, and decay for the better part of a decade. Cammell directed three more films and killed himself in 1996. Keith never forgave him. Asked about *Performance* decades on, Richards said, "The best work Cammell ever did, except for shooting himself." He was still harboring resentment more than four decades later, taking pains to point out in *Life* that his partner has a "tiny todger." This is yet another in-accuracy, stoked by Keith and embraced by those with a stake in furthering the idea of "Brenda." While it's Warhol star Joe Dallesandro, and not Mick, whose enviable endowment graces the cover of 1971's *Sticky Fingers*, there are photos, taken by Anita, that show a fully naked Mick Jagger, prostrated in bed, his hand occasionally covering his modesty and occasionally not. Let's call it average, as far as rock-legend penises go, no larger or smaller than Lennon's flaccid member on the cover of *Two Virgins*. Jerry Hall, who after twenty-three years by his side, should probably get the last word, argued: "Mick is very well-endowed. Keith is just jealous."

Turner is the only character who dies onscreen in *Performance*, murdered by Chas before he's whisked off by the thugs who've tracked him down. (His last words: "I don't know . . .") And yet it would seem "Old Rubber Lips" (as Chas calls Mick on film) was the cast's only nontragedy in real life.

It's not as clean a getaway as he might have liked, however. The essential Jagger-Richards songwriting partnership would continue to thrive. It had yet to even peak, but the friendship that drove it was never the same. "It probably put a bigger gap between me and Mick than anything else," Keith would write in *Life*. "Probably forever."

In *Lord of the Flies*, after all, the asthmatic Piggy is killed while trying to cling to the conch, crushed by falling rocks after making a last-ditch attempt to restore order. You can't hold on to the conch and navigate the rocks at the same time. With the conch in pieces, the Stones camp returned to a state of savage anarchy. Mick and Keith used to be 100 percent for each other, and against the world:

Mick devoted and deferring to Keith and Keith encouraging and protective of Mick. In the studio now, things had to be agreed on by both Mick and Keith, beginning a long period of debate which would produce masterpieces (Mick's "Moonlight Mile," which closed *Sticky Fingers* and is wholly Keith-free, and, of course, *Exile on Main Street*) but would ultimately account for a long and order-free "lost" period in the mid-'70s. Mick could not have known what long-term damage his decision to take the role of Turner would cause, essentially plunging Keith into a decade-long smack addiction and creating a tear in the tightly loomed fabric of the Rolling Stones. Keith, after all, already knew what it was like to sleep with Marianne, spending a night with her before she and Mick began dating seriously, and again, he admits in *Life*, as a sort of revenge fuck, which in itself is pretty provincial (and it takes a lot to make Keith Richards appear this way).

As records of madness, decay, betrayal, and lust go, *Performance* stands alone. Mick, all lips and pale skin and dark hair, has never looked more beautiful, with his muscular arms exposed in a suit vest. In one scene, he dances while wielding a tube of pure, white light. "The only performance that really makes it is the one that achieves madness," Jagger declares toward the film's climax. While Jagger's film career would never again reach such heights, his first time out, he really made it.

"All My Friends Are Junkies"

Parse Mick's lyrics from late '69 and early 1970 and you will find the recurring theme of someone who's had the hurtin' put on him by life, someone in bad need of a new friend.

"She said . . . you can rest your weary head on me," Mick sings in "Let It Bleed," the countrified title track of their follow-up to *Beggars Banquet*. "Gimme Shelter," written largely by Keith, opens the album with a plea for sanctuary, sung without a mote of Mick's usual ironic distance. "Nineteen sixty-nine was not a happy year for Mick," says Sam Cutler, who would road manage their triumphant, then tragic North American tour in support of the forthcoming *Let It Bleed*.

The Redlands scandal of '67, the collapse of "Flower Power" into violence and hard drugs in '68, and the inevitable decaying of Brian Jones' body and soul left the Rolling Stones reeling and weary. Jones had stopped contributing to the group creatively, and soon wasn't even pretending to be a factor by coming around the studio. On one occasion, he asked Mick, "What can I play?" as the Stones were preparing to run through a new song, and Mick famously quipped, "I don't know. What *can* you play?" With a lucrative American tour in the works, it was both Mick and Keith who made the decision to fire Brian Jones. It was, as they say, just business. Allen Klein, the very man who promised to liberate them financially, and succeeded in elevating their royalty rate astronomically, had funneled the band's publishing into an American dummy corporation with the same name as their English one, Nanker Phelge. They no longer owned "(I Can't Get No) Satisfaction," "Ruby Tuesday," or any of their era-defining hit singles. But they still owed the taxes on their sales. Jones, gone flabby, was distracted by plans for renovating his new estate. He would loudly grumble at the direction the Stones were moving in and spoke frequently of splitting to form his own combo, one with a much stronger tether to the roots of rock and roll. The implication was that Mick and Keith had sold out, gone pop, and he was the once and future soul of the band. He was a liability, a potential competitor, and they required a soldier to help them kick against the pricks. He had to go. On the morning of June 8, 1969, a sheepish Mick, Keith, and Charlie Watts drove out to his farm to break the news. They'd already hired a replacement, teenage blues virtuoso Mick Taylor, and were prepared to offer Jones (who founded and named the band) a large (at the time) cash settlement. Jones took it with resignation, but it slowly began to rattle him.

This was a time of furious planning, recording, and tour organizing; they were mounting an assault that would restore the band to fighting weight and speed. They would debut the lean, mean Stones mach-two in front of the largest rock concert England had ever seen in Hyde Park on July 5. Two days before Jones got sacked, Mick had attended a massive gathering for Eric Clapton, Ginger Baker, and Steve Winwood's new super group, Blind Faith, in the park and wagered the Stones could draw more. Blind Faith threw a gauntlet of sorts by performing a rendition of Mick and Keith's own "Under My Thumb" but they were prone to long jams. The Stones were a full live experience, with Mick as a peerless showman.

The band was recording a B-side (their mighty take on Stevie Wonder's pained "I Don't Know Why I Love You") at Olympic Studios on the night of July 3 when they were informed that Brian Jones had been found at the bottom of his swimming pool by a girlfriend and a construction worker and hanger-on named Frank Thorogood (who later made a dubious deathbed confession that he'd murdered the troubled star).

The Hyde Park show was going to go on as planned, but now it would be a wake for the their late founder. Cardboard cutouts of Jones were ordered (the ones used were from the promotional photo shoot for *Beggars Banquet* and showed Jones at his drug-fuzzy worst, but it was the thought that counted). Mick also requested a thousand white cabbage butterflies after doves were considered then rejected. This would be, as devised, both the Stones explosive return to live performance and a poignant requiem for their founder; it would end up being neither. As if the pressure weren't high enough, they'd entered into an agreement with the TV network Granada to film a documentary on it. Logistically there was a lot that had to go perfectly, and nobody was really together.

On the day of the concert, the crowd was there, but by most accounts, the groove was not. Mick's reappearance as a live attraction was a strange one. First of all, he wore a white puffy shirt (not unlike the one from the classic 1993 *Seinfeld* episode) and garish drag queen makeup. Only his long dark hair seems princely, but otherwise, he did not present as a formidable leader. In a horrible foreshadowing of events to come, he scolded the crowd, attempting to quiet them so he could recite a poem for Brian Jones. "Are you gonna be quiet or not?" he whined, then attempted to read "Adonais," Percy Shelley's eulogy for John Keats. The crowd simply wanted to rock. The dark irony that Shelley, like Jones, was a victim of drowning, was not even on the communal transom. Mick got through the recital, but it's hard to gauge what emotions if any he brought to the party. Mick did not attend Jones' funeral, and commented to reporters that he had no intention to "walk the hills" dressed in black, because he didn't believe that death was the end of existence.

It rendered his grieving suspect, but he'd become, overnight, the band's de facto manager; once again the class prefect, only now the stakes were enormous.

Faithfull can be seen beaming in footage from Hyde Park, but it's misleading. Convinced that she'd seen a premonition of Jones' demise, she was unraveling mentally as fast, if not faster than even he did. After seven months of pregnancy, they lost their unborn daughter. "The miscarriage did both of us in," she has said. Faithfull indicates that Mick seemed to handle the tragedy better than she did. As he had when Robert Kennedy was shot, Mick the songwriter and band leader simply worked his way through it. The unhappy event even found its way into his lyrics. While Donald

Cammell was editing *Performance*, Mick was finishing its musical centerpiece, "Memo from Turner," without any input from Keith. "The baby's dead, my lady said," became a part of the song's chilling, closing line.

Her own musical career had stalled in the years following the Redlands bust. Frustrated by the prospect of spending eternity as Miss X, the woman with the Mars bar (or at best, a sexual and creative second banana to Mick), she was, by '69, easing her pain over the miscarriage and frustration with her standing with smack. It worked faster and more completely than the pills and liquor that she'd initially turned to. Heroin use had gone quickly from an acceptable dalliance among the decadent Chelsea scene to a full-blown habit. Still recognizable as the angelic ingénue of "As Tears Go By," she had, spiritually, become a harder, darker creature entirely, one who'd come to resent her role as the already indelible Stones myth. "Being the kept plaything of a great rock star wasn't my destiny," she would later confess. To this day, Faithfull bristles at her inability to escape the larger Stones myth. When I spoke to her for *Vanity Fair*'s site, she complained, "Most of it's lies. It's the tabloid version of me. And that's just not me. You know that. If you know my work, you must know that. It hasn't been good for my career at all. What was good for it was 'As Tears Go By' and 'Sister Morphine,' but the tabloid aspect was not good and that's how I'm remembered unfortunately by thousands of people. As ex-girlfriend of Mick Jagger, blah blah blah."

At the time, like Pallenberg, she selected a handful of film roles designed to carve out some kind of submyth within the Stones' universe, a cinematic identity to afford her some independence and self-respect. *Girl on a Motorcycle*, one of these films, is certainly kitschy—one of those '60s fetishes that's best left to a dorm room wall—but its theme, tone, and script articulated Faithfull's real-life frustration. She stars as the titular "Girl," a sexually frustrated wife of a professor. At night, while he sleeps, she creeps out of bed naked, zips herself into a skintight leather one-piece suit, and rides the countryside straddling a snorting hog and recalling a tryst with the French film icon Alain Delon, who is almost as pretty as she is. Full of blunt innuendo (the nozzle of the gas pump going slowly into the open cycle tank), pop philosophy ("Rebellion is the only thing that keeps you alive"), and pulpy come-ons ("Your body is like a violin in a velvet case"), it somehow manages to capture Faithfull's fragile, emotionally hemorrhaging state and flirtation with death (motor girl indeed meets her maker in the windshield of an oncoming pickup, James Dean style).

She also appeared in a London production of Chekhov's *The Three Sisters* and starred as the doomed Ophelia in *Hamlet*, hitting her marks and reciting her iambic pentameter while smack ingested backstage coursed through her bloodstream. She, too, had become bad news, only Mick could not bring himself to leave her. He still adored her and hoped to start a family. He'd had a happy childhood and as he grew older and the decadence started to feel repetitive, he'd fostered a strong urge to become a parent and lavish the same love, care, and wisdom on his progeny that Joe and Eva did on him and his brother. But he couldn't get Marianne to clean up.

There was no culture of intervention in 1969. Drugs were still seen as tools for enlightenment, and as a consequence, rock stars and artists would soon be dying left and right: Hendrix, Joplin,

Morrison . . . Jones. Unable to save his lover, Mick turned his tension inward and channeled his emotions into the Stones, using modern blues and little else as a catharsis. "I'm a flea-bit peanut monkey!" Mick would write in "Monkey Man," another key track from this fertile period. "All my friends are junkies!" It was true in spades and it was starting to suck out all the fun of being a star. "I don't find it easy dealing with people with drug problems," Mick told *Rolling Stone* in 1995. "It helps if you're all taking drugs, all the same drugs. But anyone taking heroin is thinking about taking heroin more than they're thinking about anything else. That's the general rule about most drugs. If you're really on some heavily addictive drug, you think about the drug, and everything else is secondary. You try and make everything work, but the drug comes first."

Faithfull's son with John Dunbar, Nicholas, was now in school. Mick had come to consider the boy a part of his own family, and leaving Faithfull would be tantamount to losing touch with her son as well. Hoping some time outside of London might be helpful, they kept their plans to fly to Australia for the *Ned Kelly* shoot (Faithfull had been cast by director Tony Richardson as Kelly's beloved sister). It would be a working vacation, a getaway from the scene, and the specter of Brian Jones. This was the fresh start they needed at the close of a tumultuous decade. Jones' ghost would not be calmed, however. That very night, jet-lagged and sedated, Marianne Faithfull attempted to join Brian Jones in the abyss. She woke up and went to the bathroom in their hotel room, stared at herself in the mirror, and imagined she saw Brian staring back at her. "Welcome to Death," the fallen Rolling Stone supposedly greeted her. She kept swallowing pills to calm her nerves, and after a point, she knew she was taking a potentially fatal amount, but did not stop. She lay down to go to sleep and in her dreams, she was walking with Jones through purgatory. "I had my overdose in Australia and that was the beginning of the end for Mick and me," Faithfull writes.

American-born Marsha Hunt, then twenty-three, was the face of British fashion in '69, all big brown eyes and a full afro. She was an actress and aspiring pop singer in addition to her career as a model, and had been romantically involved with a pre-glitter Marc Bolan. She was also, relative to Faithfull at the time, sane. Mick had noticed Hunt from a nude photo session she shot with David Bailey and sent word that she would be perfect as the model for the sleeve of the Stones' upcoming single "Honky Tonk Women." "The picture was going to be of a girl dressed like a sleazebag standing in a bar with the Stones and they wanted me to be the girl," Hunt writes in her memoir, *Real Life*. She had misgivings. "The last thing we needed was for me to denigrate us by dressing up like a whore among a band of white renegades, which was an underlying element of the Stones' image. I tried to get in touch with Jagger to say, 'Thank you, but no thank you.' He returned my call very late and suggested I come around."

When they met, Hunt was shocked to find Mick was not the cocksure rock star that his public image might have suggested. His complexion was bad, his hair dirty, and he seemed tired and undernourished. "To think that he was the same person who had such a wide-boy image intrigued me, because there was nothing of this wrangling poseur about him," she writes. Mick began an affair with Hunt while Brian Jones was still alive. She was at Hyde Park, famously clad in a white leather suit. Their affair was a secret carried out in Hunt's modest flat in St. John's Wood, but when Faithfull finally discovered it, she made sure that her revenge affair with Italian photographer Mariano Schifrino was public.

One day, while waiting for a shot to be set up, Mick, in period dress as the Victorian-era outlaw, stood in a field strumming his guitar, when he came up with a riff. He played it over and over and soon started writing lyrics. "Black pussy," they went. "How come you taste so good?" At first they made him laugh, but the riff was strong, and soon he was taking the song seriously, writing allegorical lyrics about the slave trade. He changed the title, a sort of double entendre addressed at Keith, Marianne, Anita, and all of his friends who'd willingly given up their lives to heroin: "Brown sugar, how come you taste so good?" It perfectly taps into the "Black Is Beautiful" zeitgeist but is politically incorrect and raw enough (even with the altered title) to keep with the Stones' new, hard model.

As with integrated relationships, planned parenting between unmarried young men and women was also popular at the end of the decade, and Mick and Marsha Hunt were certainly in vogue as they discussed the idea of conception, but once it was too late, Mick found himself torn. This was a classic rebound situation following his serious relationship with Faithfull, after all. "He vacillated between approval and disapproval of the oncoming birth," Hunt recalled. "It was too late for reconsideration, as I reminded him, but it alerted me for the first time that he was already forgetting that the baby was his idea." Mick would question whether or not the child was his, ordering a paternity test. Following the baby's birth (a girl named Karis), Hunt would take him to court for failure to pay child support. Eventually he settled into the role as loving and available father, but at the time, love and availability were met with suspicion and aloofness. He'd been hurt badly.

America had changed in the three years since the Stones had last toured the country. It was hungrier for more substantial distractions after assassinations and nightly footage of the Vietnam War. The business changed as a result. During their early British Invasion tours, all the band had to do was make it to the venue on time, play twenty minutes, and collect their pay. The white noise of fifteen thousand screaming girls drowned out the P.A.s that couldn't really overpower them anyway. Now they had to actually perform for two hours and the crowd could hear every botched note or missed cue, every breakdown of time: everything that made them less than perfect. "It was like learning how to play again," Richards recalled.

Once the darlings of the underground press, they were now under fire for the price of their tickets, as they tried to replenish their purloined fortunes. The pressure from all sides was enormous as they prepped a return to the road, while continuing to record and mix *Let It Bleed*, their follow-up to *Beggars Banquet* due out around the Christmas season. If it failed, the Stones could have easily become, for all their talent and charisma, a band of the '60s, buried in time like the Beatles, who only made it a few months into the '70s before breaking up.

The band convened in Southern California in October after Mick's Australian experience shooting *Ned Kelly* and splitting with Faithfull. They piled into a rented Laurel Canyon mansion called "Oriole House." The property belonged to Stephen Stills, late of Buffalo Springfield and now a member of Crosby, Stills and Nash (who'd played Woodstock). They rehearsed in the Oriole House basement but the set didn't come together. "We'd been in America for two weeks and although everyone realized the band wasn't in good shape, no one had actually played together yet," tour manager Cutler later wrote in his memoir, *You Can't Always Get What You Want*. Sensing some urgency, they moved operations to a soundstage at Warner Brothers studios in Burbank to rehearse in an environment more like the giant venues they were now filling. The stage had been used in the upcoming Sydney Pollack film *They Shoot Horses, Don't They?* starring Jane Fonda, and the dance-contest clock still hung above as if to remind them that they didn't have forever to find the magic.

"The Rolling Stones have always in a sense been in danger of imploding," Cutler writes. "They always sound rocky to begin with and then they struggle through the barriers together and end up making amazing music. They are the most human of bands, one can sense them holding it together—just. It's something I've always loved them for, their 'vulnerability' as a band and their musical courage when you can sense them struggling and working their butts off to make the music happen."

From L.A., the band flew to Colorado to launch the tour. The lights went down, the group, featuring Taylor and new sax man Bobby Keys (who'd first met the Stones during the state fair circuit of their debut U.S. tour in '64), began to take the stage. Just then, Cutler—an archetype of the decadent but loyal rock and roll road companion of the pre-corporate era, got on the microphone and spontaneously announced, "Ladies and gentlemen, the greatest rock and roll band in the world, the Rolling Stones." Keith strummed out the chords to "Jumpin' Jack Flash," and with that the Stones were back. But were they really the greatest rock and roll band in the world? Was that a prudent thing to say just before their first U.S. date in three years, and after the shambolic set in Hyde Park?

After the show, Mick Jagger found Cutler and asked for a word. "We have to talk," he said. "Sam when you're introducing the band, please don't call us the greatest rock and roll band in the world." Cutler, without missing a beat, shot back, "Well either you fucking are or you ain't. What the fuck is it gonna be?"

"At first Mick hated this phrase," Cutler would later tell me, "but after a while he seemed to mellow with it and accept it. I think he enjoyed rising to the challenge!"

Mick contemplated this in silence and skulked off deep in thought. "I think that Mick simply thought initially that it was an absurdist claim. Hyperbole run amok, which it was, but then I think he thought, 'Well it's a hell of a job title, but someone's gotta have it, so why not us,' and then he set out to claim the title for his own," Cutler says. Each following night on that tour, when the lights went down, he would introduce the band the same way, and by the tour's end, Mick stopped correcting him. The Stones were in a groove; they were proving it. Everyone figured the tour's final date in San Francisco would be the pinnacle of their career.

What people don't really talk about when they talk about Altamont is just how sad it was. They say "tragic," but really it's just sad: sad for the Hells Angels, sad for the Rolling Stones, sad for rock and roll and its fans to this day; the specter of Altamont *still* hangs, forty-two years later, over live rock concerts from the most intimate bar back room to the Stones' 2006 concert on Rio's Copacabana beach (for a live audience of more than one million). It's the reason every large venue is teaming with cops and every small club has security standing in front of the stage with walkie-talkies. "It will always be something for critics of rock and roll to use," legendary San Francisco promoter Bill Graham wrote in his memoir. "You can't let all these people gather here for a concert. They may hurt each other. Look at Altamont." It was saddest of all, obviously, for the friends and family of Meredith Hunter, aka Murdoch, the eighteen-year-old kid who was murdered under the stage as the Rolling Stones played for three hundred thousand people. If he'd gone to see *Bob and Carol and Ted and Alice* instead that weekend, there's a chance Meredith Hunter would be turning sixty years old in October of 2011. As it stands, he is forever eighteen, forever clad in a horrible lime green suit, matching hat, and black, silk, ruffled shirt. The facts of Altamont are well-known. As with the Blind Faith concert in Hyde Park in July, the three-day Woodstock Festival in August was credited with taking rock and roll and youth culture into previously uncharted realms. Rock and roll had become a massive concern, a hugely powerful and influential force, and the Stones, who did not play Woodstock (their rivals for the "world's greatest" title, the Who, turned out a memorable set), wanted to show that they could control that force, bend it to their will. They wanted a Woodstock of their own. Yes, it was an ego trip, as many of the critics of the Stones pointed out in their coverage of the event. *Rolling Stone* magazine called it "the product of diabolical egotism, hype, ineptitude, and money manipulation." But it was also a classic case of peer pressure. They dispatched their team, including flamboyant local lawyer and television personality Melvin Belli (who is *Gimme Shelter*'s sorely needed comic relief as he plays to the camera in his oversized spectacles), to set about looking for an appropriate venue in San Francisco to host it.

San Francisco's Golden Gate Park was chosen for obvious reasons: it was the global epicenter of hippie culture, right in the middle of a major city, guaranteeing the band the attention they wanted. But it was also a way for the Stones to tell the people that they were still in touch with the street; they hadn't crawled into the bubble and isolated themselves from their brothers and sisters. *Rolling Stone* was founded and is still based in the city. The magazine's cofounder and *San Francisco Chronicle* music journalist Ralph J. Gleason had strafed the band in the newspaper for their then high ticket prices and advised that if they were really a people's band, they would do a show for free. Remember, Woodstock had only become a free concert after tens of thousands of fans crashed the gates. The Stones would do one better: They would conceive and execute the Golden Gate Park show as a symbol of brother- and sisterhood, of peace and harmony, and, most of all, of love for their fans (who Gleason felt were being treated with contempt). It was unavoidably a loud, long photo op for counterculture cred restoration. The true questions were: How much did Mick believe it? Was he using "love your brother" as a gesture to buy off the press, who, at the time, the Stones were certainly not invulnerable to? He certainly kicked the tires of the '68 revolution before deciding it wasn't for him. But in Stanley Booth's breathtaking account of the '69 tour, *True Adventures of the Rolling Stones,* he talks about Mick requesting that someone find him mescaline for a planned postshow trip. He wanted to come down from the high and think about what had just happened, what it had meant, how it had furthered humankind. You mustn't take the philosopher and the searcher out of the Mick equation, even though it's now become routine to do so. He was certainly warned against examining the possibility of people coming together to be "as one." Graham, for one, claims to have warned them, "You can't do a free concert. Not without planning. As big as you are, you can't do a free show. Free was the dangerous word." But "free" was the only word that mattered as far as the Stones' image and possibly Mick's ideals were concerned.

The city eventually nixed the idea of giving up the park for fear of rampant damage and liability, so the high-concept, long, loud photo op began leaking air as it began its sad troll toward finding a host. It was briefly to be held at the Sears Point Raceway, and finally found a taker at the Altamont Speedway, twenty miles outside of the city. Unlike Hyde Park and Woodstock, Altamont was mostly concrete. It was a cold place, not conducive to the kind of crowds they'd expected, impossible to police, and most readily accessible only via helicopter should disaster happen to strike. Altamont had been a place for gambling, and the Stones took a big one on it. They had reason to be confident. Michael Lang, the promoter who'd pulled off Woodstock, a hippie with an uncanny knack for logistics, was on board, as were local heroes Jefferson Airplane and the Grateful Dead, whose manager, Rock Scully, suggested they bring in the local chapter of the Hells Angels to protect the expensive stage gear and crucial power generators and create a practical yet counterculture-appropriate barrier between the band and their fans. There had been Angels at the Hyde Park show. The English chapter was remarkably polite. It seemed like a good idea at the time, as they say . . . The Angels were hired, according to legend, for "five hundred dollars worth of beer."

There are some who say that the band set the Angels up to be the bad cops. Mick, after all, refused any police intervention or escort for fear of being seen in the company of the local police (still regarded as "pigs" by the counterculture). When he was punched in the face by a crazed fan upon first surveying the crowd at Altamont, he made sure the kid (who'd shouted "I hate you!") was unharmed. That the Angels, equipped only with a scattering of weapons (pistols, knives, sawed-off pool cues) would have been able to somehow control what was fast becoming a crush of humanity, many of them surging on shitty West Coast speed (an autopsy of Hunter found meth in his bloodstream) and very bad acid (that some, like Sam Cutler himself, according to his memoir, claim was leaked into the population by a government agency to discredit the hippie movement) was evidence of an utter lack of thought rather than a scheme. The Angels, in their leather jackets, were, despite their strength in numbers, not invulnerable to fear and panic and adrenaline surges . . . and quick, sometimes bad, decision making. Throw in a very long wait for the Stones to come onstage (the reason for the holdup is yet another element of the eternal "Who is to blame" debate) and you have a perfect storm. Those attending Altamont were a lot of things; white, black, free, repressed, rich, poor. What they weren't, not for one second, was cool. "Woodstock was a bunch of stupid slobs in the mud," the inimitable Grace Slick once said. "Altamont was a bunch of angry slobs in the mud."

The footage of the murder itself has become rock's Zapruder film. Hunter, in his garish green duds, is easy to spot in the crowd. He licks his lips, a classic speed-user move. His girlfriend, a fair-haired teen named Patti Bredahoff, seems equally agitated, trying and failing to calm him down. Patti was a white girl. There are some who claim that the initial altercation with the Angels was racially motivated. Others say it was just random; wrong place/wrong time. Hunter clearly draws a revolver. You can see it, famously, against Bredahoff's light crocheted dress. Was he telling the Angels to back off? Letting them know they weren't dealing with a punk? Was it self-defense? Or was it, as Rock Scully claimed, the product of a kid insane on speed and intent on doing some damage? "There was no doubt in my mind that he intended to do terrible harm to Mick or somebody in the Rolling Stones, or somebody on that stage," Scully has said. Hunter doesn't stay alive long enough to clarify. The crowd quickly gyrates outward, creating a kind of bullring at the first appearance of the gun (Hunter's) and the knife (Hells Angel Alan Passaro's). Hunter appears to realize, way too late, that the skirmish between himself and the Angels has escalated and seems to try to flee as Passaro, then several other Angels, grab him and take him down for good. His last words, "I wasn't going to shoot you," indicate that perhaps it was all a bluff. It's impossible to watch footage of the murder without returning to that sadness. It wasn't antithetical to the '60s; Altamont was so . . . un–rock and roll. It empowered nobody, and this is the true collateral damage that affected the Stones' spirit even as it glamorized and darkened their rep. And so, 1969, an annus horribilis for Mick Jagger (despite releasing some timeless music), ended with another ghost straight out of Macbeth, which would circle him for the rest of his life. The day after Altamont, Mick and the band's new business manager, Prince Rupert Lowenstein, flew to Geneva to deposit the profits of the North American tour in a Swiss bank account. It was money that the alternative press considered highway robbery, and those outraged by the violence of Altamont considered blood money. The Rolling Stones had become both the greatest rock and roll band in the world, as Sam Cutler had so boldly declared, and not a rock and roll band at all. They were something else now; beyond rock and roll in a way, but also a little lost without it.

10

"The New Judy Garland"

"Some would say that Bianca Jagger is nothing but a creation of the media," Bob Colacello writes in his November 1986 cover profile in *Vanity Fair*. The Bianca Jagger that still lives in the public consciousness despite decades of activism and philanthropy on behalf of oppressed people from the Amazon to Afghanistan, her association with the International Red Cross, various green ventures, and her own Human Rights Foundation is often that media creation: decadent, gold-digging, shallow, a hag for the swish designers of the disco era. That Bianca Jagger is frozen in time atop a white horse, bareback in couture as she is led into Studio 54 by a naked man with a porn-star mustache. That Bianca sits astride a white horse. It's her birthday party. Despite centuries of "women on horseback" imagery and mythology, Jagger looks impassive, even bored by the spectacle. Her smile is faint, not broad. It's the lack of reaction that makes the image enduring, a great symbol of the disco daze. "If Bianca was mediagenic and muse appropriate in the time of disco," says author Anthony Haden-Guest, who chronicled the rise and fall of Studio 54 in his book *The Last Party*, "it was a combination of her own nature, at once opaque and hungry for attention."

Getting older is a bitch it's true, and you can't really begrudge someone for wanting to blur their vision with spectacle to avoid looking at the hard truths of growing up, but this was 1977. Down at CBGB, the grubby young punks were reinventing the music that Bianca's husband had made so exciting a decade and a half earlier, and here she was, the finale of a grand production number arranged by 54's owners, Steve Rubell and Ian Schrager, doing absolutely nothing. What did that Bianca do exactly, besides party and allow fashion designers to drape her skinny frame with new frocks?

Today of course, in an age of Hiltons and Kardashians, we can consider her fabulous idleness pioneering. Bianca was the first apparently tradeless celebrity. She was simply . . . Bianca, with a smear of red rouge on her full lips, draped in a Grecian dress, a regal shoulder bared and Halston or Andy Warhol whispering a bon mot into her bejeweled ear. She was, by now, one-name famous. But when combined with her husband, like Jack and Anjelica or Woody and Mia, she entered the zeitgeist with blunt force, leaving many confused and a few hostile. Jack Nicholson and Anjelica Huston were actors; they made films. Bianca flirted with the idea of becoming an actor but never did. Mick Jagger was an actor and a rock performer; he also was virtually managing the Rolling Stones operation the year that they met. Bianca was . . . what exactly? A very pretty vacuum with caramel skin, dark hair, dark eyes, a glamorously flat chest, a vaguely contemptuous bedroom gaze? The media that created her adored her, but everyone else injected resentment, jealousy, envy, and cattiness into that void. At first Mick suffered collateral damage, as did the Stones. What were they thinking?

But Bianca, as we will examine more closely a bit later, was likely part of a larger plan, one that would actually help the Stones in the bigger picture and carve a niche for them that a rougher-edged (if equally brilliant) band like Led Zeppelin could never hope to occupy. The arrival of Bianca Jagger, it should finally be said, made the Stones a little bit lame, sure—especially in an age of Patti Smith, Richard Hell, and Johnny Rotten, but like Marianne and Anita before her, she deepened them. Bianca gave the Stones a celebrity sheen and an air of high society that mixed very nicely with their nitty-gritty, torn, and frayed image and created, essentially, a brand-new rock and roll aesthetic. She marks the apotheosis of Mick's quest for a combination of high and low culture, penthouse and pavement. Studio 54, which would become their playground, was where sounds, fashions, and personalities from each echelon clashed in one sweaty clinch under neon. Unlike Marianne and Anita, Bianca is *still* not cool, and therefore never gets any credit for her crucial contribution to Mick's building of a '70s Stones model, only the lashing blame for exposing them to toxic celebrity culture. "Say what you will, but Mick did very well putting the Rolling Stones into this world of celebrity," says Peter Rudge, the band's Cambridge-educated road manager during this Bianca-guided phase. "It benefitted Keith, too. Now Keith could be the dark guy sitting in this world of celebrity-studded rooms, and that was fascinating to people. Mick knew it was. He knew the value of Keith being Keith. Now the band worked on many levels. It differentiated them from Page and Plant, Daltrey and Townsend, Roger Waters and David Gilmour [of Pink Floyd]—they lived completely different lifestyles to the Stones now."

The "real" Bianca Pérez-Morena De Macias was born into a well-to-do family in Managua, Nicaragua, in 1945. Her father was a wealthy businessman, but when Bianca was a child her parents divorced and Nicaraguan culture at the time didn't really protect the female divorcée. This is likely the nexus of Bianca's complex relationship with both wealth and austerity: the partying in night-clubs and the mercy missions to climates torn by war and natural disaster. She knew what it was like to have money but in an instant, money became an issue. It's also why she was initially flagged as an opportunist, after Mick's fortune.

"I saw how difficult life became for my mother from that moment on," she has said of her parents' divorce when she was seven. "And how my life changed as well. After having an easy life suddenly my mother had to work and suddenly my mother was treated completely differently. I saw the fate that women in countries like Nicaragua were condemned to have to be: second rate citizens. I didn't want to have the same future that my mother had."

Like Mick, Bianca had a great curiosity for how things worked: She read about economics, political hierarchies, and systems, having received a scholarship to the Paris Institute of Political Studies as a teen. By the late '60s she found herself in the London of protest marches and the waning psychedelic age. A fling with the actor Michael Caine placed her at the right parties, where her beauty and fierce intellect impressed. She knew Donald Cammell, the perverse director of *Performance,* as well as Turkish-born soul music impresario Ahmet Ertegün of Atlantic Records. Ertegün was, as the '70s began, very busy courting the Stones, as their deal with Decca had recently ended. They owed the label one final single after completing work on what would be their final Decca album, the live *Get Your Ya Ya's Out.* Mick offered the label an acoustic folk song with no hook and profane lyrics. The title was "Cocksucker Blues," taken from a chorus that asked: "Where can I get my cock sucked? Where can I get my ass fucked?" The label let the Stones go. They signed to Atlantic and hired Marshall Chess to head their own imprint, Rolling Stones Records. "They had a real problem," Chess says. "They were broke. It was fucked up. They didn't like their manager. Didn't like their label. There were many new acts that had been eaten up by barracudas in the business. [In the early '60s] no one thought it would explode like it did." Through his London social circles, Mick found a private banker, the aforementioned Prince Rupert Lowenstein, to completely restructure their finances. "He worked for a private merchant bank, Leopold Joseph and Sons [Ltd]," Chess says. "He was a virgin [as far as the music business went]. He'd never made a record deal." As with the launch of any venture, early plans for Rolling Stones Records were wildly ambitious, but it soon became apparent that the only real project was survival. "We were going to sign other artists to the label. We were negotiating with Hendrix— and then he died. He could have been our first artist. Then one day they called me into a meeting and said, 'We have no budget. We have this tax bill.' So I had to make a decision. It would be just about the Stones. And I loved it. Sex, drugs and rock and roll. It was fabulous."

Ertegün closed ranks around the band as well, determined to help them make the jump into the new decade as a viable rock and roll entity. Placing Bianca in Mick's life seemed to be part of this master plan, somehow. In addition to an unmatched ear for great music that led him to nurture the careers of Ray Charles, Aretha Franklin, Solomon Burke, Wilson Pickett, Eric Clapton, and Led Zeppelin, Ertegün was also a matchmaker who knew she would inspire Mick. Ertegün's father was the Turkish ambassador to various European nations as well as the United States. He knew how to work people and instinctively felt that Bianca and Mick, still smarting from Marianne Faithfull and his brief but eventful affair with Marsha Hunt, would make a good couple, not least of all because she was his virtual doppelganger. "When Mick first saw me, he had the impression he was looking at himself," Bianca recalled in 1974, three years into her marriage to Mick. "I know people theorize that Mick thought it would be amusing to marry his twin. But actually he wanted to achieve the ultimate by making love to himself." Like Marianne Faithfull before her, Bianca wasn't as initially impressed with Mick and, upon being introduced to him that March at the after-party following the Rolling Stones' sold-out show at L'Olympia in Paris, commenced playing hard to get. Again, as with Faithfull, Mick found this both a challenge and a turn-on. Bianca, then just twenty-one, attended the party with French record industry impresario Eddie Barclay, who'd worked with iconic chansons artists like Johnny Hallyday, Juliette Gréco, and Jacques Brel. The colorful mogul was more than twice her age. She was attracted to Mick, but well aware, like Marsha Hunt, of his reputation.

She turned down several lusty invitations to leave the party with him. He finally gave up, but as the tour moved on, he continued to pursue her via telephone, offering to fly her to the next venue in the next city on the tour. Bianca finally relented, convening with the band in Italy, and from that moment, they were inseparable. While Marsha Hunt was giving birth to Karis, Mick and Bianca were living together at his posh new estate outside of London, Stargroves, and plotting out their future. Bianca recently discovered that she, too, was pregnant.

When the media got word of Mick's new lover, and the baby on the way, they began to froth. "She was pregnant at the time of the wedding, and almost nothing was known about her background. That combination of scandal and mystery is sure to set the press aflame," Colacello wrote. The wedding reception was arranged in secret, with word sent hastily to various celebrities (Paul and Linda McCartney, Keith Moon of the Who, plus Mick's parents, who flew in from England on a chartered jet), and promises of secrecy requested, but it was likely all a ruse. The press hounds were hardly thrown off. Reporters choked the narrow streets and clashed with police. It was front-page news worldwide, a cultivated event: the first tabloid wedding of the new decade; a virtual debut for Bianca. It was not without wit. Bianca was dressed, like Mick, in virginal white, and the pair exchanged vows and rings to the theme from the hit film Love Story. The pageant was intended to lift Mick out of the increasingly common world of rock stardom and place him somewhere else entirely. "He'd settled himself down nicely as an international gossip column face," British journalist Nik Cohn writes. "To be photographed each time he got on a plane. He was seen at the theatre and opera, made friends in the very highest circles, and was responsible for establishing an entirely new vision of male beauty, based no longer on muscle or tan but on skinniness, outrageousness, belle-laide oddity. With the breakup of the Beatles, he became the most superstar superstar of all, after Elvis Presley, and media accepted him unquestionably as the oracle of all Western youth, to be consulted on whatever new issue might arise. Twelve months in a year, he traveled in search of amusement and got his face on front pages, haunted the smartest restaurants, guest starred at the choicest parties. Finally, he got married in St. Tropez and held a party for hundreds of beautiful-person guests, the assembled press of the world and the cream of the Rock establishment—a true Hollywood fantasia, at which he threw so many tantrums that his guests, half-admiringly, declared him 'the new Judy Garland.'"

Keith and Anita were aghast at the St. Anne's spectacle (which was followed by an opulent reception at the chic Café des Artistes). "It wasn't so much the marriage," Peter Rudge recalls; "it was the way Mick handled it. St. Tropez. Paparazzi. It was not the way they did things. Not the way Keith liked to be perceived." The very idea of a Rolling Stone doing something as bourgeois as getting married was anathema. As late as 1967, Mick was dismissing marriage as "all right for people who wash." Sure it was fine for Charlie and the older Bill Wyman, but it compromised all their hippie ideals of a new culture, a new political structure. Instead, Keith and Anita (who never married) now had to reckon with the Liz and Dick of rock and roll; recipients of cocaine as a wedding gift, and honeymooning on a yacht in Sardinia. Keith didn't hate Bianca, as Anita, who'd allegedly cast various black spells her way, initially did. He merely didn't get her. Four decades later, he writes in his memoir, still bemused about his inability to get her to laugh at a joke. He acknowledges being impressed by what Bianca would become; her campaigns for human rights get high marks from the elderly Keith, but the young pirate's style was cramped. He was unable to breathe for all the jet-fuel fumes.

By '71, the personal and cultural gap between Mick and Keith, begun on the set of *Performance* three years earlier, was even wider. They no longer kept the same hours, and a surplus of interlopers prevented either of them from enjoying any real fraternal intimacy. Keith had Anita, and Gram Parsons, the great southern aristocrat in a pills- and loose joints-bedazzled Nudie suit. And all three had heroin. Mick may have experimented with heroin at this time, wondering what the fuss was about, what had taken away his brother and creative partner, but he could do nothing about Parsons. Now permanently ensconced in the Stones' traveling retinue (following them on his own dime and constantly strumming and doping with his new best friend, "Keef"), Parsons made Mick beside himself with jealousy, according to Richards' memoir.

"I don't know that Mick was jealous of Gram," says Chris O'Dell, who worked for the band at the time (and later chronicled her life with the Beatles and Stones in her 2009 memoir, *Miss O'Dell*). "If anything, Mick might have disapproved of the fact that both Keith and Gram got so loaded! And it was probably more so when Gram was around."

Far too together to do smack (Mick's experimentation with heroin might have been nothing but a fact-finding mission: "What is this thing that's tearing me away from my brother?"), he almost perversely went as far in the other direction as possible—the land of cocktails and coke spoons, town houses and jets—as if to thumb his nose not just at Keith and Anita, but at the newly ruptured and exhausted Beatles. "Lennon and Jagger were seen as more intriguing figures than your run-of-the-mill hotel suite–trashing rock star," Anthony Haden-Guest says, "but Lennon disdained the attention so Jagger became the focus."

And Bianca was the ideal travel companion through this new demimonde. Flashbulbs didn't seem to blind her.

The arrival of Bianca also marks the moment the Stones ceased to be a truly British band. By the spring of 1971, Mick and his fellow Rolling Stones were permitted to spend no more than ninety days in England, lest they pay 90 percent of their income to the government. Lowenstein instructed the band to establish residency and begin work on the follow-up to *Sticky Fingers* in France.

There may be elements of racism or at least nationalism in the curiosity—and certainly the hostility—that was aimed at Bianca as packing ensued. Marsha Hunt would have probably suffered the same fate, even with her rock and roll credentials. Yoko Ono certainly did when she fell in love with John Lennon and "lured" him away from his white, English wife. "The press turned me into something I was not. They wouldn't accept the fact that Mick had married a foreigner. So from that moment on I was a bitch," Bianca told *People* in the mid-'70s. Bianca, a citizen of the world, was, however, at home in France, London, or New York, having left Managua as a teen to study and explore. She'd always intended to be a woman in power; she figured she'd become a diplomat or a film director. Instead she became the wife of a Rolling Stone. The power is the same, the means unusual. Mick's second daughter, Jade, born to Bianca, arrived in October of '71; her birth, like the wedding, generated pages and pages of tabloid coverage. The Stones were bigger than ever. The wedding, the children, the odd courtship and canny shunning and baiting of the tabloids, changed Mick Jagger and changed the nature of rock and roll.

With more people than ever before watching his moves, his fashion risks, and his creative decisions, it behooved Mick and the Stones to produce a masterpiece. By mid-1971, the band could not be less united in their task to do so. "I think [Bianca] has had a bigger negative influence on Mick than anyone would have thought possible," Keith has said. "Mick, Anita, and I used to go around an awful lot before he met Bianca. Mick marrying Bianca stopped certain possibilities of us writing together because it happens in bursts; it's not a steady thing. It certainly made it a lot more difficult to write together and a lot more difficult to just hang out."

Ultimately, marrying Bianca—marrying anyone at all for that matter—was perfectly in keeping with Mick's almost perverse unpredictability and determination to not be shackled to the rules of rock and roll like his ideologue partner. When questioned about the odd juxtaposition of being a raunchy rocker as well as a (for a time, anyway) happily married man, Mick gleefully quipped, "Everyone's life is contradictory, innit?"

11

"Infamous"

"The 1972 tour was the first great viral campaign," says Peter Rudge of the band's return to the North American touring circuit and to an infamousness that even the Stones of 1967 could not imagine. The lasting myths of '72 are largely due to a lengthy magazine article and a film project, both designed to document the tour, and both never officially released: Robert Frank's *Cocksucker Blues* (named after Mick's notorious contract-breaking would-be single) and Truman Capote's sequel of sorts to his classic *New Yorker* tour reportage, *The Muses Are Heard*. Frank's film was shelved. It's still never been formally viewed, although I don't know one Stones fan who hasn't seen the bootleg at least once. Capote's article, assigned by Jann Wenner, editor in chief of *Rolling Stone*, was never finished or published. Both have contributed immeasurable to the Rolling Stones' lasting notoriety, and both may have been manipulated into glamorous exile by Mick. "You let everyone know they *can't* see it or read it," Rudge says. "Mick got all that."

The Stones' arrival in America, eight years after their first landing at JFK, drew the kind of mainstream attention not seen since the early days of the British Invasion. "I can't even *remember* the Beatles," Mick told *Life* magazine in 1972. "It seems so long ago. That *was* another era." The three-year gap created a hunger to see them live. *Sticky Fingers*, which they did not tour in the States, had been a major hit. Stevie Wonder, then absolutely on fire, both creatively and commercially thanks to the chart-topping "Superstition" single, was going to open the shows. As with the "Would you let your daughter marry a Rolling Stone" scandal of '65, Mick's wedding to Bianca exposed him to people who didn't own a single rock and roll record. "The baby boomers were now getting older," says Robert Greenfield, then a *Rolling Stone* reporter who was embedded with the Stones for their 1972 American tour (Greenfield's account of the tour would produce the Stones-lit classic *STP*, or Stones Touring Party). "The band had not been in America in three years—an enormous amount of time in those years. Everything was changing so rapidly. All of a sudden the straight media has perceived the Stones as something that is newsworthy and legitimate. Their arrival in every city on that tour was front-page news." The tickets, assigned to those who presented postcards for a lottery, sold out instantly.

Harnessing this new media power and control that Mick and Keith's generation was now enjoying in their thirties was part of the band's 1972 campaign. Perhaps Elvis was more famous and Elton John and Led Zeppelin sold more records, but in '72, nobody in rock and roll would court more media attention than the Rolling Stones; simply put, it was the year that the Stones opened their doors to the mythmakers. "This is their just desserts. They're more than happy to do the publicity, do the interviews. You can't have all these media guys on tour without them giving them access, which they did," Greenfield says. "They'd hired Gibson and Stromberg, the rock and roll publicity firm; they were traveling with their own press corps. Every magazine was there. Ken Regan and Annie Leibovitz taking photos. I'm there for *Rolling Stone*. The world has changed and the Rolling Stones are now crossing over into show biz. They're it. Ahmet Ertegün and Marshall Chess are behind the scenes engineering everything he can to make the band as big as possible. And then Jann brings Truman on board."

Like the Stones, Capote was a commercial phenomenon as well as a genuinely edgy property. This wasn't exactly Rona Barrett or some other lightweight entertainment reporter coming out to tag along. "It was a fusion," manager Peter Rudge recalls. "Although we attracted the so-called celebrities, they were in their own right counterculture celebrities. These were not people considered mainstream culture or who were regarded by middle America as thoroughly good people. Robert Frank. Truman Capote. There was a like-mindedness. They had the same principles. The same references." The straight media's attention, if anything, gave the Stones a harder ride across America. Even more people knew they were coming to town, and the local police forces and hotel managers prepared in advance. Entire floors needed to be booked in order to guarantee any kind of lodging at all. Transporting drugs was a constant challenge. They were, as Keith describes them in *Life*, a "pirate nation." "The manifestation of evil to many people," Rudge says. "They wanted to lock your daughters up. The police harassment, trying to find a hotel to take us, they genuinely didn't understand what we represented."

Capote, however was the wildcard. His classic 1957 *New Yorker* profile of Marlon Brando, "The Duke in His Domain," did more than anything to puncture the myth of the lean, beautiful, mumbling star who'd changed the way Hollywood actors operated. Brando was furious with "The Duke in His Domain," which depicted the star heavier, with thinning hair and a slew of neuroses, binging on apple pie in a lonely Japanese hotel room. Surely Capote would turn this same unsparing, unsentimental eye on the Stones. How could they possibly benefit from letting him in? And what would the Stones really offer someone like Capote? Unlike the Stones, who were, with the release of the double album *Exile on Main Street*, at the top of their powers, the literary hero shined brightest a decade earlier. The 1970s were not shaping up to be kind to him, with blown deadlines, creative blocks, drink and drugs, and depression. He was in trouble. He needed real material, not more folly; but the less-disciplined Capote could not resist. The two forces were drawn together by a stronger pull. "I'm gonna give you the answer in two words: star fucking—it's an interesting concept and it occurs at the highest level," Greenfield says. "Mick certainly knew who Truman was." Jagger was willing to take the risk of being exposed, because even a debunking would put him in the same strata as a Marlon Brando or Marilyn Monroe, and 1972 was all about posterity. "I think Mick was fascinated by them and they were fascinated by him," says Chris O'Dell.

Capote was a friend of Ertegün as well as Andy Warhol, who'd designed the cover for *Sticky Fingers*. He was bemused, if not by the Stones, certainly by the attention of the magazine editor. "Wenner kept sending me these telegrams about it," Capote remembered later in an interview with Andy Warhol for *Rolling Stone*. "And then I just sort of thought 'Oh well,' and then I just got kind of caught up in it."

Wenner assigned photographer Peter Beard, husband of Capote's best friend, air kissing princess Lee Radziwill (sister of Jackie O.), to shoot the tour, and after premiering in *Rolling Stone*, it would be released as a splashy book.

Capote could not have concocted a better opportunity to reintroduce himself in the 1970s. He wouldn't even be the only dissolute writer in the touring party. Capote would convene with the Stones' touring party in New Orleans and chronicle the goings-on at the venue, at the hotel, and aboard the band's converted DC-7, aka the Lapping Tongue, as it was emblazoned with the new Rolling Stones Records logo. The idea was to do a modern version of *The Muses Are Heard*, Capote's book-length 1956 *New Yorker* piece on the Everyman Opera Company's mounting of Gershwin's *Porgy and Bess* in Moscow.

The notion that Capote might have ever repeated such a heroic piece, much less in his older and dissipated state, was optimism of the highest level. But he certainly did have a history of mining the best detail from a chaotic entourage. The Everyman party had contained, according to *The Muses*, "fifty-eight actors, seven backstage personalities, two conductors, assorted wives and office workers, six children and their school teachers, three journalists, two dogs, and one psychiatrist." Not to mention the American State Department and Russia's Ministry of Culture. Surely a few British rock stars, their girlfriends, a traveling physician, some roadies, security guards, a film crew, and a few other literary titans wouldn't be too much for him.

William S. Burroughs was going to cover the tour, but those plans fell through; still, if Capote's famous photographic memory failed him or he needed to bond with a fellow famous journalist, there were others to pick up the slack. Novelist and screenwriter Terry Southern, Keith's erstwhile drinking buddy, was embedded with the Stones as well, covering the tour for the *Saturday Review.* "Terry Southern became a Rolling Stone that week," Rudge recalls. "The Stones actually let people come in and live the same life that they did. And they got caught up in it." For Capote, the '60s were a much kinder decade to him, and by the '70s, his health and business affairs had begun to deteriorate. He was mired in hipster speak, almost a caricature of the sharp cultural satirist he'd been in the previous decade. And everything was being recorded. Robert Frank, the Swiss photographer and filmmaker who'd designed the cover sleeve for *Exile on Main Street,* was also traveling on the tour, shooting everything, including, famously, the "plane fuck," for a proposed documentary, which would never be released officially but would enjoy a long life as the cult bootleg *Cocksucker Blues.* Frank, like Rolling Stones Records president Marshall Chess and Capote, had a great pedigree as a chronicler of America; famous for shooting the beat film *Pull My Daisy* and publishing the landmark photo book *The Americans,* which, according to Kerouac, captured "that crazy feeling in America when the sun is hot on the streets and music comes out of the jukebox." Frank seemed to approach it with an immigrant's sense of work ethic.

Mick, more erudite than most knew at the time, was honored

and flattered that artists and socialites would be following the Stones around as they did their thing. "Ahmet Ertegün understood the power of celebrity," says Rudge, "the power of the media, and he also knew how much it attracted Mick." It seemed too good to be true . . . and it was.

Capote met the tour in New Orleans and immediately feted Mick with an elaborate dinner, assuming the role of hometown host even though he'd not lived in New Orleans for decades. Once the heady mix of drink and anticipation faded, the author sensed he'd made a mistake. Capote, who had seen plenty of examples of fame changing people the closer they got to it, was bored and depressed by the Stones' entourage, cavorting and mugging for the cameras as if they were as interesting as the band themselves. "I was twenty-six years old and really conscious of not ever wanting to be part of the movie—and I don't mean the documentary; I mean the 'movie,'" Robert Greenfield says. There was playacting going on at every stop, rock stars and their retinue mugging for the cameras and building a myth for the new world. "That famous photo of Keith posing in front of a sign that said KEEP AMERICA DRUG FREE," Rudge says; "that wasn't by accident."

Capote, it was inferred by every sour look, had seen this movie before. He'd done decadence first and had done it better, from his persistence in Kansas, covering the murder of the Clutter family (immortalized in *In Cold Blood*) to his famous Black and White Ball at the Plaza Hotel, during the initial rise of the Vietnam conflict. And here they were, the war still going on, Nixon in the White House, jetting across the country with their own doctor, entire floors of hotel rooms closed off, two former policemen hired as security guards vetting everyone, an endless supply of pharmaceutical cocaine, and cameras everywhere. Capote alone found it depressing and decided, before informing anyone, that he would never write this story. Like a numb sleepwalker, he kept on with the trajectory, sharing hotels with the band but retiring early, and making sure that everyone around him was aware of his displeasure. "We didn't get along," Marshall Chess recalls. "You know how you meet people in your life who just don't rub you right? He was so queeny. Overly queeny. He had a horrible, queeny, bitchy attitude from the moment he came on tour."

"Truman got a little intimidated at a certain point," Rudge recalls. "It was quite wild—and got quite loud late at night. He wasn't young. He thought 'It's three in the morning and people are still going crazy. It's not somewhere I feel comfortable.'"

Worse, the question of why exactly to write this piece became an issue. The way Capote saw it, there were stakes when it came to *The Muses Are Heard*: It was a genuine cultural exchange in which changing notions of eroticism, race, and popular music on both sides provided rich material. The Stones' tour of '72, unless you were twenty-five and strung out, just seemed like a long, sloppy party. This, the crestfallen writer soon realized, was merely decadence, and more of that was not what he required.

The Stones didn't know what to make of Capote either. Only their brawny Texan sax player Bobby Keys seemed to charm him. Sensing perhaps his dispassion, Keith would sometimes try to rile him, pounding on his door one night, inviting him up to a party. "Keith said, 'Oh come out we're having a party upstairs,'" Capote recalled years later in a *Rolling Stone* interview. "'I'm tired, I've had a long day and so have you, and I think you should go to bed.' 'Aw, come to it and see what a rock group's really like.' 'I know what a rock group's really like Keith, I don't have to come upstairs to see,' and apparently he had a bottle of ketchup in his hand. He had a hamburger and a bottle of ketchup and he just threw it all over the door of my room."

Answered Prayers, the purported follow-up to *In Cold Blood*, was already taking on the legend of a great lost work, and Capote knew the ramifications of failing to complete yet another piece. When asked about *Answered Prayers* during the late '60s, Capote, no longer the fire-eyed, spry terror he'd been in the '50s and early '60s, would sigh heavily and inform them it was "two-thirds" done. Some rumored it hadn't been one word written. Based on the sensation of *In Cold Blood* and the hit film version of his novella *Breakfast at Tiffany's*, 20th Century Fox had snatched up the film rights. Now they were asking for their advance (reportedly two hundred thousand dollars) to be returned. Out on the road with the Stones, the writer responded to the building pressure by slowly growing as mean as a snake. "He was loaded," Greenfield says. "Nobody knew this, but he was taking prescription drugs. At first he couldn't get close enough on the tour, he was all atwitter, but he definitely became one of the most mean-spirited people I've ever met in my life—nasty about everybody."

Capote was two decades the twenty-eight-year-old Mick Jagger's senior, not of the rock and roll era, but he liked what he called "beat music." One might expect him to be impatient with the rock star. Jagger, after all, played at being a southerner; Capote was the real thing.

Jagger played at being gay. Capote was one of the few true celebrities of the era who was out of the closet. More likely, Capote understood what Mick was offering too well to work up any interest in unraveling a second layer. He, too, after all, had become famous in his very early twenties; the dust jacket photo for his first book, *Other Voices, Other Rooms*, created a minor scandal, as it showed Capote, beautiful and androgynous and haughty, much like the young Mick. The Capote portrait was shot by Cecil Beaton, who years later found *himself* fascinated by Mick. He would photograph Mick and paint his portrait in the late '60s.

Capote, with his thinning hair and booze-doubled chin, would stare at Mick Jagger in his blue eye shadow and sometimes merely see that youthful hauteur evaporating. They were, in a way, both navigating a vulgar age they didn't really understand anymore.

Mick was an actor, he determined. "One of the most total actors that I've ever seen," he'd later tell Andy Warhol. "He has this remarkable quality of being absolutely able to be totally extroverted. Very few people can be entirely absolutely altogether extroverted. It's a rare, delicate, strange thing. Just to pull yourself out and go—wham! This he can do to a remarkable degree—but what makes it more remarkable is that the moment it's done, it's over."

By the time the tour hit New York on the eve of Mick's twenty-ninth birthday that July, Capote's commitment to the gig was over as well. You can see a lack of warmth when he enters the backstage area with Radziwill in *Cocksucker Blues*. The idea of some kind of synergy of legends quickly proving to be a huge flop, Mick cooled to Capote as well. He had other, more practical concerns, after all. Mick was doing lots of good coke daily (you can see him snort a rail in *Cocksucker Blues*). He was on edge, indulging in fears of assassination, both abstract (the zeitgeist, shootings, politically motivated everywhere) and concrete (the Hells Angels took a post-Altamont hit out on him). "We had a doctor come on tour to keep any of us alive if we were shot onstage. We had a specialist travel with us, carrying a big suitcase."

After years of touring, Mick had also suddenly developed an anxiety about flying. "I remember flying with him and when the plane took off, he'd tell me, 'This is the power turn. It's the most frightening part.' He wasn't phobic, but a bit nervous about it." He couldn't hold Capote's hand and stroke his ego. It was bad enough having to follow Stevie Wonder every night.

S.T.P. ended with a sold-out engagement at Madison Square Garden and a posh after-party at the St. Regis Hotel (attended by Bob Dylan, Dick Cavett, and Tennessee Williams). After the tour wrapped, the Stones flew to France. Capote retreated to Sagaponeck to sort through his notes and see if he might complete something. Drinking, staring at the ocean, trying to get inspired. The abortive piece had a title: "It Will Soon Be Here." It was the title of a painting Capote had liked depicting a rural family preparing for an oncoming storm. According to Capote's biographer, Gerald Clarke, "The title had an ironic symbolism. In the twentieth century, things had been so turned around that instead of rushing from the storm the Stones and the chaos they represented—the young descendents of those god-fearing farmers were running toward it—despite to be engulfed in the maelstrom." He'd appeared on Johnny Carson, where he contemptuously referred to the Stones as "the Beatles." The quip that Mick was "about as sexy as a pissing toad" took on a life of its own, but privately Capote was again unable to produce. He finally telephoned Wenner to tell him that he wouldn't be submitting the story. "I hadn't really made up my mind. I had all the material there, and it was sitting there and it was bothering me and I kept thinking, 'Well it would be so easy really to do it.' Finally the time came that just made up my mind that I wasn't going to do it and I just told him." It's truly our loss that Capote was never able to apply his great gift for presenting physical detail, dialogue, and pretense to another lengthy feature. Reading the minutia present in *The Muses Are Heard* ("he took off a pair of horn-rimmed glasses and polished them with a handkerchief") provokes an almost painful sense of lament when one thinks of what could have been.

Seven years later, in 1979, *Rolling Stone* sent Warhol to interview his friend for an extensive feature essentially about why he didn't write the piece. In that story, one line has more truth about the Stones than anything Capote could have penned: "I just don't know where it goes from here. Because I don't know where the Rolling Stones go from here. I don't know if that particular group and the particular thing that they do can go on for more than a year or two. I think Mick's whole career depends on whether he can do something else. I'm sure he'll go on. I just don't know in what area."

The Frank film had been shelved as well, some of the footage surfacing two years later in the quadraphonic virtual concert event *Ladies and Gentlemen, the Rolling Stones*, which toured movie theaters in America in 1974. "Marshall Chess realized they'd never be able to release *Cocksucker Blues*—they already at that time couldn't get into three countries because of their drug bust—they didn't need any more problems you know—and to verify a lot of what people heard about the Stones—Marshall asked me if I could do anything with this footage," says director Rollin Binzer. "Robert is a wonderful guy and his vision was always sort of on the dark side."

The absence of any real scrutiny allowed the tour to pass into legend and ultimately fuel the Stones' bad-boy image without ever showing people any anticlimactic activity. Frank and his two-man crew shot every bit of onstage transcendence plus backstage debauchery, but, more tellingly, captured the crushing boredom of tour life as well. Yes, Keith Richards and Bobby Keys toss a TV over the balcony of the Continental Hyatt House in West Hollywood. Yes, Mick and the band play shakes and percussion instruments while a roadie lifts a naked girl up to his mouth aboard the band's jet, dubbed "the Lapping Tongue." But really it's the waiting, the ordering room service ("Do you have any apples? Blueberry?") and the hours before and after sound check that take up most of the road time. It's frequently not the drugs that cause bands to burn out, to overdose, to break up; it's all that waiting.

When talk show hosts inquired about his experiences on tour with the Stones, Capote, even deeper into his dissolution, made several damning remarks, and contemptuously referred to his subjects as "the Beatles," implying that all British rock icons were interchangeable. And yet, none of this would have been as damaging as a full-bore "The Duke in His Domain"–style feature; which might have genuinely tarnished the Stones' cool at a time when it was most crucial to solidify it. Is Mick Jagger responsible for this birth of viral culture; where scandal and novelty, even a failure to produce a work of art, gain more media traction than the art itself could have ever hoped to? And if so, why now? Did Mick somehow realize that the Stones, as the '70s progressed, were moving at jet-speed towards a creativity-compromised state where they would need all the help that they could get?

12

"The Ballad of a Vain Man"

Sometimes the difference between a hit single that will be played somewhere, on some radio station, every single day until the end of time, and a hit single that will almost never be played again once it slips from the charts is simply a matter of our continued ability to wonder about it. The most enduring hits are mysterious. We ask, "What is it about?" "Who inspired it?" Phil Collins "In the Air Tonight" jumps immediately to mind. They're pretty rare in pop. "You're So Vain," Carly Simon's No. 1 hit single from 1973 (and nearly forty years later, her signature tune) is one of these songs as well. It even sounds a little sinister if you break down its sonic components. The bubbling introductory bass notes, the result of studio bassist Klaus Voorman (a friend and favorite sideman of the now separated Beatles) limbering up his fingers.

The spitting of the muffled "son of a gun."

The strummed acoustic chords, perfectly rhythmic but sinister enough to avoid being coffeehouse folky.

The piano offering countermelody.

A gentle drum beat holding it all down.

Then the first verse, in which Simon, then only twenty-seven, sounds as world-weary as Fitzgerald's Nick Carraway as she watches her mystery subject walk into a cocktail party where all the female guests fantasize about being the one to take him home and win his heart: "And all the girls dreamed that they'd be your partner . . ." She repeats the last lyric for emphasis but it's unnecessary as the wistful "clouds in my coffee" bridge and the hear it once/know it forever chorus are about to power the ballad into eternity. Mick appears on the second verse, just after the guitar solo. The backing vocals are uncredited but unmistakably Mick Jagger's. "His voice cuts through like a shot," remarks Keith Altham. And this presence got the mystery going. "How did this relatively new artist manage to get Mick Jagger, the biggest rock star in the world, to sing on her album?" And from there listener's first wondered, "Is he the one who thinks the song is about him?" Had "You're So Vain" been half as beautiful and masterfully arranged and executed, it would still be a cause célèbre. But it also happened to be one of Mick Jagger's best vocal performances of the sometimes fallow early to mid-1970s.

This also marks the beginning of a long period where Mick first begins to wander from the Rolling Stones. Over the next decade and a half, he would record duets or add significant vocals to records by John Phillips (whose lost classic *Pay Pack and Follow* would also feature Keith Richards and Ron Wood), John Lennon (the funky bootlegged favorite "Too Many Cooks," recorded during a 1973 jam), Bette Midler, Michael Jackson, David Bowie, and Daryl Hall of Hall and Oates. Ten years into his career as a professional singer, Mick was the perfect singing partner. He knew what notes to hit and when to pull back.

Mick and Carly Simon were drawn to each other much in the same way that Mick was drawn to Bianca. People kept remarking that they looked alike.

"Apparently he'd seen a picture of me on my first album," Simon tells me. "I don't want to call it narcissistic but he was intrigued by that. That made him want to meet me."

Carly Simon was considered a new artist, but she'd been performing since the early '60s as one half of the family act the Simon Sisters. Raised at the northern tip of New York City, the privileged child of the publishing magnate Richard Simon of Simon and Schuster, she honed her perceptive lyrical skills at Sarah Lawrence. She knew the swinging London scene of the mid- and late '60s, living with British scenester Roger Donaldson in a flat on Portobello Road. When that relationship ended, she moved back to New York City and pursued opportunities in journalism before signing with Elektra Records at the height of the singer-songwriter era of the very early '70s. She had a brief affair with Cat Stevens, the muse for her first big hit, "That's the Way I've Always Heard It Should Be," and opened for Kris Kristofferson, whom she'd also been rumored to be involved with. Her second Elektra album, released in 1971, produced a classic in its own right, in the title track "Anticipation" (later a popular commercial jingle for Heinz ketchup). Jingles had actually been an early way for Simon to generate income, so she had an innate knack for getting to the salient point with speed and certainty that was uncommon among some of the more star-gazing figures of the early '70s singer-songwriter scene. "When you are writing about beef jerky you have to write about why beef jerky is so good," she says today. "I was less into the right side of my brain at that point."

Simon was performing and touring all over the country. Backstage after a show at Carnegie Hall, she met the talented but very troubled James Taylor, who was struggling with fame and heroin addiction. Watch Monte Hellman's existential West Coast car culture classic *Two-Lane Blacktop* for a taste of the quiet, haunted, all-American charisma of Taylor, who costars with Beach Boys drummer Dennis Wilson and the grizzled Warren Oates.

By the time she finally met Mick at the launch party for the Stones' "Brown Sugar" single in early May of '71, Simon and Taylor were an item. "I'd just fallen madly in love with James. Mick was married, therefore we were not in a position to have a relationship, but there was an attraction on both sides." Enlightened "open marriage" was part of the early '70s zeitgeist, but Simon was an old-fashioned type. "It was certainly not what I'm like at all. And not what James was like, or if he was he was careful not to tell me. I was extremely intrigued by the idea of meeting Mick Jagger and that he would want to meet me. It's not as if I was wrestling with anything but certainly it was a feature that I was a woman and Mick was a man. That was certainly a part of it."

Simon kept thinking about Mick in the period that followed. "It was a thrill for me to meet him. When you meet somebody who was an idol of yours, it's hard to remember that they go home alone too." Simon felt that she'd seen this Mick, a real guy with emotional depth, not just a symbol of the '60s. She was determined to find a venue in which to explore this and came up with the idea to interview him and pitched it to the editor of the *New York Times* Arts and Leisure section. "[Section editor Seymour Peck] said if Jagger was willing, it would be great," she told *Rolling Stone* two years later. "Somebody got in touch with Chris O'Dell and she got in touch with Mick, who really liked the idea. So I casually went out to L.A. and ended up hanging around there, waiting for Mick." Simon knew O'Dell through James Taylor and found it easy to set up a meeting with Mick. A bit more difficult was actually getting him in the room. She loitered in Los Angeles for nearly a week before Mick finally rang her and said he was in town. Mick was still living in the South of France and was too jet-lagged to discuss anything besides being jet-lagged. "We talked about how we both hated airplanes," Simon said. But there was a chemistry and the pair made plans to keep in touch.

By the time she and Mick met again, she felt they'd grown too close to entertain the idea of examining him journalistically but it would be a journalistic lyric that would bring them together and unite them for all time.

With her air of unspoiled privilege and cultural smarts, coupled with earthy clothes and long hair, Simon was an icon of early '70s femininity; smart, witty, talented, with a clear, ringing voice and a signature piano style, but most of all, a way with a pop lyric that was true, like a piece of Woody Allen dialogue: urbane affairs, deceptions, searching, vain and neurotic people with too much money and too much intelligence. Simon once opened for Woody during his nightclub years. But at heart she was a writer; a true journalist ironically; always writing, always taking detail at parties. She socialized with the elite and the glamorous but she also mentally recorded them; and by '72, following a party among the opera-attending elite in New York City, she had the sketching for "The Ballad of a Vain Man" (a check on Bob Dylan's 1965 indictment of a changing culture, "The Ballad of a Thin Man"). The song came together, like a great piece of writing, piecemeal over time. "There was a plot line that went through all three verses. This vain man does all these things that he can get away with. I had the chorus—'You're so vain, you probably think this song is about you,' a year before I had the song."

During a flight from Los Angeles to Palm Springs, she came up with the images of "clouds in my coffee," the only abstract bit of "You're So Vain." "I was sitting with a friend of mine on an airplane— and he was looking at the view. He pointed it out to me, 'You have clouds in your coffee.' I was always writing down great lines, the way a reporter might." Everything else is straight if occasionally adverb-happy reportage, and like a good journalist she never publicly revealed her source. Who, in his apricot scarf, inspired that first jot in the notebook?

Meanwhile the Stones were as shambolic as Simon was creatively on point. By the end of 1972's North American tour, Keith had tried and failed to clean up many times. Keith has written about turning to heroin to deal with the scrutiny and glare of being a Rolling Stone, and there was more scrutiny of the band than ever before. The early and mid-'70s would find Keith visited by tragedy after tragedy, which made kicking it for good even more difficult. He had time to clean up, but his increasing discomfort with the Stones' fame and tragic events, like the accidental overdose of Gram Parsons and the crib death of a son he and

Anita had named Tara, compelled him to remain in an opiate co-coon for much of the early to mid-'70s.

The Stones, still "exiles," moved operations down to Jamaica to attempt a new studio album (later released as *Goats Head Soup*) but finding the old magic became increasingly difficult. "I don't think Mick and Keith were getting together, sitting in a room with guitars," says Marshall Chess.

Mick would struggle with a track, only to abandon it and have Keith stagger in ten hours later, pick up his guitar, and produce a riff that would occasionally be the song's salvation (in the case of strong new material like "Coming Down Again" or "Heart-breaker"). But too often, these songs remained in the shallow end, smack riffs with tossed-off coked lyrics. "*Exile* may seem flawed compared to the albums that preceded it," Robert Palmer once observed, "but it sounds positively concise compared to the ones that followed. As Keith grew increasingly preoccupied with and sapped by his drug habit, and as Mick coped with his social re-sponsibilities and celebrity, the Stones' music seemed to unravel. Their next three albums—*Goats Head Soup* (1973), *It's Only Rock 'n' Roll* (1974), and *Black and Blue* (1976)—are actually a single, rambling work." When people play the resulting *Goats Head Soup* today (and to be sure, it divides fans; there are those who love it), they play it to achieve a groove. They seldom play it for the songs. They were not, as widely accused, sucking in the '70s. The trilogy that preceded their *Some Girls* return to form sounds great today, but they're personality records; "Stones" records. They're great because, like certain Jack Nicholson or Robert DeNiro films, the root artist is appealing and the work of art marks a fascinating time in pop history, not because they contain, as with their late '60s run, one killer song after another. They're *The Passenger*, or *New York, New York*, not *Five Easy Pieces* or *Taxi Driver*.

In '73, they'd become what they were never before: a band full of rich and famous people, not playing or writing as well as they used to, but looking perfectly decadent in their floppy hats. Worse, glitter rock, reggae, and krautrock were offering critics and real music fans something genuinely new. The Motown hit factory that provided all of their early material had moved from Detroit to L.A. and now released complex pop suites that the band could no longer compete with or even hope to cover. Peers like Stevie Wonder, David Bowie, and Marvin Gaye were eclipsing them with wildly ambitious and visionary releases that the Stones didn't even try to compete with.

"That's it, we've done it," Mick is quoted as saying at the close of the Stones blockbuster '72 live dates. "It was definitely the most celebrated and most talked about tour ever," says Chris O'Dell. "In some ways it was more the beginning of an era for touring. They set the bar and most bands followed. But perhaps it was the end of that crazy time. They seemed to settle a bit after that." The prospect of having to top the triumphs of '72 year in and out seemed like some hell ride for the pragmatic rock star. He sensed, given Keith's wretched state, that it simply could not be done. The band that he expected to last two years had lasted a decade and would now have to alter its standards. He was about to turn a very blunt thirty. Good would have to do. He still recognized great, however, when he heard it, and found himself attracted, more than ever, to those who seemed hungry.

Carly Simon was recording her third album, *No Secrets*, at

Air Studios in London. Richard Perry was producing. The major instrumental tracks for the album's centerpiece, now retitled "You're So Vain," were finished. Perry's friend and collaborator Harry Nilsson (Perry had the previous year made Nilsson's baroque pop hit *Nilsson Schmilsson*) popped in to contribute some backing vocals to the song. Nilsson was in the studio when Mick placed an impromptu call to his look-alike. "Mick said he was in the area and I said come over. He came over very fast." When Mick arrived and heard what Simon and Perry were up to, he wanted in and focused on Nilsson as a potential rival. "Mick does not want to let other people step on his territory," Simon recalls. "There's another rooster in the cage. He will come in and join the rooster and then probably oust him. God knows why I was considered the right hen to do this for." Initially, Mick joined Nilsson and Simon, but after three takes, a frustrated Nilsson said, "You guys clearly don't need me," and left. "Harry bowed out," Simon says, "probably because he wanted to have a drink or something." Although he's really only singing the chorus, Mick did his small part on "You're So Vain" with such conviction that he simultaneously suggested that he knew what it was like to be both the narrator and the subject of the track. His voice mingles with Simon's in a fashion that certainly recalls their sexual chemistry, but there's also great empathy there. "His part is fantastic," Simon remarks. "It's iconic. It brings the record over the line." Simon was so inspired by Mick's contribution that she later rerecorded her lead vocals.

Mick isn't credited on "You're So Vain" and has not discussed the track. "We talked about it," Simon says. "He thought it would be more interesting if he wasn't credited. It would add to the mystique." By 1972, a credit was not needed in order to inform the listener that Mick Jagger was on the track. Still, when Mick volunteered to sing backing vocals, the savvy self-promoter knew he would also be inserting his name into pop's own riddle of the Sphinx: the "Who exactly probably thinks this song is about them?" question. "A lot of people think it's about Mick Jagger and that I have fooled him into actually singing on it, that I pulled that ruse," Simon told *Rolling Stone* in 1973. "You're So Vain" is not about Mick Jagger. "He's excluded as a possibility," she tells me, simply because he is on the record. Mick is not the man in the apricot scarf. Still, a few hours in the studio forty years ago prompted millions to ask and continue to ask, "Did Simon carry on an affair with Mick?"

Bianca Jagger certainly thought so, placing a call to James Taylor the night before he and Simon were to marry and warning him, "My husband is having an affair with your wife." All these years later, Simon has not spilled the beans about the song's muse but swears there was no affair. "Bianca was really jealous but she had the facts wrong," she says. "She believed there was more between Mick and me than there was. She passed that information on to James the night before we were going to be married. James was wonderful. He knew that he trusted me and trusted my version of the story. That my relationship with Mick was purely musical. Unfortunately, there was an awful mistake that I made in my life at one point when James had hurt me very much. I retaliated by telling him what was actually a lie. That there had been something going on. I used it as a weapon. I used Bianca's story to hurt James, purely to hurt him, and when I see that in myself, when I see the fact that that kind of violence sprung from me, it shocks me and makes me very ashamed." Still, the only funny business was . . . funny business, according to Simon. She and Mick worked on another song in the studio that night, fooling around at the piano in between takes, and nearly came up with another duet. "We wrote a song together that became a song on the Stones' next album called 'The Next Time We Say Goodbye.' I thought that that was going to be a joint venture, but I'd never heard from Mick about how he'd like me to share the royalties." The track, entitled "Till the Next Goodbye," is credited to Jagger/Richards. "It's the very least I can do to thank Mick for turning what could have been an ordinary record into an iconic huge song for me over the years—so, my god, let him take all of my songs and say that he wrote them."

"You're So Vain" marks the first time Mick Jagger sees real musical vitality beyond the realm of the Stones. Released in early 1973, "You're So Vain" was an even bigger hit than their own No. 1 single of '73, the beautiful but fan-polarizing ballad "Angie." Musically, it's breathtaking, written by Keith, with Charlie's gentle drumming and Mick Taylor's evocative piano. The "vibe" is perfectly '70s mellow gold, but "You're So Vain," unlike much of the *Goats Head Soup*, *It's Only Rock 'n' Roll*, and *Black and Blue* trilogy, is timeless. Kate Hudson couldn't even ruin it serenading Matthew McConaughey in *How to Lose a Guy in 10 Days*. Commercially, it was unstoppable, topping the charts on both sides of the Atlantic and selling millions of copies and driving *No Secrets* to No. 1 for a month and a half. More important, it remains one of the few moments of true intrigue at the start of what Lester Bangs would come to dismiss as the Stones' "flakey" period.

13

"The South's Answer to the Rutles"

Let's temporarily suspend the well-worn rock writers' notion (examined earlier) that the disastrous free concert at the Altamont Speedway on December 6, 1969 (or even the Tate-LaBianca murders on August 8 and 9), marked the "Death of the '60s." Mick dispensed with it long ago, telling a journalist: "Perhaps it was the end of their era, the end of their naïveté. I would have thought it would have ended long before Altamont." Even Sonny Barger, the president of the Hells Angels, when contacted for this book, declined to revisit December 6, 1969, dismissing it with a curt e-mail: "it's just too stupid."

This isn't an attempt to be iconoclastic or dismissive. The murders of Sharon Tate and six other innocents in Southern California that summer and the senseless death of Meredith Hunter were obviously tragedies, and certainly burned up a lot of utopian energy, leaving in its place fear and confusion, and, worse, cynicism and selfishness, but a tragedy alone cannot truly put something so sinister to rest. It would take a *comedy* to truly finally allow us all to move on. And so I suggest to you that the 1960s truly ended on the evening of March 22, 1978, at 9:30 p.m., when NBC first broadcast *The Rutles: All You Need Is Cash* in prime time.

A full-length spin-off of a sketch that began on Monty Python cast member Eric Idle's solo BBC comedy series *Rutland Weekend Television* three years earlier, *All You Need Is Cash* neutralized both the naïveté and the hauteur of the youth-quaking generation with one brutally witty punch line after another. This was a different kind of acid.

It was born, of course, from the first of many powerful waves of '60s nostalgia. "What spawned the Rutles was the fact that somebody was offering the Beatles a colossal amount of money to get back together," says Python-affiliated songwriter Neil Innes (aka Ron Nasty, the "John Lennon" of the group). "It was getting so silly that something silly needed to be done; the moment was right."

On the April 24, 1976, episode of *Saturday Night Live*, show creator and producer Lorne Michaels offered the Fab Four a check for three thousand dollars to reunite.

"Here it is right here," he deadpanned sincerely. "A check made out to you, the Beatles, for three thousand dollars. All you have to do is sing three Beatles songs. '*She loves you, yeah, yeah, yeah.*' That's a thousand dollars right there. You know the words—it'll be easy." People didn't want to let go. Michaels' generation were straining to move on into the new. When Eric Idle hosted *S.N.L.* for the second time on April 23, 1977, and he brought Innes in as musical guest, debuting the Rutles' "Cheese and Onions" as well as some skits from *Rutland Weekend Television*, "the mailbag was huge. People sending in albums with Beatles crossed out and Rutles on it—so really the public at large were ready for a joke."

All You Need Is Cash (the title alone indicates that some much-needed wound licking has begun) was shot in the summer of 1978. Nearly a decade removed, nobody wanted to get past it more than the people who made the myths themselves: the '60s icons, trying like the punks to make new music themselves, to finally move ahead.

"George was the one that wanted to put the suit in the cupboard," Innes remembers. George Harrison worked closely with Idle and Michaels on the Rutles film, and his involvement brought perhaps the biggest '60s icon to the mix.

Codirected by and starring Idle, and featuring uncanny Beatle-style parodies by Neil Innes:

> "Ouch" for "Help"
> "Piggy in the Middle" for "I Am the Walrus"
> "Let's Be Natural" for "Let It Be"

The Rutles' creators astutely determined that their audience would be as steeped in Beatles iconography (*A Hard Day's Night's* running, *Help's* hazy, cannabis-filtered tropical locales, John and Yoko's avant-garde forays, the rooftop concert) and peripheral characters (Leggy Mountbatton, for late manager Brian Epstein, Ron Decline, played by a neckless John Belushi, for Allen Klein), and with each recognition they would find themselves breathing a bit more freely, like some elaborate, candy-colored exorcism.

"It actually was the best, funniest, and most scratching [of all the Beatles-related films]," George Harrison later said. "But at the same time, it was done with the most love. The Rutles sort of liberated me from the Beatles in a way."

One cannot, after all, successfully skewer something one doesn't first love and understand perfectly. The Beatle-like melodies were already such a part of Innes' songwriting DNA that he didn't have to relisten to any of them to turn the *Ed Sullivan Show*–Fab Four singles into "Hold My Hand" (complete with ad libs like McCartney's "Woo hoo" at the end, pulled straight from "All My Loving"). The "Pre Fab Four" were Dirk, Stig, Barry, and Nasty (five if you count Leppo, "The Fifth Rutle." These were crucially Rutles songs, sung and played in a universe where the Beatles never existed. "It was really like we were little kids playing cowboys and Indians—or some game that children can play," Innes says. "They're going to be pirates—we were going to be Rutles—and the Beatles did not exist. But Mick Jagger and Paul Simon did."

This is the second masterstroke. The Stones were no longer the Beatles' greatest rival through the '60s; they were now "the South's answer to the Rutles," as a gleeful Mick Jagger (the real Mick Jagger, two full decades before the real John Malkovich anchored Spike Jonze's *Being John Malkovich*) describes his band. "It was hugely important to have Mick and Paul," Innes says.

Identified in a caption as "Mick Jagger: Rock Star," Jagger, then thirty-five years old, doesn't look remotely flamboyant. With shoulder-length hair and a clean button-up striped shirt, he calmly sits on a couch and gamely answers mock questions about the era he came to personify. "I thought, 'He's very good,'" says Gary Weiss, an *S.N.L.* short-film director who helped Idle make the film. "Then I realized he meant every word of it. All he was doing was placing Rutles instead of Beatles."

"The first time I met the Rutles," Mick the "Rock Star" recalls, "they came down to see us at Richmond. We were just completing a number and suddenly they were just standing there in their black suits. They'd just come off a TV show and they were standing there checking us out—the opposition. And then they introduced themselves, you know Dirk, Stig, Nasty, Barry—they were very nice."

Mick proceeds to target certain key points in the Stones' history. On the filthy Edith Grove apartment he shared with Keith Richards and Brian Jones while getting the Stones together (and still attending the London School of Economics): "We were living in squalor, didn't have any money, there were the Rutles on TV with girls chasing them. We thought this can't be that difficult so we thought we'd have a go ourselves."

On being offered and recording "I Wanna Be Your Man" in 1964 (written by John and Paul and soon to become the Stones' first British Top 10 single): "They said 'Do you want a song?' We were really open for songs because we didn't write our own and of course the Rutles were really well-known for their hit-making potential ability—and so they ran around the corner to the pub to write this song and came back with it and played it to us and—it was 'orrible and so we never bothered to record it."

On the Beatles playing Shea Stadium (or "Che Stadium" as it is referred to): "[They took] a helicopter back to the Warwick Hotel. Two birds each."

On exploring transcendental meditation in Bangor, India, with the Maharishi, which Jagger and Marianne Faithfull explored as well (in "All You Need Is Cash" this is Ouija-board-tapping "Bognor"): "We were just as eager to find out what was going on with the board-tapping 'Bognor' as anybody." Even the Stones' notorious drug bust is mocked in a flash of newspaper headline during the segment when the Beatles and Stones fall under the influence of "tea": "Stones arrested. Nude girl and teapot!" Altamont is not spared either, with Ron Wood appearing as a clueless Hells Angel. Mick is even given the last word. When asked by Idle's journalist, "Why did the Rutles break up?" he responds, "Women. Just women. Getting in the way. Cherchez la femme." "Do you think they'll ever get back together?" Idle continues. "I 'ope not," Mick replies.

Even Bianca Jagger, whose lack of a sense of humor Keith was still puzzling over in 2010, gets in on the fun as one of the aforementioned rock wives (as McQuigley's muse Martini, a French woman who spoke no English and very little French).

"When I saw his footage, I remember thinking 'This is coming over really well,'" Innes says. "He was happy to take the piss out of the myth of the '60s. It's why he came off so well." Another reason is more elemental: Mick is naturally funny, perhaps the most gifted mimic and comedian of his rock and roll peers. "He had good timing. Very natural, yeah," Weiss agrees. There's an extended scene in Peter Whitehead's 1965 tour documentary, *Charlie Is My Darling*, in which Jagger, standing at a piano with Richards, does a spot-on Elvis impersonation.

Mick Jagger had been witty at press conferences perhaps, but he had not been *funny* on film before. He'd written some humorous lyrics about rock and roll as it was slowly becoming big business ("The Under Assistant West Coast Promo Man") and was already a master at skewering the hypocrisy of his elders ("Mother's Little Helper"), as well his own London-ruling hipoisie ("19th Nervous Breakdown"). In the year that *All You Need Is Cash* aired, he would turn this keen eye on nearly bankrupt and punked-out Manhattan with "Shattered," but up until that point, his '60s, and certainly the Beatles', ever the alpha to the Stones' beta, were sacred. Michaels and the original *Saturday Night Live* crew and writers, many from the *National Lampoon*, had broken through by casting their critical eye on the generation in which they came of age, as they now struggled to make money and hold on to their ideals, and reckon with things like the breakup of the Beatles, the escalation of the Vietnam War, and Watergate. The humor as a result became tougher and harder, and on occasion crueler. It became less Beatles and more Stones in its essence, which is why Mick Jagger jibes perfectly with the zeitgeist, and in the '70s takeover as the culture's undisputed alpha band.

Mick's long association with *Saturday Night Live* and friendship with Lorne Michaels, its creator, begins with *All You Need Is Cash*. The Stones would perform on the show on October 7 of '78 and Mick would appear as himself alongside Dan Aykroyd's Tom Snyder.

DAN AYKROYD (AS TOM SNYDER): "Get Off of My Cloud." It was one of the best singles you guys ever did, and I'll tell you why. I was working within Westinghouse Industries back in the fifties, not in the coaster division, in the broadcasting division. And there was a unit manager, he used to get me so teed off! I used to feel like saying to him, "Get the heck off my cloud!" You ever feel like saying, "Heck! I'm Mick Jagger,

I've got a few hit records. I can afford to take some time off and do whatever the heck I want?"

MICK JAGGER: I suppose I do. I mean, we did a tour that was really successful and I went crazy, I guess, a little crazy afterward—I put a barbecue and a swimming pool in the back-yard.

Over the years, Mick would parody Keith in both a Weekend Update sketch alongside Mike Myers' "Mick," and, at the start of the new century, he would again take the piss out of himself (on the opposite side of a Marx Brothers–style vanity "mirror" with Jimmy Fallon's equally excellent Mick. ("Here we are *S.N.L.* again, what am I gonna do? Did it in the '70s, the '80s, the '90s, now I'm doing it in whatever you call this decade.") Tearing down youth culture idols is de rigueur, and by the end of the '70s, Jagger, now pushing forty, had become the butt of such jokes. If you were in-clined, you could find a YouTube clip of now Senator Al Franken imitating Mick (with partner Tom Davis as Keith) on *Solid Gold* (doing a live lip-synch version of "Under My Thumb" in '81 tour drag of yellow tank top and tight football pants). Richard Belzer's Jagger impression ("a rooster on acid") became one of his signa-ture bits. Eddie Murphy observed in his breakthrough standup special *Delirious*: "Being a comic ain't like being no singer—the singers get all the pussy. You don't even have to look good—you can sing and get pussy. Mick Jagger is an ugly motherfucker with big ass lips. Mick Jagger's lips so big, black people be going 'You got some big ass lips.' But he singing." And yet, Jagger's ground-breaking appearance as himself in *All You Need Is Cash* did it first, did it best, and in that small sitting, Jagger managed to liberate his generation for a second time. In playing himself, he also introduces the concept of meta-performance. Once they could laugh about it all, the '60s finally had a context and its relics were if not a little bit younger, a lot more free. In Woody Allen's 1989 dark comedy *Crimes and Misdemeanors*, Alan Alda's pompous Lester lectures Woody Allen's less successful filmmaker Cliff that comedy is nothing more than "tragedy plus time." With blood on the ground in Benedict Canyon and at Altamont, there was nothing to do but wait.

14

"Punker Than Punk, Ruder Than Rude"

On a promotional flyer from a concert at the Whisky a Go Go in Hollywood dated June 8, 1978, the bill features art brats the Weirdos and the Dils, led by the near militant Kinman Brothers. It depicts Mick Jagger, long-haired, imperious; his bedroom eyes looking askance occupied the center. Someone has drawn a Fu Manchu mustache and goatee on him with what looks like a Sharpie marker, like Marcel Duchamp's Dada-defacing of the I. The Rolling Stones' fourteenth album, *Some Girls*, designed to restore them to good rebel standing, would be released the following day. They had a lot of work to do.

How did the Stones lose their edge and menace? Where'd the teeth go? When did discerning listeners stop believing what they were hearing? Through the mid-'70s, the riffs were still frequently punchy ("If You Can't Rock Me" and "Dance Little Sister," off

It's Only Rock 'n' Roll, "Crazy Mama," on *Black and Blue).* Ron Wood, who replaced Mick Taylor in 1975, had been the guitarist in the Faces, whose albums were great, boozy fun, hardly the stuff of Emerson, Lake and Palmer, or Genesis. Kids could play these riffs. But none of the new breed wanted to know the Rolling Stones.

I decided it wasn't about the music at all. Why had a band whose first manager, Andrew Loog Oldham, built their fame almost entirely on a bad-boy image, become so reviled by an entire generation of rebels on both sides of the Atlantic Ocean? It was about the friction, or in the case of Mick, Keith, Bill, Charlie, and Ronnie, lack of friction. Perhaps the Rolling Stones simply got too big to be an oppositional band. You can't own English country estates that you're only allowed to visit three months a year by law, vacation homes in Mustique, and a pad or two in upper Manhattan (as Mick did) and lay claim to be an oppositional band. And it's fine to not be one. Who doesn't love Paul McCartney's '70s band, Wings? Or Led Zeppelin for that matter? The problem with the Stones, why they inspired vandalism among punk-rock gig-flyer designers, was that they claimed to still be oppositional.

Pete Townsend got a punk pass because he was self-deprecating; listen to the lyrics on the Who's final album with Keith Moon, '78s *Who Are You.* They're ale-sodden, miserable, and true. The punks determined it would be uncouth to kick Pete when he was doing it himself so successfully. Freddie Mercury of Queen would just sass them right back. He didn't care about punk cred. He cared about midgets with silver tray hats. He'd play Sun City. Nothing was going to keep him from a stage. John Lennon went into hiding, stripping off his radical-chic garments and learning to bake bread. David Bowie went to Berlin and started returning Iggy Pop's calls again. Mick Jagger became the main target. He assumed people would appreciate that he wasn't only penthouse, he was pavement too. It got him far through the late '60s, and early '70s, but a seventeen-year-old kid on speed doesn't see subtlety. He or she just sees a thirty-five-year-old millionaire in a white disco suit. Someone should commend Mick for having the balls to stay and fight; to insist that he was still punk, still oppositional, still relevant. It was tremendous chutzpah and he nearly pulled it off.

It surely must have galled Mick that the Stones virtually handed the punks a musical blueprint. Devo stripped the iconic "(I Can't Get No) Satisfaction" down to a syncopated, barely recognizable herky jerk, wresting it from the oldies bin. It's not unaffectionate or unfaithful, but it's a radical revamping that nearly claimed the song for their own. The previous year, the San Francisco art rockers the Residents recorded their own muted, nightmarish, hilarious version of the song. The Strand, an early band featuring future Sex Pistols bassist Glen Matlock, guitarist Steve Jones, and drummer Paul Cook, built their rehearsal set around '60s classics by the Stones, the Who, and the Small Faces. Punks on both sides of the Atlantic drew their inspiration from the *Nuggets* soundtrack, which basically featured American bands copying their British Invasion heroes (listen to the Stones' "She Said Yeah," and you more or less have American garage rock in less than three minutes). In his classic punk treatise *England's Dreaming*, writer Jon Savage observes: "In ignorance of the music that was on their doorstep, most of these groups were copying white British pop groups—like the Rolling Stones or the Yardbirds—that were themselves attempting to capture the spirit of black American R&B— this double refraction resulted in a purely white, blue-collar style in which any black rhythmic influence was bleached out in favor of pure noise and texture." The sensational punk trio the Jam even dressed like a streamlined version of the '60s mod Stones. They, of course, no longer dressed this way. If they had, ironically, they might have been rewarded for their sartorial stasis. Look at the way the Ramones or Motörhead's Lemmy (or Keith Richards for that matter) are held up as bastions of integrity, largely because their iconic look has given them a dependable, action-hero air. You could draw Lemmy. Mick was too slippery. He changed clothes, looks, sounds. Like the punks, he was very easily bored.

Watch any documentary on the advent of the Sex Pistols, like Julien Temple's excellent *The Filth and the Fury*, and you will see sounds and images of social strife, racism, and economic repression (and indifference on the part of the government and the monarchy). The Pistols formed out of desperation, a product of their environment, like N.W.A. and Nirvana after them. When Malcolm McLaren took three major labels for healthy advances, it felt like Robin Hood returning to Sherwood Forest. When the Stones took money for lackluster albums like *Black and Blue* and shambolic tours, hobbled by Keith's hit-or-miss presence, it was the wrong kind of rock and roll swindle. Around this time, Sex Pistols manager Malcolm McLaren, his then partner Vivienne Westwood, and future Clash manager Bernie Rhodes designed a T-shirt bearing a manifesto of sorts. It was headed with the slogan: "You're going to wake up one morning and know what side of the bed you've been lying on." Beneath it there were two lists, which divided people and things into Loves and Hates; i.e., icons both approved and reviled by the punks. Marianne Faithfull appears midway down the "loves" list under Joe Orton, Lenny Bruce, would be Warhol assassin Valerie Solanis and "zoot suits and dread-locks." Mick nearly tops the "hate" list, coming in at number two, just under "Television (not the group)."

"The straw that broke the camel's back and galvanized the punks was the Earls Court run in 1975," says veteran British music writer Kris Needs, referring to the Stones decadent tour in support of *It's Only Rock 'n' Roll*, which climaxed with the band playing "Star, Star," as a giant, inflatable penis was erected by a wind machine. "It was attended by Clash and Sex Pistols. The sound was poor, the band sluggish, and the vanity overwhelming as Mick straddled a blow-up knob. Tacky."

By '77, Keith had bigger problems than irrelevance. He was kicking heroin, again, only this time it was mandatory. After being busted in Canada with enough of the drug to land him in prison for seven years, he finally began to get his act together, open his eyes, and have a good look at the lay of the land for the first time in a good half decade. To Keith, punk was just the flavor of the month; the same old chords, dolled up in torn T-shirts, safety pins, and bondage pants. "Punk was built to alarm Mick but inspire Keith, who saw it as another trend to beat at its own game. With the punk bands, he just saw himself fifteen years before," says Needs today. But then nobody asked Keith about punk.

Everybody asked Mick. A rumor had spread that Mick had dipped into Sex, Malcolm McLaren and Vivienne Westwood's notorious bondage couture boutique on the Kings Road, intent to kit himself out in the new drag, only to be told to "Fuck off" by Johnny Rotten, the Sex Pistols' iconoclastic singer and lyricist.

"Just complete and utter fantasy," Mick countered, dismissing the rumor bluntly in an interview the following year. "Nobody ever slams the door on me in the Kings Road. They all know I'm the only one who's got any money to spend on their crappy clothes . . . though even I would draw the line on spending money on torn T-shirts." Perhaps he'd seen the McLaren/Westwood/Rhodes–designed shirt? Rotten clearly had no patience for the likes of Mick. Years later, in his memoir, *Rotten: No Irish, No Blacks, No Dogs*, he recalled: "I saw a lot of old rock stars—and lots of jealous rock stars too. One of the most verbal instances was Mick Jagger. 'The Sex Pistols are awful, and they can't play!' Shame on you Mick. The Stones were one of the most notoriously inept bands in music, and here was this old coke hag pointing fingers and calling us disgusting. The Stones were into patting themselves on the backs and being self-congratulatory like many of those old timers. The Pistols were an absolute threat to that nice little world they had all built for themselves."

Still, the media, which had abided by the Stones' antics for more than a decade and seeing an opportunity to exact some revenge, embraced the idea that Mick was out and punk was in. You can see the seeds of this media-concocted war during the Pistols' infamous appearance on the *Today* show on December 1, 1976. Introducing the assembled Sex Pistols and some of their outlandish entourage (including a pre-fame Siouxsie Sioux), an inebriated and un-amused Bill Grundy observes, "These aren't the nice, clean Rolling Stones." On cue, the Pistols proceed to curse and outrage, prompting screaming headlines ("Filthy lucre!") the following morning. When writer Charles M. Young was in London in the summer of '77 covering the Pistols for *Rolling Stone*, word came across the transatlantic lines that Elvis Presley had died. "Elvis Presley died? Makes you feel sad doesn't it?" Pistols manager

Malcolm McLaren (who ironically took his cues from Stones manager Andrew Loog Oldham) quipped to Young. "Like your grandfather died. Yeah. It's just too bad it couldn't have been Mick Jagger." It was excellent copy, as they say.

The Pistols' new bassist and the ultimate symbol of the new nihilism, Sid Vicious, weighed in as well: "I absolutely despise those turds," he said with a sneer, lambasting the Stones and their generation. "The Stones should have quit in 1965. You never see any of those cunts walkin' down the street. If it gets so you can't see us that way, I don't want it."

The street was key to the Stones counterattack. The album they were recording in Paris at the time of the Pistol's *Rolling Stone* interview would contain countless references to the street, like 53rd and 3rd, Manhattan's gay male hustler spot that the Ramones sing about on their self titled debut in "When the Whip Comes Down." "Shattered" described a maggot-filled "Big Apple" full of two-faced hangers-on and people wearing garbage bags as "some kind of fashion." Even "Miss You," Jagger's "disco song," was raunchy, describing a late-night hang full of lots of wine (a whole case!) and some enthusiastic Puerto Rican girls. "We're gonna mess and fool around, like we used to!" Mick cheers, conjuring the spirit of the old, bad Stones.

Musically, *Some Girls* offered magnificent bluesy pop ("Beast of Burden"), camp country ("Far Away Eyes," a showcase for Mick's gift for mimicry), soul (a cover of the Temptations' aching "Just My Imagination"), and the aforementioned disco, but it is dominated by short, punchy songs, not like the previous three albums, which were anchored by a lot of searching jam songs. "Lies," was designed to be as brutal as anything by the Pistols or the Adverts or the Clash. On "Respectable," Mick acknowledged the band's standing with a quip: "We're talking heroin with the president . . ." Did they pull it off? Yes, in that it's hands-down the best Stones record since *Exile on Main Street* (a popular opinion because, well, it's true). No, in that by the time they released it, punk had already started to become something else: post punk and new wave. *Some Girls* was a great album, but it was an old-fashioned album; the Stones were "good again," but breaking no new ground, seeking nothing but a return to form, the very concept itself a hackneyed one. "The 'punk' songs were basically faster Stones songs," Needs observes.

The band was much more in tune with the times when it came to their association with Peter Tosh, who would open the North American tour in support of *Some Girls*. While West Indian culture had long been an important part of postwar England's identity, seemingly overnight, the British youth had gone mad for reggae and dub. The Pistols disintegrated in the winter of '78 while on tour in America. Rotten and his old friend Jah Wobble formed Public Image Limited along with guitarist Keith Levene and began setting more sophisticated and expansive songs of angst and anger to Wobble's dub-inspired bass lines. The Clash had recorded a version of Junior Murvin's "Police and Thieves," on their debut. From the Midlands came Coventry's the Specials, whose label logo, a skanking rude boy named Walt Jabsco, was a cartoon rendering of Tosh from an early '60s album cover. Reggae and dub had always been the music that the punks listened to, thanks to the Roxy's DJ Don Letts. "It was so early in the scene that there wasn't any punk-rock records to play," Letts told me during an interview for *Spin* in 2009. "So I played what I was into: Big Youth, Prince Far I, Toots and the

Maytals. Lucky for me, the audience liked it as well. England had a long tradition of white, working-class youth gravitating toward black music. What were the Beatles and the Stones listening to but black music from the Mississippi Delta? The difference with the Jamaican music of the late '70s was that kids were fascinated by a music and a culture that weren't really removed from their day-to-day life." Signing Peter Tosh to Rolling Stones Records in 1979, the year the Special's "Gangsters," Madness' "Madness," and the English Beat's "Tears of a Clown" stormed the British charts, did more to return the Stones to the right track than anyone could have imagined. "I think they liked the mutual credibility," music journalist Vivien Goldman says. "Both parties thinking they're authentic together. Peter thought they were pretty interesting too. I guess they were squaring their authenticity by linking."

Bob Marley had broken in America, selling out arenas after splitting with Tosh, who'd become bitter and jealous that the man he considered his "student" had surpassed him. He'd already alienated one label (Columbia, which had released the excellent *Legalize It* and its also even stronger follow-up *Equal Rights*). It was decided that the best way to reach a larger audience was to record a duet with Mick. In their early years, Tosh, Marley, and (third Wailer) Bunny Wailer had recorded a sweet, rocksteady version of the Temptations' 1965 hit "(You Got to Walk and) Don't Look Back," penned by Smokey Robinson.

Tosh was invited to perform on *Saturday Night Live* after the release, and footage from the duet shows both the esteem the two held for each other and the uneasiness of this partnership of convenience. Mick looks stiff. He dances nervously, and lapses occasionally into reggae mimicry, something he so skillfully avoided on those early blues albums but, often it seemed, for his own amusement, he would indulge in later in his career. Occasionally the men smile at each other warmly, but Tosh literally and figuratively dwarfs Mick, the much bigger star, and one gets the feeling there's a different kind of clash they now have to reckon with. "Peter was a man with a massive ego. You need that if you're gonna be a messiah and he was very messianic," says Goldman, who wrote extensively about both Tosh and Bob Marley. "He was very much of an alpha male and I'm sure things like the Rolling Stones daring to tell him that he hadn't sold, he would not be a happy camper and that would strike him to the core. He was very proud."

Sid Vicious was already gone by the time the Stones began work on *Emotional Rescue,* their follow-up to *Some Girls.* Tosh returned to Jamaica to live in Keith's vacation home, Point of View, in Ocho Rios until a dispute over the actual ownership of the residence (which has since passed into Stones legend) ended that as well. Ironically, he scored one of his biggest hits after his association with the Stones, on a Chuck Berry cover, no less. In 1983, his reggae version of Berry's "Johnny B. Goode," was heavily rotated on MTV. His final album, *No Nuclear War,* released in 1987, won the Best Reggae Album Grammy, but Tosh died violently, murdered in a mysterious home-invasion robbery by an associate.

If Mick took anything away from his war with the young punks and his all-too-brief alliance with the rudest rude boy of them all, it was that perhaps being "bad," like being on the right side of the barriers in '68, was not really worth the sacrifice. Bad boys die young. The '80s were drawing near and Mick was about to choose life in a big way.

15

"It's Nice to Have a Chick Occasionally"

The "chick" in question was 1969 tour opener Tina Turner. In *Gimme Shelter*, Mick delivers the potentially sexist line with a perfect sense of camp that renders it instantly inoffensive. It's a decent metaphor for his entire modus operandi with regard to the pursuit of the opposite sex. Warren Beatty wasn't camp. Neither was Wilt Chamberlain. Gene Simmons was camp but didn't realize that he was camp. Of all the legendary ladies' men of the post-pill/pre-AIDS era, Mick Jagger was the only one who had that out: "It's all a laugh. I don't really mean it." Irony may redeem some of his behavior, which, when conducted without a wink, could be and has been construed as pretty abhorrent.

Like the time Mick supposedly lured eighteen-year-old Mackenzie Phillips, daughter of his old friend John Phillips, away from a cocktail party and into his kitchen with the pretense of fixing a few tuna fish sandwiches for everyone. According to Mackenzie, Mick asked John to go out to fetch some mayonnaise (he had run out). While John Phillips was shopping, Mick allegedly took Mackenzie to the bed he shared with Jerry Hall and had his way with her. "My dad came back and started knocking on the door, yelling, 'You've got my daughter in there!' " she recalled. How about the time when "sex mad" Mick emerged from the shower of a Brussels hotel room, stark naked, to introduce himself to the new nanny, hired to look after his and Hall's kids. "I didn't know where to put my eyes," the nanny told UK tabloid the *Daily Mirror*. "The next thing I knew he put out his hand and said, 'Hi, I'm Mick.' To be honest, I didn't know which hand to shake!"

Mick Jagger is a go-er, but his beauty is both male and female, and since the '60s, he's appealed to both sexes equally. There's that famous line from Milos Forman's adaptation of the musical *Hair*, where the blond Woof is interrogated by a prison shrink. "You have any sexual attraction toward men?" he's asked. "Well, I wouldn't kick Mick Jagger out of my bed but I'm not a homosexual." Young, male music fans were attracted to Mick for a different reason than the one that attracted them to Keith. It was a seduction, by someone telegraphing absolute sexual confidence. Humor—camp humor—is a key ingredient to this highly appealing energy. In writer Christopher Isherwood's recently published '60s diaries, he recounts a moment where Mick confides in him that the true reason that the Beatles left the Maharishi's ashram abruptly was because the holy man allegedly made a pass at one of them (and not, as has been widely reported, the actress Mia Farrow's sister Prudence). "They're simple, north-country lads; they're terribly uptight about all that." With the exception of his

Screening the footage from the disastrous Altamont concert with Gimme Shelter directors the Maysles brothers. (1970)

The odd man out—with Keith, Anita, and their infant son Marlon in Sweden. (1970)

Honeymoon in Venice with Bianca Jagger, Italy. (1971)

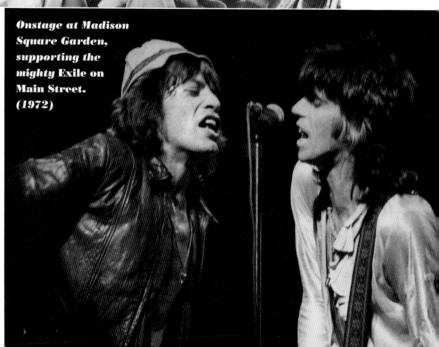

Onstage at Madison Square Garden, supporting the mighty Exile on Main Street. (1972)

Jamming with John and Yoko at the Record Plant—New York City. (1972)

The underrated guitar player, strumming in Vienna, Austria. (1973)

In Paris with new girlfriend Jerry Hall after stealing her away from the elegant Bryan Ferry. (1978)

With Bob Marley and Peter Tosh—backstage at the Palladium, NYC. (1978)

"Gimme Mick!"
with Gilda Radner.
(1978)

Bearded and incognito with younger brother Chris; his mother, Eva; and father, Joe. (1979)

"Dancing in the Streets" with partner in high camp, David Bowie. (1985)

The new old video stars take Live Aid. (1985)

Working his "evil face" on the set of Freejack. (1992)

With England's newest '90s hitmakers, the Spice Girls. (1997)

Live at the 53rd Annual Grammys in Los Angeles. (2011)

very early sexual encounters and the urban legend of Angie Bowie catching him in bed with her husband, David, there's really not much to suggest that Mick has been anything but a chaser of skirts. And yet, even while living in Edith Grove in the very early '60s with Keith and Brian, he would sometimes astound them with acts of extremely camp prancing; puzzling when one ponders the very long list of beautiful women he has pursued, sometimes loved, and sometimes hurt. Brigitte Bardot, Marianne, Patti D'Arbanville (muse of Cat Stevens and Warhol star), Marsha Hunt, Bianca, Pamela Des Barres, Bebe Buell (muse of Todd Rundgren and Elvis Costello), and in middle age, Angelina Jolie and Sophie Dahl.

Maybe Mick's failure to commit to sincere emotion when it comes to relations with significant others accounts for his occasionally painful and certainly pain-inducing lack of fidelity.

Has it always been this way, since his first serious girlfriend, Chrissie Shrimpton, had to reckon with screaming fans and road affairs? Certainly the Stones' witty blues track "The Spider and the Fly" plays upon what was, by 1965, already a questionable reputation. "Keep fidelity in your head," Mick sings with camp lasciviousness, as if to convey to the listener "Yeah, there's no way that's gonna happen." In his memoir, Keith talks about how his shirt was wet from all the girls who came to him, cried on his shoulder, and asked him to explain Mick. If women didn't understand Mick, part of his arsenal was a seemingly effortless appreciation for them. "Most men aren't very good at feelings," his ex-wife Jerry Hall has said. "Mick had a talent for it."

"I think his lyrics are the lyrics of a conflicted man," says musician Liz Phair, who responded to Mick's lyrics on *Exile on Main*

Street with her own *Exile in Guyville,* now regarded as an indie-rock classic. "Which is what makes him so timeless. Like he's one of those misogynists that loves women too. He's the prototypical. He gets us completely. Those lyrics. I don't think anyone could ever understand me as well as Mick understands me. And yet I don't think he's going to treat me well at the same time."

Indeed, lyrically, Mick has a penchant for berating a woman trying to control him: See "Slave" off *Tattoo You.* Or how about the title track from his solo debut, *She's the Boss:* "When I first met you, you looked so soft . . . What a fool I was." It's interesting to read into his lyrics if only because they frequently counter the public perception of Mick as the one who does dirty. If you believe what you read on the sheet, it's Mick who's heartbroken; hence the "put-down" songs, as Keith calls them, that they manage to put out at least once a decade: "Tell Me" in the '60s to "I Got the Blues" in the '70s to "Worried About You" in the '80s to "Anybody Seen My Baby" in the '90s and "Streets of Love" in the 2000s. Women think he's tasty but they always try to waste him. His first marriage, to Bianca, was marked by public infidelity on both sides; Mick initiating counterattacks from Bianca, who would take care to be photographed on the arm of handsome movie stars like Ryan O'Neal and the German matinee idol Helmut Berger. They would divorce in '78.

In Andrew Morton's 2010 unauthorized biography of Angelina Jolie, he recounts numerous, often hilarious instances of a lust-crazed and dignity-challenged Mick pursuing the then up-and-coming actress all over the world. Jolie stars in the video for the above-mentioned "Anybody Seen My Baby" and later sings a tone-deaf version of "(I Can't Get No) Satisfaction" while reporting from a picket line in the little seen 2001 romantic comedy *Life or Something Like It* ("I don't know if you're aware of a popular song by a little band called The Rolling Stones," she asks the angry crowd, "but it talks about these very same issues and it goes something like this . . ."). The actress's late mother, Marcheline, was smitten with Mick since the '60s and reportedly wanted them to get married. If Morton is to be believed, Jagger, still married to Jerry Hall when they met, was willing to give up anything for her. Instead, she toyed with his emotions and led him on, perhaps exacting revenge for her entire gender.

Ultimately it's not women who need to administer payback. Mick's "this isn't really happening" camp abandon has given him tacit permission to ruin the lives of just as many men. It's one thing to have your girl stolen by a macho man, but probably doubly maddening to watch her slink off with an eye-rolling, androgynous rock and roll cuckhold maker. Among his fellow musicians, the guy is universally regarded as dangerous.

In the early '60s, according to Keith, he slept with Brian Jones' girlfriend.

"Mick had come back drunk one night to visit Brian, found he wasn't there, and screwed his old lady," Keith recalled. "This caused a seismic tremble. Upset Brian very badly." We've already covered his dalliance with Pallenberg. Also in the late '60s, he stole famous groupie Des Barres away from Jimmy Page, making out with her in the corner of the Whiskey a Go Go for all to see. In the late '70s, Margaret Trudeau, the young trophy wife of Canadian prime minister Pierre Trudeau, glommed onto the Stones as they were recording parts of the live release *Love You Live* at Toronto's El Mocambo nightclub. In truth Trudeau just wanted close proximity to the band, a "groupie" as Keith later dismissed her, but the press made it seem like Jagger stole her away from the politician. In the late '80s, he stole the future first lady of France, Carla Bruni, from Eric Clapton. By then, he had such a reputation that Clapton dreaded bringing Bruni to a stop on the *Steel Wheels* world tour. "We went to the show and afterward I took her backstage to meet the guys," Clapton remembered in his autobiography. "I remember saying to Jagger, 'Please Mick not this one. I think I'm in love.' In the past he had made several unsuccessful passes at Patti, and I knew Carla would appeal to his eye. For all my pleadings, it was only a matter of days before they started a clandestine affair."

Even his relationship with Jerry Hall, the longest of his life, began with a cock block.

Even aggrieved guys need to give Jagger credit for one of these acts, as it's something that heretofore seemed impossible: He actually stole a woman away from Bryan Ferry, the most debonair and tasteful gentleman in rock. When Ferry was introducing himself in the recording studio, he couldn't have known that the devil would one day slink in and steal his woman. Although he had his omens. The Texas-born Jerry Hall, then a sought-after fashion model (and once the Paris roommate of Grace Jones) appears on the cover of Roxy Music album *Siren*. Ferry approached the big, blond, loud, and fun-loving Hall as an art project. He altered her. She devoured the books in his library. "Getting the education that I had missed by not going to university," she writes in her memoir, *Jerry Hall's Tall Tales*. Ferry suggested she dress in tweed suits and enjoy afternoon tea. When her inner Mesquite came through, she'd get drunk on tequila and punctuate loud stories with "fatter than a hog on a fence." Ferry was horrified, according to Hall. "Bryan always seemed to have two sides to him too. Part of him liked it that I was a model. He thought I was glamorous and funny. And then there was this other side of him that wanted a wholesome, aristocratic country life and wanted me to be a different kind of girl." They certainly looked great together.

In 1976, flush from *Siren's* success, he offered up "Let's Stick Together," a soul-powered remake of the old Wilbert Harrison track. Hall appears in the video, and she and Bryan began appearing in the British tabloids a lot. This is probably where Mick saw her.

That year, the Stones were touring Europe in support of their *Black and Blue* album. Mick called up Ferry and asked him to see one of the band's six sold-out shows at London's Earls Court (the very engagement that, according to Kris Needs, drew and severely disappointed the Sex Pistols). After the show, Hall joined Ferry, Mick, and Ahmet Ertegün (who'd also signed Ferry) at an after-party at the Ritz hotel. As was his method, Mick flirted openly with Hall, right in front of the flustered Ferry. Camp. "This isn't really happening." Ferry was too polite to say anything and burned silently. Their relationship was never the same after that. They continued to live together but Mick stayed on Jerry's mind. Ferry went on tour of the Pacific Rim (where Hall maintains that he had an affair with an Asian model). Hall left London to visit friends in New York. There, on May 21, 1977, she ran into Mick at a dinner party thrown by the fashion photographer Francesco Scavullo, and that was that.

Ferry, in Montreaux recording his next solo album, *The Bride Stripped Bare*, heard through the grapevine of world travelers that

Hall had been spotted with Mick. Soon it was in the gossip columns. He froze up. When Hall's father passed away from cancer, he sent her his condolences via telegram. "Brian took me leaving him very badly," Hall recalled. "He kept all my clothes."

Eric Clapton never did much with the heartache that Carla Bruni left (he gave at the office there with "Layla"). Roxy's next album featured his own "she did me wrong" song, the kind that Mick was an unlikely master at. The gorgeous "Dance Away," like much of *The Bride Stripped Bare*, was written for Jerry Hall, and about the man who stole her away: "Yesterday, when it seemed so cool," Ferry croons, until he sees his Texan beauty "hand in hand with another guy." She's dressed to kill, but he's the one who's dyin'. That is, until he feels the beat. Ferry danced his pain away (the cover of Roxy's album *Manifesto* has about eight girls on the cover) but ostensibly learned from his mistake: bringing the girl he adores to a Rolling Stones concert. "I had left a book by the bed called *The Mists of Avalon*, about Druids," Hall writes of one of the possessions she left behind in the home they shared. "Bryan wrote a beautiful album called *Avalon* that was a huge success." That album, released in 1982, had a bird of prey on the cover. "Mick could out-irony Bryan anytime," says music journalist Rob Sheffield. "I love 'Dance Away.' One of the best late Roxy songs. The thing is, Bryan always meant it . . . he never had the ironic escape clause that Mick always had."

Jagger and Hall stayed together longer than expected: twenty-two years and four kids, culminating in a later-contested ritual wedding in Bali (which involved the sacrificing of a chicken), but their relationship was ultimately a victim of the same thing that vexed Chrissie Shrimpton and Bianca (and potentially several dozen others). In 1989 he began seeing Bruni, and has continued to chase women, including the young Angelina Jolie.

"Making love and breaking hearts, it is a game for youth," Jagger sang in 1981 on "Waiting on a Friend." It's probably one of the things that indeed keeps him young, but certainly in exchange for a lot of collateral heartache. Hall finally kicked Mick out after he had a baby with model Luciana Morad (he is now linked with fashion designer L'Wren Scott). She has since gone on to star in a reality show in which she picks a boyfriend from a group of contestants. She's currently a Levitra spokeswoman, which is, in its own way, pretty darn camp.

16

"State of Shock"

The 1980s were about big dreams and wild, ultimately fruitless, ideas: trickle-down economics, *Star Wars* nuclear missile defense shields, time machines built out of DeLoreans, *Cop Rock*, and the notion that Mick Jagger as a solo artist might have more pull than Mick Jagger, front man of the Rolling Stones, the greatest rock and roll band in the world. One can't really fault Jagger, who turned thirty-seven in the summer of 1980, for starting to feel a little restless and thinking that it may be more dignified to go it alone. In September, John Lennon gave what would become one of his very last interviews to *Playboy* in promotion of his comeback *Double Fantasy*. Lennon had spent the '70s on a spiritual journey that took him from wounded, primal-screaming ex-Beatle to inebriated Lost Weekender to househusband and father and now, at forty, a wise, mature rock and roll adult; perhaps the first of his kind. With typical Lennon acid wit, he turned his eye toward the Stones, who released their seventeenth album, *Emotional Rescue*, in June. "You know, they're congratulating the Stones on being together 112 years," Lennon said. "Whoopee, you know . . . whoopee. At least Charlie and Bill still got their families. In the '80s they'll be asking, 'Why are these guys still together? Can't they hack it on their own? Why do they have to be surrounded by a gang? Is the little leader frightened someone's gonna knife him in the back?' That's gonna be the question. They're gonna look at the Beatles and Stones and all those guys as relics . . ."

The words reportedly stung Mick deeply. Lennon was the Beatle both he and Keith felt closest to, the band's leader and a sort of older-brother figure. On the Stones' *Rock 'n' Roll Circus* DVD from their shelved 1968 concert special, Mick calls John "Winston" (his given middle name, although he later changed it to "Ono"). John calls Mick "Michael." The Beatles gave the Stones their first Top 10 British single and carved a path they could follow through America. Now it seemed John was again clearing brush and building roadways into adulthood and daring Mick and Keith to follow him there—if they could.

Ironically, the Stones were finally in a good place creatively, better than they'd been through much of the '70s. *Some Girls* yielded three hit singles in the chart-topping "Miss You," "Beast of Burden," another all-time classic, and the punky, tough "Shattered." Even Lennon admitted that their first single of the new decade, "Emotional Rescue," was a beautiful song. "Emotional Rescue," is perhaps the most eccentric Stones single ever released. Like Lennon's own "Happiness Is a Warm Gun," it's a song suite.

Mick sings the verses in falsetto, addressing, yet again, a woman in trouble, a gold digger locked up in a tower. The groove of "Emotional Rescue," like "Miss You," is built around a club disco bass line, heavily indebted, like most singles from that era, to Chic's Bernard Edwards. Charlie plays the beat with a swing; four on the floor and as light as smoke-machine vapor. Mick wrote the song while sitting alone at an electric piano, which gives it a late-night, urban-soul feel as well. In the studio, Bobby Keys's snaky, vaguely porn-soundtrack sax is another highlight. It's avant-garde pop that you can roller disco to; not at all out of place with the post-punk era's early pop hits like "Money" by the Flying Lizards, "Pop Muzik" by M, or "Rock Lobster" by the B-52s, and points the way to where Mick might have wanted to take the band. Keith, off heroin since the late '70s, couldn't see why being a killer blues-rock combo was not enough. It was a new wave, and only one of the Glimmer Twins seemed eager to ride it.

The Stones still looked great, too. Between March and July of 1980, they shot two video clips for the title track, one in a strobe-lit "Thermo-graphic" mode, calling to mind the cover sleeve for the album, also entitled *Emotional Rescue*, and a second with the band performing in a red, black, and white backdropped room, with snatches of the Thermo-graphic footage edited, but mostly with nothing but their personalities as pyrotechnics. This would be the first footage that a new generation would see of the Stones. The band adapted well to the new world of video thanks largely to the miles of attitude they brought to the set. Most of the '60s-born artists who pioneered the video clip look either sullen by design or perturbed by having to lip-synch (check out the early Moody Blues videos). Only a few seemed ready for the camera: Rod

Stewart, the solo Robert Plant, Paul McCartney, and, of course, the flamboyant Elton John.

In the "Emotional Rescue" clip, the Stones not only look like the "gang" that Lennon indicted; they seem at peace and then some when faced with this new marketing burden. They giggle at each other as if to say, "Crazy, man. We're making a . . . 'video.' Wot? We used to call these 'promos.'" Keith is in full rock and roll lion mode, healthy, fit, with a little silver in his hair. Ron Wood looks like he's just heard a good dirty joke (but then he always looks that way). Even Charlie manages a smirk. The video for the follow-up single is even better, with Keith resplendent in leopard-print and Mick in red and black singing into a très new wave checkerboard microphone in what appears to be the freezer compartment of a small Frigidaire. "When I touch her, my hand just froze!" he shouts while staring with mock alarm at his clawlike fingers. The videos off *Tattoo You*, their classic 1981 release, were better still, with Mick in a skintight purple tank top and white sweats doing Joe Jagger–style calisthenics for "Start Me Up." "Hang Fire" featured inexplicable cuts to giant, oiled breasts squeezed into a red bikini top; "Worried About You" and "Neighbors" were fun and feisty; and, best of all, "Waiting on a Friend" perfectly captures an aimless day in Lower Manhattan, featuring Mick literally waiting on Keith on a stoop in New York's East Village. They *got* music video. They were still making one hit after another.

The '80s were going to be great for this band! Weren't they?

Mick was the first superstar to tape an endorsement for MTV. In the late summer of '81, the channel was a fledgling network that was desperately trying to pad out its list of affiliates. The network's founders flew to Paris, where Mick was living and working at the time, to ask him to recite the start-up channel's slogan in an effort to get affiliates across the country to agree to sign on to carry it. Mick protested that he didn't do commercials but eventually agreed (for the price of one dollar) to say, "I want my MTV," in a bumper promo. While being accepted by the MTV audience would, inside of a few months, become key to every single marketing campaign no matter what an artist's status or stage in their career might be, at the time, it felt like a typically canny risk. MTV might have seemed an utter folly to a less savvy pop star. Mick instantly legitimized them and the affiliates soon multiplied. In return, he was given an informal pass. He was about to turn forty, but he would always have the loyalty of the network, aimed squarely at the teenage dollar: the very same currency that made the Stones in the '60s. Could he have the audacity to court it again two decades on? Yes he could.

Meanwhile, the '60s oldies were becoming more and more lucrative every day. In 1983, as the Stones were about to release their next album, another strong effort entitled *Undercover*. "You Can't Always Get What You Want," their 1969 hit, was featured (as part of a hysterical and wordless joke) in the funeral scene at the beginning of the classic baby boomer film *The Big Chill*, along with a revival of Motown hits. Even as he appreciated the money, Mick absolutely hated the notion of being a retro act. "I think MTV has done something great—although quite by accident, I'd imagine. It's shaken up all the radio people and made 'em realize that there's more to life than all those bands that they were playing over and over and over. Like the Rolling Stones," he told *Rolling Stone* that year.

As he had been with a pre-fame Prince (whom Keith Richards dismissed as fluff for never paying his dues on the circuit like he, as well as other prodigies like Stevie Wonder, had), Mick found himself smitten by several other future titans of the MTV generation, including Duran Duran, who were to become Keith's bête noires. The "Fab Five" were too pretty, too airy, a redux of Mick's early '70s fascination with David Bowie. Keith could abide punk rock, derivative as it was, but new wave rubbed him the wrong way. He couldn't understand what Mick saw in these kids, or how it could possibly be good for the Stones.

"Keith's not a flavor-of-the-month person," Ron Wood has said. "He's not a great trend follower. Keith knows what he likes. Mick is always interested in what's new, which is very good for the band because it gives us this push and pull." By the mid-'80s it was mostly push. "He'd get involved with these groups like Duran," says Bill German, who founded the Stones newsletter *Beggars Banquet* and later wrote about his experiences with the band in the memoir *Under Their Thumb.* "It really got under Keith's skin. Hanging out with Paul Young. God, it's right there in his name. Paul *Young!* Mick wanted to be affiliated with these people and it just drove Keith crazy. Mick'd worry 'Oh the Stones, they look like a bunch of pensioners.' He wanted to distance himself from being perceived as a retro act."

Mick carefully distanced himself from his own legacy in his forties. The Rolling Stones started as fan boys, collecting and studying records, and there's always been a bit of that in their fans as well; even today there are websites that archive every B-side, tour date, set list, or bootleg ever. In interviews, Mick would now play dumb with regard to the band's history. The trainspotting detail of Stones album minutiae which drove fans like German to fervid distraction were beneath him. "I'm not a historian," he has said. "I have no idea about our history. I don't even know which songs appear on which albums. I have to go and look it up."

"Keith knows where his bread is buttered," German says, "Mick forgets that. Sorry Mick, but you're stuck with us schlubby fans." Such displays of insecurity, Keith fretted, reflected poorly on the whole band. "Keith would say, 'You don't need anything from these younger groups. Why are you coming to them?'" German recalls. "He liked things that stand the test of time. Whereas he saw these guys as flavors of the month, Mick would invite them up to the studio when Keith wasn't there."

As MTV gained power and influence, the Stones' videos become more elaborate, expensive, and plot driven; mini movies, really. Their big-budget "Undercover of the Night" premiered on MTV in the fall of '83, the year of *Scarface*, and featured (at that time) a controversially violent plot, with Jagger portraying multiple roles: a wealthy South American businessman, a rock star kidnapped by masked terrorists, and, in a video within a video within a video conceit, Mick Jagger, fronting the Stones, as a young couple on the couch channel surf from the original movie to MTV. Keith, in an act of unmistakable symbolism, fires a bullet through the screen.

The network showed the video with a warning and it became a catalyst for a new "video violence" controversy spearheaded by worried parent groups. The Stones may be forty, but they were still dangerous, the implicit message ran. "Too Much Blood," another single with a Duran Duran (via Chic) style new wave funk bass, was even more "controversial." During the song's break, Mick sits at a table, wearing dark shades. He pours a glass of wine, and casually relates the (real-life) tale of a French case of murder and cannibalism that inspired him to write the song: "He took her to his apartment, cut off her head. Put the rest of her body in the refrigerator, and ate her piece by piece . . ." It's quite nearly a rap, which must have galled Keith even more than the new wave conceits of *Emotional Rescue*. It also should be briefly noted that no matter how outrageous, dark, and ambitious these videos are, they all, without exception, manage to squeeze in a fleeting close-up of Charlie Watts rolling his eyes, unimpressed as he keeps the beat. Mick was about to make his biggest gambit yet for the hearts and minds of the video kids, and it would be a move that nearly destroyed the Rolling Stones forever.

In 1984, both the Rolling Stones and Michael Jackson were label mates, under pressure to deliver follow-ups to hit records, in Jackson's case, the biggest hit record of all time. The Stones' contract went up for renegotiation after the release of *Undercover*. Their 1981 tour had established them as the biggest live draw in the world. They were a hot property and were brought to CBS Records by wildman executive Walter Yetnikoff, who promised them anything they wanted. Mick, allegedly unbeknownst to Keith and the other Stones, saw this as an opportunity to finally experiment with a career outside of the Rolling Stones. As it's now widely known, Jackson was looking to establish himself once and for all as a solo artist, but felt similar obligations to those who helped make him. He was pressured by his family to refill the coffers and capitalize on the unprecedented success of *Thriller* by agreeing to a stadium tour with his brothers in support of a hastily recorded Jacksons album, *Victory*. He assented, but carried his own trump card.

"State of Shock" is a pretty good song, but its greatness lies in synergy.

There have been few instances of guaranteed hits in rock and roll. Many albums that seem predestined to be smashes simply flop. Labels end up shipping way too many copies and these get sent back in droves. But in 1984, Michael Jackson could have guzzled a liter of Pepsi and belched the alphabet and it would have moved units. A song from his teenage years, "Farewell My Summer Love," was a Top 10 hit. He'd sung the hook on Rockwell's "Somebody's Watching Me" (later immortalized in a Geico insurance commercial) and the track went to No. 2. It would be good for Mick to notch a huge solo single, and good for Jackson, who'd only recently broken the color barrier on radio and at MTV to score a rock and roll hit (his mother and older brother Jermaine allegedly lobbied hard for a Michael-Jermaine duet to be the centerpiece of *Victory*).

The song had actually been kicking around for three or four years when Jackson approached Mick about a possible duet. His initial partner had been Queen's Freddie Mercury. There are demos of the Mercury version available on YouTube. Jackson had already done rock-aimed duets with Traffic's Dave Mason and Paul McCartney. Both "Save Me" and "The Girl Is Mine," respectively, had been ballads. "State of Shock" was a limber, raunchy, horny rocker. "It was a perfect Stones riff, which was an extremely popular trend on R&B radio at the time," says music journalist Rob Sheffield. "It was like Ray Parker Jr.'s 'The Other Woman' times Shalamar's 'Dead Giveaway' plus Prince's 'Let's Go Crazy' divided by the Time's 'Jungle Love.' It was pretty basic, yet it sounded more like an old-school go-for-the-throat Stones riff than anything on the most recent Stones albums. It showed that Michael Jackson could imitate the Stones at least as well as the Stones could imitate hip-hop (all over *Undercover*)." The song was put in storage because it was begging for Mick Jagger. "It's basically a song about how much fun it is to be Mick, or be near him." True enough, Michael Jackson seems to catch the fever as the track unfolds, gleefully shouting, "We're doin' it!" "It's why the Freddie Mercury version doesn't work at all. Who wants a three-note melody from Freddie Mercury?" Sheffield asks. The fact that "State of Shock" (issued as a single in July of '84, shortly before Mick's forty-first birthday) was so "Stonesy" certainly vexed Keith. That it charted higher than the past three Stones singles (eventually hitting No. 3 on the *Billboard* charts) added salt to the wound.

"State of Shock" laid the groundwork for Mick's 1985 solo debut, *She's the Boss*. MTV was in. CBS was in. Chic's Nile Rodgers, who'd just produced Duran Duran's smash *Seven and the Ragged Tiger* as well as INXS's *The Swing* (and who kept David Bowie afloat during the MTV deluge with the smash *Let's Dance*), was in. The best session players in the world were in: Sly and Robbie, Herbie Hancock, Jeff Beck. The only men out were the Rolling Stones.

"The album is further proof that Jagger, unlike most forty-plus performers, can stake out contemporary musical territory without embarrassing himself," *Rolling Stone* raved. Unfairly lumped in with Mick's lesser solo material (or compared with the Stones' best) *She's the Boss* is indeed a good record, in that the singing is good, the songs have hooks, the production is peerless. What's really missing if anything is us . . . the listener. We have nothing to do with it and that's its fatal flaw. When we listen to the Stones, we always think of the larger "we." When we listen to Mick (or Keith, for that matter) solo we only think "he." We are all Rolling Stones. "The Stones still have the strength to make you feel that both we and they are hemmed in and torn by similar walls, frustrations, and tragedies," Lester Bangs wrote. But there is only one Mick. We cannot embody him without Keith and Charlie around.

We also forget, when seen now within the context of a solo career that's seen quite a few commercial flops, just how big these singles were in '85. Mick gets very little credit for actually achieving his goal. He absolutely succeeded at crossing over to the MTV audience. He was a video star at forty-two years of age.

In a post-"Thriller" universe, it wasn't enough to simply do a three-minute video clip. Real superstars issued mini movies to MTV and the channel heralded them as events. Bowie had made the lengthy slapstick *Jazzing for Blue Jean* in '84 with Julien Temple, whom Jagger hired to make his. Mick's 1985 foray into video bloat would be longer than *Thriller*. Longer than *Jazzing for Blue Jean*. Longer than *The Color Purple* (but perhaps not as long as *Out of Africa*). *Running Out of Luck* had ambition. What it lacked was a script.

"There were notes on a bar napkin that only Mick and Julien saw," Rae Dawn Chong, Mick's costar, tells me. It's ostensibly a make-believe account of Mick Jagger, his wife, and lovers navigating the very real chaos of the new video age. Mick and Jerry Hall (playing themselves) are bickering on the Brazilian video shoot for the *She's the Boss* song "Half a Loaf." Dennis Hopper, shortly before his sobriety and *Blue Velvet* comeback, plays the video director ("You're ready to rock, right?"). Dozens of dancers, tons of lights and equipment, and hours of footage were expended in the service of . . . *what* exactly remains unclear. "It was posh chaos,"

Chong says. "Dennis Hopper was this wild, scary dude who would ask me to go out and photograph drag queens with him. I declined. Something about Rio was dangerous. I was a kid, really. I had a small child and I wanted to make it home in one piece. Brazil was no joke, especially Rio."

True enough, Mick is rolled by some Brazilian trannies, and ends up in the back of a meat truck before finding himself in a workers' camp, a jail cell, and, later, a London nightclub, singing his single "Just Another Night" in a spangled coat and very heavy makeup.

There were Hollywood movies in the '80s with even flimsier plot hinges (most of them starred Andrew McCarthy).

Running Out of Luck was Mick selling the "idea" of Mick. The funniest scene is also metaphorical for his '80s plight. He stumbles, hungry and tired, into a general store and asks to use the "telephone, you know, the blower," and tries to get the proprietors to recognize him by pulling out an album (the best-of *Through the Past Darkly*) in which his face is obscured, pressed against glass) and miming to "Jumpin' Jack Flash." A neat trick, reminding people who he is, while not resorting to the oldies power. "I felt he was anxious for his record to do well. He was pretty nervous," Chong says.

Mick opted to play Live Aid that summer separately from the other Stones backed by fellow veteran rockers turned MTV superstars Hall and Oates. In case nobody got the message, he also brought on '60s survivor turned MTV superstar Tina Turner to sub for Jackson on the duet. After Live Aid, Mick reunited with the Stones to record a new studio album, their first for CBS Records, but spent much of the sessions at odds with Richards, who was still quite put out by the secret solo deal. The *Dirty Work* set produced a Top 10 hit with a great cover of the 1963 R&B hit "The Harlem Shuffle" (originally by Bob and Earl). Keith wanted to tour in support of the album but Mick preferred to resume his pursuit of a solo career. He recorded yet another synergistic track, the theme to the Danny Devito and Bette Midler hit *Ruthless People*, with Hall, and began work on the follow-up to *She's the Boss* with Dave Stewart of yet another MTV-dominating act, the Eurythmics. Stewart had modernized Tom Petty and the Heartbreakers' sound with "Don't Come Around Here No More," and promised to do the same for Mick. Keith went apoplectic, and this time, his worry that Mick would be swallowed up by fashion had some weight to it.

Primitive Cool is extremely '80s-generic, with the wailing guitar-face licks, *Miami Vice* synths, and forward-mixed but oddly canned rhythms. It could be a Pointer Sisters record with the vocals wiped and recorded over. "I'm so greasy, I'm so slick, I leave no traces, I just get out quick," Mick sings on "Throwaway," and for the first time his nitty-gritty confessions aren't attractive. The title track is pretty and satisfying in its lyrical candor. Mick sounds his age: "It all seemed so different then," he admits. The lead single, "Let's Work," however, seemed wildly insensitive and any irony is lost in its implicit message (the poor just needed to work harder?). At least the video was hilarious. Mick runs up a street trailed by various examples of the common workforce. At one point, a chef follows him waving a dead pig.

Primitive Cool also marks the beginning of Jagger's unfortunate untucked-shirt phase, in which he tops an array of sherbet colored T-shirts with a loose-fitting buttoned-up shirt, open all the way. It seemed to take him forever to ditch that look, and thankfully he finally has, preferring a tight black T-shirt and trousers, which suit his still trim frame nicely. The hair, too, is a problem. Whereas on the pugnacious video for the Stones single "One Hit to the Body" the previous year, it is lush and Steven Tyler–like, by the late '80s it seems oddly cut, almost a mullet. He's still in great shape, but whereas Keith seems to ease into his graying hair and slightly sagging flesh, its jarring to see Mick age. In 1987, the year "Let's Work" failed to stay on the charts, Mick and Keith's cronies in the Grateful Dead scored a surprise radio and MTV hit with "Touch of Gray," which honestly and affectionately addressed the issue of boomers becoming middle aged. The Dead were giving up the ghost with a little grace, and were rewarded for it. Mick refused to do the same and eventually suffered.

Ironically, the synergy that broke Mick the solo star and nearly killed the Stones would make them stronger and more lucrative than ever once their lost decade drew to a close.

In August of 1986, Nick Kent wrote a *Spin* magazine cover story showing Mick, circa the early '80s, bare-chested and grimacing, with the headline "It's Almost All Over Now," which spoke of the band's imminent breakup. After the crash and burn of *Primitive Cool*, Mick would resort to a "State of Shock"–style superstar duet to restart his career after the failure of his *Primitive Cool* solo effort. This time, however, his superstar duet partner would be . . . Keith Richards.

17

"Look in My Eyes, What Do You See?"

Opening for the Rolling Stones, while great exposure, can often be a thankless gig. Just ask Marty Balin of the Jefferson Airplane, coldcocked by a Hells Angel at Altamont in 1969, or the aforementioned Prince, sandwiched between George Thorogood and the Destroyers and the J. Geils Band and bombarded with bottles and garbage until he was forced to flee the stage in '81. Some bands try to blow them off the stage, like Lynyrd Skynyrd did at Britain's massive Knebworth venue in 1975, and barely enjoy the experience of playing to an ocean of rock and roll fans. If they choose you, it means, in part, you've arrived—but good luck enjoying the moment. Most of the time, you are allowed to meet the Stones for fifteen minutes, exchange good lucks, and pose for quick photos before you go on and do your set as the arena or stadium slowly fills. There's no pyro, no backing band

and horn section to help the sound fatten and travel to the back rows, 150 yards away. And yet, for forty-plus years, it has remained a coveted gig.

There are other bands that the Stones support more aggressively; the bands who are permitted entry into their inner circle. Usually it's a rhythm and blues hero like B.B. King, Ike and Tina Turner (who opened the 1969 tour), Buddy Guy, or ZZ Top. More recently Sheryl Crow and Jack White have been adopted by the Stones, but in the history of the "Rolling Stones support act culture," only one band has been truly nurtured by them and placed in the eye of a media storm. The band was Living Colour. The year was 1989 and the Stones' return to the road would see them navigating a country if not as fraught with racial tension as the one they first visited in 1964, then certainly addressing some serious questions about race, free speech, and responsibility. Eventually, the Rolling Stones would liberate the Eastern Bloc, playing at the invitation of new president Václav Havel ("Stones Roll In, Tanks Roll Out") but the roots of this new restoration of equality would begin down on the Bowery in Lower Manhattan.

Vernon Reid, Living Colour's intense and thrilling guitar player, not yet thirty, with a hawk-like gaze and a ringed explosion of dreadlocks piling up from his skull, already knew Mick Jagger. He'd auditioned to play on the ill-fated *Primitive Cool* in 1987. A fan of blues, jazz, pop, punk, reggae, heavy metal, and hip-hop, he already knew the weird paradox that a black man playing heavy rock and roll guitar was looked upon as strange by both fans and the music industry. For many, Jimi Hendrix and his white rhythm section were the first, and the last, to be accepted as such. Funkadelic had moments of shining guitar brilliance like Eddie

Hazel's solo on the title track of their trippy, creepy *Maggot Brain*, and the Bad Brains were produced by Ric Ocasek, a major new wave rock star, but these feats were often appreciated by small, knowing cults of rock fan boys or willfully isolated punk communities. Things are so cross-pollinated in 2011 that it seems silly, but the prejudice was so rigid in '87 that it went both ways. Hip-hop, under the guidance of future Mick Jagger producer Rick Rubin, was borrowing rock and roll guitars from heavy metal and classic rock: people like AC/DC, Led Zeppelin, and even Billy Squier, but even that was looked upon suspiciously. Run-DMC famously blanched when Rubin suggested they remake the entire song they'd been cutting up and rapping over—with Aerosmith themselves. The result was a visionary hit. Artists like Schooly D, and Boogie Down Productions enjoyed hits in its wake. But the divide between the reality of black rock and the public perception was such an issue that Reid cofounded (with journalist Greg Tate) a group of black musicians, the Black Rock Coalition, to take it on.

"The difficulty that a band like Living Colour presented was in the eyes and ears of those people who make decisions was no small thing at the time," Reid recalls. "Things were still very compartmentalized. Prince doing 'Little Red Corvette' was considered edgy and revolutionary. Now 'Little Red Corvette' is a nice song. But it couldn't be a milder rock song. And it was one guy who had this one song that kind of sort of broke through. It was still incredibly rare. We already had interest (before meeting Mick). We had people who passed on the band. We had a really close call with Elektra Records. We got all the way to the top to the president at the time. And he said nope."

Mick, who was grappling with such issues as what a black

man can play and what a white man can play credibly before Reid ever picked up a guitar, was not aware that he was about to again have a hand in correcting an unjust perception. He was just look- ing for a badass guitarist. In typical Mick fashion, he'd grown weary of the abundance of ace session men who were available to him. He sensed that the future sound would be a bit rougher, more jagged and street. Via Doug Wimbish, who was playing bass on the record and was a founding member of Living Colour, Reid got the call. "Mick wanted to step outside of the normal guys he would just call," Vernon Reid says today. "There's a bunch of cats [who only work] with upper-echelon people; they always get the calls. [Mick] wanted to hear other stuff, wanted to hear other people—he reached out to several folks to ask who was cool. Doug and Kurt Loder suggested me." Reid was a lifelong fan of the Stones. "It was unsettling to have heard 'Brown Sugar' on the radio and there he is in front of you. I don't think I'd been more nervous. It was kind of nerve-wracking. It was like a cattle call at the studio. A lot of people waiting to go in to play with them. He basically just jammed with people. We played 'Just My Imagina- tion' and 'I Heard It Through the Grapevine.' I think he wanted new voices—certainly wanted younger people and also, aside from younger people, he just wanted people with a different take on it. He said 'I heard you have a really cool band. I think I'm gonna come see you play.'—I was like 'Ah, OK.'"

When we think of Living Colour today, distracting visions of spandex bike shorts first come to mind and we tend to forget what a thrilling dervish they were, how heavy and melodic their songs truly were three years before Nirvana took that formula to the world. The lead singer, Corey Glover, muscular and aggressive like a metal frontman, with long, thin braids clumped together like a great rope, had a gospel-worthy voice he could take high or low. Reid shredded his multicolored guitar like Steve Vai or Eddie Van Halen, and the rhythm section, Wimbish and drummer Muzz Skillings, didn't play just nimble funk or jazz riffs but also connected on a heavy, Zeppelin-like stomp. In 1987, the band held an unofficial residency at CBGB. At the time they seemed utterly unique among New York City bands. "We were all going to CBs to see them play," former *Vibe* and *Spin* editor Alan Light (then an intern at *Rolling Stone*) recalls. "They were phenomenal in an enclosed space. They had the energy and the look, what they were drawing from hip-hop and from culture in New York City. They weren't signed yet, but that was the band everybody was talking about and everybody was watching. Those shows were packed with critics and media and everybody was asking, 'Why can't these guys get a deal?'"

Mick had been going down to CBGB since the days when the Ramones and Richard Hell played there. He was always checking out new music whenever he was in New York; disco at Danceteria, new wave at the Mudd Club; always searching for inspiration and a new sound. He slipped in one night in the company of guitarist Jeff Beck (a fellow '60s blues-rock icon who'd become a pal and collaborator during the Keith freeze) and took in the band's set. Vernon Reid got word that he'd be coming down but took care not to inform the band for fear they'd crumble with stage fright. "I made a conscious decision to not mention it to the band," Reid says. "Our manager at the time said 'Jeff Beck and Mick Jagger are in the audience,' and I said, 'OK, got it,' and immediately proceeded to tell myself they didn't show. I did it so thoroughly I completely managed to forget that they were there. Some part of me knew that it would have been disastrous. We played one of our better CBGB shows that night."

Mick was blown away by the set and met Reid and the band after she show. "Would you let me produce a demo?" he asked. "And it wasn't false," Reid recalls. "It wasn't like 'I can do things that you can't do.' He was really like 'Would you let me?'" *Primitive Cool* was about to be mixed and Mick sometimes found this process a bit boring. He was looking for something to excite him. "I'm going to be here for a while," he told the band. "It was like a request," Reid says, "musician to musician. A lot of the guys of that generation, the rock royalty that I've met, it's amazing how they operate on a couple of different levels. They are rock stars—but they're also weirdly humble. They know 'this is really fragile,' and they tend to be less arrogant about music. I thought he was a great producer. One of the first things he did was make a mix tape for our singer Corey Glover. Really old rarities. Blues. He made him a mix tape!"

The two-song demo (featuring future hit "Glamour Boys" and the politically charged "Which Way to America?") was taken to Mick's label at CBS Records, who on the basis of their famous champion and the quality of the tape, offered Living Colour a deal, and the band quickly began work on their debut, *Vivid*. Mick, who opted not to tour the last Stones album, *Dirty Work*, agreed to a tour of the Pacific Rim in support of *Primitive Cool*, further infuriating Keith, who took issue with a set that would feature Rolling Stones classics essentially played by lookalikes, with a scattering of solo material. "I had no idea the level of what that was," says Reid. "Mick, for his part, never said anything bad about Keith.

The subject of the Rolling Stones never came up. When I met Keith a bit later he couldn't be warmer or more friendly. I mentioned Mick's name and it was almost as if I'd never seen a transformation on a person's face at the mention of a name—literally darkened like Larry Talbot turning into the werewolf. It couldn't have been more grim."

Things would look up for both the Stones and Living Colour. *Vivid* was a brilliant debut. The association with Mick Jagger contributed to an early buzz and got the door open, but the quality of the songs and the ferocity of the performances (and yes, those biker shorts) would kick it down. Sales built slowly at first. Radio didn't know what to make of the band. They dressed like David Lee Roth but sounded bluesy and bold. The more intelligent rock press loved them. Influential *Los Angeles Times* critic Robert Hilburn (an early champion of both Bruce Springsteen and U2) listed them alongside Sonic Youth and Metallica as one of the "twenty bands that matter," and perfectly encapsulated the race issues with the band. "This fast-rising New York quartet's place on the list is no more tied exclusively to the fact that its members are African-American than Los Lobos' place is based on the fact that the majority of its members are Mexican-American. Still, the success of both bands represents an undeniable sociological breakthrough."

No young band wants to bear this burden, but this was the beginning for Living Colour. "We've done interviews where not a *tune* has been talked about," Reid told the paper the following year. It was a time when hip-hop lyrics were becoming increasingly angry, profane, and violent, and the still powerful Tipper Gore led P.M.R.C. (Parents Music Resource Center), which succeeded in stickering certain objectionable bands. N.W.A., who released their debut *Straight Outta Compton* in late 1988, were, by decade's end, being publicly targeted by the F.B.I. "We were coming out of the Reagan years and '88 was the year of the Willie Horton ad and Jesse Jackson running his second, bigger campaign for president. There was a debate going on about race at that time that was different than what had been there before," says Light. "It was a couple of years after crack, and Reagan-tolerated urban decay. A lot of that stuff was on the table. 1989 was also the year of Spike Lee's *Do the Right Thing*. I remember reading an article in *New York* magazine saying 'This movie is going to cause rioting in the streets.'" Public Enemy had recorded the opening theme to Spike Lee's scorching tale of an explosion of racial tension between blacks, whites, and Asians in one Brooklyn community on one of those mind-meltingly hot New York City summer days. *Do the Right Thing* was prescient cinema. That summer sixteen-year-old Yusuf Hawkins would be shot on the streets of Bensonhurst, Brooklyn, by a gang who were randomly targeting blacks and Latinos. Two years later, in 1991, Public Enemy's "Welcome to the Terrordome" single would come under fire for allegedly anti-Semitic lyrics, and the Crown Heights riots would pit blacks against Hasidic Jews following an automobile accident that claimed the life of a seven-year-old child of Guyanese immigrants. Reid had played on the Public Enemy's 1987 debut *Yo Bum Rush the Show*, and *It Takes a Nation of Millions to Hold Us Back* was now the go-to cassette on the bus as the band toured America in support of *Vivid*. "Public Enemy shifted the conversation massively," Reid recalls. "We started to hear the n-word. It's difficult. It's a difficult thing. Something no black artist would put on a record. You know offstage it was cats—cats going to talk the talk but the idea of putting it on a record for sale was unthinkable. It was a real generational shift in values. Part of makes the n-word in pop a very difficult thing."

As they traveled from gig to gig, Living Colour would, as they had in New York, build their reputation on their live show, a swirl of color and dexterity and passion. They performed "Cult of Personality" on *Saturday Night Live* and Arsenio Hall's talk show and slowly the song caught on and *Vivid* climbed the charts.

Meanwhile, smarting from the commercial failure and critical drubbing of *Primitive Cool* and Keith Richard's better-received but still commercially marginalized *Talk Is Cheap*, the Glimmer Twins had a summit and soon were laughing about the bitchy barbs they'd hurled at each other in the press. Inevitably, Mick and Keith began writing songs while a megatour, the first of its kind, was quickly planned. Steel Wheels, the Stones' first outing since their tour in support of *Tattoo You* in the early '80s, would be the biggest the band had ever played and the biggest rock and roll had yet seen. They had a massive band: five backup singers, a full brass section, the Uptown Horns, the return of Bobby Keys (ousted by Mick in the mid-'70s for his drug use), and two keyboardists. The stage (designed by Mick and Charlie Watts) seemed like an actual cityscape. Everything about it would be unprecedented in its hugeness, except for the scrappy support act; the band from the punk club on the Bowery, who couldn't find a record executive to take a chance on them, would now open every show.

The Rolling Stones might have been the biggest band in the world in terms of ticket sales in '89, but those who followed rock and roll knew who the real new kings were.

Guns 'n' Roses' *Appetite for Destruction*, released in late 1987, was like *Vivid*, another slow build, but by '89 it was on its way to becoming the best-selling debut of all time. The rushed follow-up, a hodgepodge of acoustic tracks and their faux live demo, was released as the EP. The lead single, "Patience," was a "Wild Horses"– indebted ballad. The last track on the album was a harder-edged song called "One in a Million." Like their breakthrough single, "Welcome to the Jungle," it's a farmboy's tale of coming to the big city and being fascinated and aghast by what he sees. Lead singer and lyricist Axl Rose cited "Police and niggers" as oppressive figures from the urban nightmare he was portraying. A lyric attacking "immigrants and faggots" made the track even more controversial. Rose did little to help the situation by agreeing to an interview for a *Rolling Stone* cover story. Asked about the inflammatory lyrics, Rose explained: "I'd been down to the downtown L.A. Greyhound bus station. If you haven't been there, you can't say shit to me about what goes on and about my point of view. There are a large number of black men selling stolen jewelry, crack, heroin, and pot, and most of the drugs are bogus. Rip-off artists selling parking spaces to parking lots that there's no charge for. Trying to misguide every kid that gets off the bus and doesn't quite know where he's at or where to go, trying to take the person for whatever they've got. That's how I hit town."

One could argue that Axl's use of the *n*-word might have been innocent. He'd heard the word used repeatedly on *Straight Outta Compton* or *It Takes a Nation of Millions to Hold Us Back* or any number of hip-hop singles and thinking it was up for grabs, he'd use it too, in an enlightened Lenny Bruce sort of way. "I don't think he's thinking that far ahead," Reid says. "And—it was hidden for a long time that Slash was a black guy—hidden top hat just became this character—says so much about the dynamics of race in rock—that that's like—it took a long time to see. He was always in sunglasses always in a top hat, took years to literally see his face— You gotta wonder about that. If Slash was two shades darker, what they would have done? Would he even have been in the band? It's horrible to think these things—to be forced to have to think these things. One of the things that bothers me about racist things in rock," Reid says, "there's almost a presumption there are no black fans. It's OK to say this because no black people are listening to what I'm saying. It's thinking in reverse. N.W.A.'s huge, Ice Cube is huge, and it's because just black people are buying it? I was a huge fan of *Appetite for Destruction*. It's one of the problems with commoditization of the n-word. It's not going to a select group of people."

Living Colour were already on the bill for the entire North American leg of the tour through the fall, and would be forced to think about these things directly when Guns 'n' Roses were added for four nights at the Los Angeles Sports Coliseum in October of 1989. They'd already been turned into pariahs. "We were supposed to play a David Geffen AIDS benefit concert," recalls then Guns bassist Duff McKagan, "We got pulled off that because of the faggots line. The song started a lot of tension."

It begs the question, why add them? "I think Guns 'n' Roses could not be denied as a force in rock and roll," Reid explains. "At that point the impact of Guns 'n' Roses couldn't be overstated. The Stones had to respect and recognize that they were heirs apparent on some level. It was a threat and it was also like L.A. was their town. There was no way around Guns 'n' Roses. They wouldn't be on the bulk of the tour, but for three days in L.A., they would be there. I completely saw the logic of it. Completely."

This was business as usual for the Stones. This is what they do; they absorb the hot new band into their orbit and in a way neutralize them, so it makes sense, but it can also be argued that Mick wanted to put them in their place. It's jujitsu: using the opponents' own fury against them and watching them destroy themselves. Guns 'n' Roses were a weird mix of Stones acolytes and punks. They almost were obliged to take potshots at the band, as the punks had a decade earlier. "Mick Jagger should have died after *Some Girls*, when he was still cool," was a quote attributed to Slash, the band's top-hatted guitarist. The truth was that Guns had been, as early as the previous year, just another club act, hustling for support slots on larger tours like Aerosmith's or Mötley Crüe's. They worshipped the Rolling Stones and were as nervous as hell to be on the bill. "The thing that stuck out was that 'This is the fucking Rolling Stones and we're playing with them.' It just kind of terrified me. This is the big leagues now. This is the real deal." Mick couldn't resist tweaking the already jangling nerves of these, his latest potential rivals. "I wore cowboy boots all the time," says McKagan. "It was raining, and Mick came up to me before we went on that first night and said, 'Hey, mate. You gonna wear those boots on our stage? You're gonna slip. I have some tennis shoes you can borrow. What size are you?' I said, 'I'm an eleven.' He said, 'Me too. We must have the same size willies.' And that was my first conversation with Mick Jagger."

The day of the show, Reid had called into local radio station KROQ to take Axl Rose to task for his lyrics, something that had gotten back to him. Backstage on that night with GNR, the Stones were in the middle of a storm, protected in their gentlemen's club while security and tour teams for all camps tried to keep everyone calm.

"After we played on that first show, I wanted to check out Guns 'n' Roses to see if they were good live," Living Colour's drummer Muzz Skillings has said. "I was standing backstage. I saw Axl coming down the stairs and he walks by. But then five minutes later somebody taps me on the shoulder. I look up and it's him."

"You got a problem with me?" Rose asked, his face red.

"What are you talking about? Skillings asked.

"It's in the media that I'm some sort of racist, man. I ain't no damn racist." He went down this long list: "I don't think you're a nigger. Anyone can be a nigger. If you're a bad person you're a nigger. I don't think black people are niggers. I don't think black bands are niggers."

"And he just went on and on," Skillings recalled. "So then he sticks out his hand and I say we should talk about it, just talk about it."

The Jagger-jujitsu worked brilliantly over the three-day residency in Los Angeles. The following night, tensions escalated. Before Living Colour played their hit "Cult of Personality," Reid addressed Guns' racist lyrics, explaining his disapproval and disappointment to the crowd. "I thought 'I gotta say something the next show'—I made my statement—we played—we came offstage and Keith was waiting for us and he shook my hand and said, 'Man that's right on.'" The Stones and the audience were clearly in Living Colour's corner.

Guns 'n' Roses, had they come on and played a killer set, might have swayed them. But this didn't happen. "The pressure of it was too much," Reid says. "They were human beings. They became kind of mawkish. It was very weird what happened with them." Guns 'n' Roses fell apart right there on that stage that night and were never really the same band again. Within a year, drummer Steven Adler and guitarist Izzy Stradlin would leave the group and Rose would be the band's sole power player. There would be riots and shows that started hours late, and then, for a decade and a half, nothing. Whereas Living Colour just went out and met the challenge by playing, Rose used the stage as a bully pulpit, hard enough when you are not playing before a crowd waiting for the Stones. To be fair the third night saw the embattled band pulling it together a little. Slash wore a Betty Ford Center T-shirt and Axl addressed the crowd: "I'd like to apologize for my actions and comments last night. I just didn't want to see my friends slip away." They played a blazing set, but it would be, as far as the beloved original lineup was concerned, one of their last true highlights.

There's a YouTube clip from a show during that tour when Axl Rose sings with Mick and Keith on the *Beggars Banquet* ballad "Salt of the Earth." Axl sings it note-perfectly. You can detect Mick absorbing Axl's power right there on the stage. He even does a split-second version of Axl's snake dance. "Mick was incredibly jealous of Axl Rose," said one observer on the tour. "Rose was preening around in his little jogging shorts and the girls were all going nuts. Mick is extremely sensitive about his age and how he looks, and here was a kid who was easily young enough to be his son, stealing his thunder. You could see from the way Mick watched Axl out of the corner of his eye that he was burning up. In that respect, Mick was sort of like a woman jealous of another woman."

While privately supportive of Living Colour, the Stones never weighed in on the controversy; not a word. They barely acknowledged that they'd played host to a melee between two up-and-coming rock attractions. Come at the Rolling Stones, the message was, and they will destroy you, no matter how many years since *Some Girls.* The *Steel Wheels* tour in '89 was not about black vs. white; it was about the Stones vs. everyone else. It was a restoration of dominion.

18

"An Evil Face"

[Mick] has a sharp sense of cinema," Martin Scorsese observed in the *New York Times* in 2010. The various working parts of filmmaking appeal to his sense of discipline and his intellect. Mick is at the top of the heap in terms of rock and roll, whereas when he makes a film, every few years, between tour and recording commitments, he can reconnect time and again with the spirit of the early '60s, when he was wide-eyed. This really picked up as he entered middle age and felt those years slip further and further from memory. Mick founded his own film production company, Jagged Films, and took more roles. "Toward the latter part of the '80s, Mick started to set his sights on Hollywood, being a producer and actor—I don't know if he wanted to be a director—he saw it as a new frontier—[I give him credit] as an artist for wanting to pursue a new [career]," Bill German recalls.

Mick's film choices are so few (a half dozen at the time of this writing) that they are even more revealing than his recording career, politicking (or lack of politicking), and certainly his sexual conquests.

In his twenties and early thirties, Mick was being offered every part in films that called for a new, young antihero. Some of those movies, like *Up the Junction*, would go on to become classics, which surely instilled some sense of regret and made him think of opportunities lost and the sacrifice he made to be the frontman for the Rolling Stones.

Mick made his second film in the chaotic year of 1969. That film, a period piece called *Ned Kelly*, matched him with famed British director Tony Richardson. While regarded as a flop, *Ned Kelly* (remade three decades later with the late Heath Ledger in the title role) is underrated and has its charms. Mick, who has Aussie roots on his mother's side, does his best as the wild colonial who ends up on the end of a noose. The movie begins at the end. Ned is in prison, preparing to be executed, to "die like a Kelly," according to his proud mum. "Such is life," Mick shrugs before going to the gallows; not exactly *Hamlet*, but it grabs the attention. Poised between 1967's *Bonnie and Clyde* and 1973's *The Harder They Come*, Ned Kelly was very much a vogue role, a modern antihero. The audiences were meant to draw parallels with the current struggles (cops are called "pigs"). The local color is intriguing (kangaroos hop across the screen), and the soundtrack by Waylon Jennings (in proto *Dukes of Hazzard* mode) and Kris Kristofferson doubles as a Greek chorus. Why didn't it work? Perhaps because Mick wasn't ever meant to be a leading man.

As his face grew less androgynous with age, it became clear

that his calling was that of a character actor: the guy who plays a great and intensely watchable villain or hero. In 1977, eight years after *Ned Kelly*, Mick remarked, "I'd like to do some more films someday and people keep on offering me nasty roles. They reckon I've got an evil face."

Mick began to consider larger parts in the '70s and early '80s. "He continues to yearn for a breakthrough in his long simmering movie career: something dignified to fall back on," Kurt Loder wrote in a 1983 profile. By then, he'd signed with the powerful Creative Artists Agency (C.A.A.), and seemed poised to solidify himself as a credible musician/movie star like David Bowie, Cher, or Dolly Parton. He also began writing scripts (*The Tin Soldier*) and optioned properties (Gore Vidal's *Kalki*) with an eye toward developing, producing, and starring in them. There was talk of him playing mad genius writer and actor Antonin Artaud (who is quoted and clearly an influence on *Performance*) and more strangely the reporter Fletch in Gregory McDonald's cult novels (the part, of course, went to Chevy Chase). He appeared in an episode of actress Shelley Duvall's acclaimed children's series *Faerie Tale Theatre* opposite Bud Cort, Barbara Hershey, and Edward James Olmos in *The Nightingale*. Mick plays a cockney-speaking Chinese emperor. He exchanges lines with a mechanical bird. ("Let no one know you have a little bird who tells you everything; then all will go well with your kingdom.") As far as one on one's go, I've seen worse. Mick even auditioned to play the title role in Milos Forman's *Amadeus* (that part eventually went to Tom Hulce).

There's a line of thought that suggests that the reason why Mick Jagger doesn't have a heralded career as an actor is because he lacks talent. He was good playing himself in *Performance*, the way Madonna was good playing a version of herself in *Desperately Seeking Susan*, and little else, or Eminem was good playing himself in *8 Mile*. At his worst, he chews dialogue (*Ned Kelly* is the hammiest of these instances). It's as if someone instructed him to wrap his teeth around every consonant. For someone so perfectly physical onstage, thespian Jagger acts with his mouth and his eyes and hardly ever seems comfortable in his body. Madonna acts this way as well, as if Stella Adler had never been born. Both can be wonderful subjects, and even in extended, filmic music videos, you cannot help but connect with them. And yet, in scripted features, they have been captured speaking in a way that says, "I am speaking now. I know my lines, and I will say them at the right time. Now you say yours and I shall respond." But both have gotten better and more comfortable over the years: Madonna in *Dangerous Game* and *Evita* and Mick in his character roles of the '90s and 2000s.

Mick's duties to the Stones have certainly interfered with what might have been a sturdier career. In 1981, he was cast in a supporting role in director Werner Herzog's *Fitzcarraldo*, playing Wilbur, the companion to Jason Robards' titular eccentric, determined to build an opera house in the Amazonian jungle. In order to fund this venture, he charters a boat and pulls it over a mountain in order to get to the rubber-rich parallel river on the other side. The documentary *Burden of Dreams* chronicles the production nightmares that plagued the set, from political skirmishes with the natives to illness and the logistical terror of actually getting a boat over a mountaintop. It also contains the only footage of Mick as Wilbur, shortly before he dropped out to hit the road in support of the newly released *Tattoo You*. In the footage from

Burden of Dreams, we see what might have been. He is a scream, playing his part jungle-twitchy and sweaty, a camp figure with rolling eyes and clicking teeth as he recites poetry alongside Robards in the bell tower of the local church.

"Wilbur, you are definitely my man!" a dissolute Robards cheers. They seem a perfect odd couple and clearly could have sustained the chemistry. Herzog, writing in his diary from that period (later published as *Conquest of the Useless*), describes Mick as a trooper as well, helping to shuttle cast and crew to and from the set in his private car and laughing uproariously when accidentally bit by one of the jungle's many monkeys. He also kept the director amused during the singularly punishing shoot. "Whenever we take a break, he distracts me with clever little lectures on English dialects and the development of the language since the late Middle Ages," Herzog recalled.

By early 1991, after yet another massive Rolling Stones tour, Mick was once again ready to commit to an acting job. He accepted the role of futuristic bounty hunter Victor Vacendek in the modestly budgeted sci-fi endeavor *Freejack* alongside Emilio Estevez, Rene Russo, and Anthony Hopkins. *Freejack* would be Jagger's first major above-the-title role since *Ned Kelly*. The project promised good company. Estevez was still a going concern as a box office star. *Young Guns*, in which he played Billy the Kid, was looking like a franchise after a successful sequel (helmed by *Freejack*'s director, New Zealander Geoff Murphy). Anthony Hopkins had just won an Oscar for playing Dr. Hannibal Lecter in *The Silence of the Lambs*, and former model Rene Russo was well on her way to becoming the decade's go-to pretty girl who can hang with the boys (she would shoot *Lethal Weapon 3* in the same year).

"Smart" science fiction was hot again thanks to Paul Verhoeven's 1990 smash *Total Recall,* the follow-up to his equally witty and nihilistic *RoboCop* (1987). Arnold Schwarzenegger was about to reprise his role as the Terminator. Things looked auspicious for *Freejack.* Like all good smart sci-fi, it purported to be an adaptation of a cult novel (Robert Sheckley's Hugo Award–nominated late '50s offering *Immortality Inc.*). It also rode the then fashionable "cyberpunk" wave, inspired by the novels of William Gibson and the advent of the World Wide Web. Cybernetics was to the mid-'80s and early '90s what the *Tibetan Book of the Dead* and the *I Ching* were to Mick Jagger's 1960s. The part offered to Mick was the showiest in the film and, in truth, he is the only interesting thing about it.

Victor, as written, is a stock villain in that he's motivated, or so we are led to believe, by money, but Mick Jagger works that "evil face" with grimaces, frowns, and camp eye-pop, giving him a moodiness and middle-aged gravity that is his own. As with Schwarzenegger, underrated as well, we feel more for the "villain" than the hero and so (and here comes a spoiler) when the cad is through circumstances inspired to behave heroically, we are validated. Every time Mick opens his mouth we are reminded that for all the gravity expressed by Hopkins, it's all a bit "silly." Only Amanda Plummer (as a nun!), who wields a shotgun, is equally pleasing. If you want to look at bad rock-star acting, compare Mick's performance with that of New York Dolls singer David Johansen, who plays Estevez's scumbag agent and is another we can imagine messing someone up. Johansen and Jagger never share any screen time, unfortunately.

Freejack is, in its way, pioneering. It charts out territory later covered by Christopher Nolan's critically adored blockbuster *Inception*. The final scene takes place, for example, in Anthony Hopkins' mind as he lingers in a dream state or coma. Thus far, Hopkins has literally phoned it in. When he appears onscreen, he's usually on a video phone. His one moment of interaction with Estevez, Russo, and Jagger takes place in the portals of his own brain: "Welcome to my mind." Jagger and Estevez never turn into buddies as they chase each other all over the decaying landscape. "Though the action is nonstop, it's so unengaging that we might as well be watching a blank screen," the *Washington Post* criticized. It was not a box office hit. All of its other stars went on to enjoy big box office in the following years. Estevez launched another franchise with the kiddie hockey flick *The Mighty Ducks*. In addition to two *Lethal Weapon*s, Russo starred alongside Clint Eastwood in the classic suspense film *In the Line of Fire*, and Anthony Hopkins would play Dr. Lecter again twice in the next decade. Within two years, Mick would be back on the road with the Rolling Stones for their *Voodoo Lounge* tour, and once again enjoying guaranteed adulation. And yet he refused to give up his pursuit of a respected film career.

Since *Freejack*, he has returned to his habit of playing much more affecting, smaller parts. These choices grew increasingly more brave, and as he entered middle age, Mick finally began to carve out something like a sustained film career, that of a character actor and not a leading man. In the 1997 adaptation of Martin Sherman's controversial late '70s stage play *Bent*, set during 1930s Berlin as the Nazis began rounding up and interring Jews, gays, gypsies, and cripples, Mick appears in drag as Greta, a respected businessman by day and a nightclub performer by night who avoids detainment by ensuring that nobody finds out about his hidden life.

Greta is the first thing we see, swinging on a giant parakeet perch, nylon stockings on his skinny legs in a decadent, prewar Berlin nightclub, singing a Marlene Dietrich–style ballad, miles away from anything the Stones had ever done. As with Herzog in the jungle, Mick was willing to rough it for the sake of the low-budget project. He attended workshops in London with director Sean Mathias and the cast, which included Clive Owen and Sir Ian McKellen. "In the first scene, when he came down from the trapeze, it was from an incredible height. He was nervous and frightened but he didn't complain," Mathias recalls. "He had an entourage with him on set, a group that protected him and looked after him, but he was very affable. He took a great interest in supporting the film." *Bent*, with its explicit gay sex and depressing subject matter, was not designed to be anything but a labor of love, and Mick, blending with the cast around a converted, un-used power station, was certainly sacrificing a measure of comfort for a project that was bound to upset some of his fans. "I think it was a brave choice; although *Bent* appeared onstage some years before, it was fairly radical as a film in the mid-'90s," Mathias says. "A lot of people who couldn't deal with these ideas in the film: gay love; a great more people other than Jews also tragically being sent to the concentration camps. And also being viewed as a historical piece through the telescope of time. AIDS was still so incredibly present in our lives. Not new but pretty frightening."

In *The Man from Elysian Fields*, his next dark and interesting character role, he plays Luther, an elegant pimp and mentor to struggling novelist Andy Garcia. He injects the role with a real sadness (we later find that Luther, a former prostitute himself, has fallen in unrequited love with one of his hires, played by Anjelica Huston). It's one of those "only in L.A." slice-of-life pictures with wooden dialogue, but the actors transcend the material and provide a quiet dignity, the kind that it'd be hard to imagine another rock star of his caliber tapping into. And yet, like *Bent*, *The Man from Elysian Fields* garnered very little critical attention, much less acclaim. *Performance*, his very first film, still stands alone as his most lauded.

"The thing that makes him so great onscreen is also, in a funny sense, paradoxically a handicap, because he's famous no matter what character he plays; he's Mick Jagger playing it," says Mathias. "But in a way, as with many famous, classic Hollywood stars, you will always identify with them as the stars themselves. Greta Garbo may play Camille brilliantly, but we always see Greta Garbo up on that big screen. Humphrey Bogart. Tom Cruise. Tom Hanks. The big stars are famous for delivering what we know they can deliver there. And Jagger has that because that face is so etched and so extraordinary—those lips are so iconic you can't get away from that."

His production company, Jagged Films, has kept going as well, producing equally little-seen period pieces such as *Enigma*, as well as the flop remake of *The Women*. He's been developing a project with Scorsese titled *The Long Play*. Jagger is an eccentric; an auteur; a product of the '70s. Look at the directors he's chosen to make Rolling Stones concert films: Scorsese and Hal Ashby, with whom he collaborated closely on the 1983 tour documentary *Let's Spend the Night Together*, one of the *Harold and Maude* director's last films. "There was definitely a greater bond between

Mick and Hal than there was with the rest of the band," Prince Rupert Lowenstein has said. "Mick was a man who was the incarnation of the band for Hal and also much more interesting in the filming side than all the rest." (According to Ashby's biographer, Keith Richards was uncooperative and irritated by the cameras.) Like any Hollywood veteran, he's been overpraised and he's been underrated, but never truly considered (you won't find any Mick Jagger film festivals). But he's stayed involved for five decades now. In 2007, Keith Richards, who has never deviated from his role as musician, made his debut as the father of Captain Jack Sparrow; it was stunt casting à la *Performance*, and while amusing, didn't require much beyond the growth of a black beard and mustache. "It's not just about living forever, Jackie," he says in his pirate croak; "it's about living with yourself forever." If film is indeed forever, then Mick Jagger has certainly done enough fine, complex work beyond *Performance* to justify continued pursuit, but it would be great to see him one day get the role that he's been longing for. He's more than just an evil face.

19

"The Red Devils' Blues"

What producer Rick Rubin would become famous for doing to other artists, he first did for himself. By 1993, more than a decade into the advent of hip-hop, certain old-school terminology had, according to Rubin, grown tired and stale. The cofounder of Def Jam Records had, by the start of the '90s, moved from New York City to Los Angeles to run the label's offshoot, Def American, which featured hit acts like the Black Crowes. Rubin noticed that the word "def," meaning "cool," had been formally added to the lexicon, included in the Webster's New Collegiate Dictionary in May of 1992. He decided that in order to keep the hip-hop that he loved fresh, "def" had to go. On August 27, 1993, the word Rubin helped popularize would be buried at Hollywood Memorial Park's Chapel of Psalms. Rubin sent out invitations to friends and peers to come pay their final respects to "def." The Reverend

Al Sharpton presided over the services. "Def was kidnapped by corporate mainstream entertainment and returned dead. When we bury def," he said in his stentorian preacher tone "we bury the urge to conform." Pals Trent Reznor, Tom Petty, members of the Red Hot Chili Peppers (whose *Blood Sugar Sex Magik* was recorded in the former's haunted castle in the Hollywood Hills), were among those gathered to pay their last respects. A coffin was filled with remnants of def, including record company literature and album covers. Rubin was thirty and on the verge of becoming the bearded Buddha of the music industry, a sort of guru of the studio, adept at getting to the nut of what was good about an artist and bringing it back to the foreground. It was something he did with young acts like the Chili Peppers and thrash metal kings Slayer, but those were new acts, young, hungry, and just finding their sound. What Rubin, like Quentin Tarantino, then in the process of reminding John Travolta what was great about himself, would come to be best known for was motivating older acts. He'd routinely take legends and franchises and get them back in touch with their sometimes squandered gifts. In the following decade he would apply this to Tom Petty and Neil Diamond, and form a legendary partnership with Johnny Cash. Mick Jagger, however, was his first.

Mick had not lost his taste for finding a solo voice, and his previous two solo albums had, by the '90s, sounded somewhat dated, especially the very '80s *Primitive Cool*. Mick was commendable for chasing new sounds, but some of his material gave Richards' "only dig what's always good" ethos some credence. While I was interviewing Jack White for *Uncut* magazine in 2008, he complained to me, "I know in my heart that music if you ask anybody, 'When do you think music, especially rock and roll, which was sounding incredible; when do you think it started sounding not very good?' that arc starts in the '80s and that same arc starts when digital technology came into play to the studios, and all that new trickery started destroying country, rock and roll, everything. Who escaped the '80s with good sounding records? Not many people. Even with a great band like Gun Club, you can hear gated reverbs and all that crappy digital stuff." A rocker making music since the early '60s is hard pressed to try to stay interested in the recording techniques, lyrical conceits of the past, no matter how good the drums sounded.

The Stones' sound, look, and attitude circa '68 to '72 had never gone out of style, but in the early '90s it seemed to be in vogue again. Rock and roll decadence with threadbare velvets and sashes instead of grunge flannel. Def American had in the '90s broken the Black Crowes, who took a Stonesy look and sound circa 1971 into the American Top 10, and Guns 'n' Roses had not been completely drained of their power. Commercially speaking, they were the world's biggest band. Again Mick was searching for the balance between the Stones and the new. He would not make one album with Rubin; he would make two: a contemporary rock record called *Wandering Spirit* and a wildcard that was not exactly old, not entirely new.

One night in the midst of sessions at Ocean Way Studios in L.A., Rubin took Mick to a local club he liked called the King King. A former Chinese restaurant, the club had been revamped into a funky, chic music venue with a small stage, black lacquered walls, and a dark, homey ambience that made celebrities feel comfortable. The bartenders were good-looking; the door was celebrity-friendly. There were various nights for various genres (ska, swing, reggae) but Monday night was the blues night featuring the Shadows, soon to be rechristened the Red Devils. The Red Devils were a scrawny, surly, tattooed combo featuring members of L.A. roots rockers the Blasters and fronted by a charismatic and not a little Jagger-esque singer and harp player named Lester Butler. "Lester had that rock star thing," says former Red Devils guitarist Paul Size, then a teenage transplant from the blues-guitar haven of Texas. "He had that thing. That kind of angel on one side, devil on the other side. Like Jerry Lee Lewis. Or Anthony Kiedis. He had the stage presence of perfection and also just chaos. It showed. His voice was unique and it just captured your attention. People loved it. It was something different and fresh." Hollywood had, for the past decade, been the domain of the glam metal bands: Ratt, Poison, Faster Pussycat. The nitty-gritty blues seemed like a breath of fresh air, and hipsters of all size were drawn to the King King. Bruce Willis, he of the harmonica-blowing alter ego Bruno, was a regular who would jam on the King King stage with the band, and the Shadows played loud. The King King's sound man was not too concerned by any local noise ordinance. If you wanted to extend your weekend by a day, the King King was the place to go in the early '90s. Rubin and his cohort and Crowes mentor George Drakoulias loved the purity of the Monday night scene and felt inspired to expose or possibly remind Mick of that good party energy to possibly loosen him up.

One night Mick shocked the King King patrons by jumping onstage to jam with Butler and the band. The Red Devils were tipped off by Rubin, who'd already changed their name and slowly drew him into his inner circle with an eye toward recording them. "They called us and told us he was coming down," Paul Size says.

Size, a purist, was not intimidated by the prospect of backing up Mick Jagger. "If they weren't black I didn't listen to them," he says today, nearly twenty years later. "I was a Blues Nazi. I had seen that tongue and the lips, but I'd never gotten into the Stones. It was just classic rock to me. Part of me was like, 'Oh just like Bruce Willis, here's another big star on our stage.' That's what happens out there in L.A.: As soon as you get something, these other guys who are dying in their career try to grab it. So I thought, initially, 'Oh great, he's gonna grab our mojo.' But I gotta say, when he got onstage, something happened." Size watched Mick move and strut. He saw the reaction from the crowd. Heard the authentic tone in his singing. "I thought, 'Wow, this guy is something else.' I guess it brought back something he hadn't had in a while."

The spontaneous blues jam proved a good release indeed. Perhaps it meant little else to Mick, but Rubin got inspired. He began lobbying Mick to record an album of blues standards with the Devils. "I said, 'Jeez, while we're doing this record, we're going to do another one?'" Mick recalled years later to journalist Alan Light. "Rick, you're a hard guy to work with!" It seemed oddly timed, as the sessions for what would become Mick's third solo album, *Wandering Spirit*, were going so well. Mick's boyhood love of the blues didn't really inform the new album sessions sonically, but might have opened him up to the power of truth. Musically there's a lot that ended up on *Wandering Spirit* that could have doubled on a late-period Stones record, such as "Wired All Night." This is likely why it has come to be so highly regarded by Stones fans; it's got the punch of a Jagger-Richards project, but it's certainly a bit more of a personal endeavor lyrically. Mick was writing songs plain-faced like "Evening Gown" and "Don't Tear Me Up." The sound, however, was very modern, "Sweet Thing" boasts a great, soulful falsetto and a future funk groove that would not be out of place on a Chili Peppers album; hardly gutbucket blues. As was his style, Mick was pursuing just that: the latest sound rendered with the newest technology, but Rubin was a persuader, and Mick sensed that he should listen to this guru in the making.

One night in mid-June 1992, Rubin placed a call to the Red Devils and told them to be at Ocean Way Studios the next day to record with Mick Jagger. "Everybody was excited, obviously—and nervous," says Size. Mick showed up with a collection of LPs, which he began playing for the band. "Mick was extremely happy. I thought he was stoned. He was in a genuinely good mood. Thrilled to be doing all these songs. He picked all the songs he'd never gotten to record in the Rolling Stones." The musicians sat and listened to each one once through, then picked up their gear and played along, and finally, with Rubin at the board, did a few takes of their own versions. The entire session lasted about seven hours, and then Mick picked up his records and left in a waiting car, leaving the Red Devils high on adrenaline but unsure of the strange events that just took place. Was this going to be Mick's solo album? Were they his backing band now? "I was under the impression we were making a record. Everybody thought it was gonna come out; definitely gonna come out. [We] waited and waited; of course it never did."

For their troubles, the Red Devils were paid two hundred dollars each. "They gave us a *tip*," Size says. The Red Devils were put out on the road, playing club dates in London, including one for Mick's birthday that July, but the pressure and the drugs soon got to them and they began to corrode. Only one song, "Checkin' Up on My Baby," ever formally saw the light of day on an anthology of Mick's solo hits, *The Very Best of Mick Jagger*, released more than a decade later. The inclusion of a never-before-heard song was designed to make an album of Mick's solo hits seem a bit more commercially viable (the rare Lennon-Jagger jam "Too Many Cooks" appears as well). Mick immediately returned his attention to *Wandering Spirit*, which was released the following year to great reviews. It's widely considered the finest of all the Stones' solo efforts, but like everything since *She's the Boss*, it was not a big commercial hit, and by the end of the year, Mick was again writing Jagger-Richards compositions with Keith for the next Rolling Stones album, *Voodoo Lounge* . . . and the next megatour.

One wonders, with the advent of the White Stripes, how a straight Mick Jagger blues album would have been received, especially now that it's become such a model. Ahmet Ertegün, a blues expert, loved what he'd heard of the Red Devils sessions and encouraged Mick to release it, but it never saw the light of day beyond being a much-traded bootleg, the result of a burned CD of the master recordings allegedly smuggled out of Rubin's possession. Some of the tracks like Howlin' Wolf's "Evil" sound a bit thin (but then it's a hard task, copying Howlin' Wolf, whose voice alone seems like a Wall of Sound). Still the listener can certainly imagine the good time had recording them, and the tom cat lament "One Way Out," on which Mick is almost unrecognizable, allowing his black blues mimicry to run wild, and the throbbing "Ain't Your Business" are brilliant. Ultimately what might have been missing despite the genuinely liberating energy was the King King. "We didn't capture that essence in the studio," says Paul Size. "I think because there wasn't the crowd there—the feedback and the live energy. It was the beginning of the end of certain things." Rubin hired members of the Red Devils to play on his next history-making project, applying his tested Jagger formula to Johnny Cash's American Records debut. The Red Devils soon returned to obscurity, minus their leader. "I was living with Lester," Size says. "I got sucked into all of that with him." Lester Butler died from a drug overdose in 1998 at just thirty-eight. Size is back in Texas, playing guitar. He saw the writing on the wall with Rubin and holds no real bitterness. "I remember seeing him one day driving a Rolls-Royce and I was on a bicycle. I said, 'What's wrong with this picture?' He waved at me." He's since discovered the ramshackle brilliance of the Stones at their peak. "I went back and learned about them after that," he says today. "I realized they loved everything I loved. I just heard *Exile on Main Street,* in fact, and I was like 'Holy shit. These guys are amazing!'"

20

"A Knight of the Realm"

There's a scene toward the end of Martin Scorsese's gang-ster epic *Goodfellas* when Robert DeNiro's Jimmy the Gent and Ray Liotta's Henry Hill wait excitedly while Joe Pesci's Tommy is about to get made. "I never saw Jimmy so happy," Henry says in the voiceover. "You'd think he was being made. Jimmy and I could never be made because we had Irish blood. To become a member of a crew you've got to be 100 percent Italian so they can trace all your relatives back to the old country. It's the highest honor they can give you. It means you belong to a family and a crew. It means that nobody can fuck around with you. It also means you can fuck around with anybody just as long as they aren't also a member. It's like a license to steal. It's a license to do anything. As far as Jimmy was concerned, with Tommy being made it was like we were all being made. We would now have one of our own as a member." It didn't work out so well for Tommy, and depending on who you ask, the knighting of Mick Jagger, who the British establishment once tried to destroy, was either a triumph of rebellion or a tragedy on par with getting shot in the face so your mother can't even bury you in an open casket. Mick Jagger, who became a knight of the realm on December 12, 2003, was not the first rock and roller to receive knighthood, but he was certainly the most raw. When the announcement was made, it instantly polarized the country, as well as the Stones' fan community and the rock and roll world in general. In this way, it was the last truly controversial act he'd commit to date. His acceptance of the honor divided the nation and got people talking in a way that a Rolling Stone had not done since 1965. Was it good for England? Was it the final insult to a crumbling empire and a laughingstock monarchy? Was it then prime minister Tony Blair's attempt to win back the rock and rollers who helped him get into office, then turned on him once he aligned himself with George W. Bush? Was Mick a pawn? Was he a poser, obsessed with class, who was vying for the title all along? Was he in on the joke?

There had been artists who'd been honored for their contribution to the arts. Mostly actors, but a few musicians. Mick's contribution to British music and culture was not in question. Forty years into their career, the mere idea of the Rolling Stones stirred feelings of great patriotism for generations of British people, but the public perception of the soon-to-be Sir Mick was that he was tight. Since his marriage to Jerry Hall hit the rocks in 1999, the British press had a field day with daily reports about his efforts to hold on to his fortune (reportedly in the neighborhood of 150 million pounds). Whether or not he gave money to charity privately,

there were certainly other artists who were more publicly committed to philanthropy. Following Live Aid, Bob Geldof was knighted:
the first rocker to receive the honor and, to date, the youngest.
Paul McCartney followed. Elton John, who'd pledged the proceeds of every one of his singles throughout the '80s and '90s to
AIDS research and helped the nation grieve the loss of Princess
Diana in 1997 by retooling his 1973 Marilyn Monroe elegy "Can-
dle in the Wind," was knighted the following year.

The line on Mick was that money was his only concern. In
1997, when the Stones were recording their twenty-first album,
Bridges to Babylon, Britpop underdogs the Verve scored their first
hit single with "Bittersweet Symphony." The track looped an or-
chestral version of the Stones' early hit "The Last Time" (credited
to the Andrew Oldham Orchestra). Allen Klein still owned the
rights to "The Last Time"; lawyers for his ABKCO firm swiftly informed the Verve that this was not their song (despite the fact that
all of the lyrics were lead singer Richard Ashcroft's and dozens of
hip-hop singles were still getting away with using obscure vinyl for
sampling and looping). When Mick and Keith's names were
added to the songwriting credits, and 100 percent of the song's
royalties were rerouted to the Stones, it only strengthened Mick's
image as rock's greatest miser, obsessed with pecuniary detail.
The aching, youthful sentiment of the Verve's lyrics, coupled with
the freshness of the music, made them seem true, whereas the
Stones, as they did in the late '70s, seemed cynical and tired. Ironically, Mick and Keith were in the same boat as Ashcroft, paying
the bulk of the proceeds from their greatest hits to Allen Klein.
While he was famous for quipping that "'Bittersweet Symphony'
was the best song Mick Jagger and Keith Richards had written in

twenty years," today, Ashcroft is philosophical. "I never had any ill will towards the band," he says. "They were one of the pivotal reasons I got in a band." Still outraged Verve fans booed when he dedicated the song to Mick and Keith, and when the track licensed to Nike for their aggressively inspirational "I can!" sneaker ad, all of the musicians simply had to take it. "We were in the same boat," Ashcroft says. "The same boat as George Harrison and John Lennon. I was in pretty good company as far as situations with Allen Klein."

The perceived lack of philanthropy however, was a minor issue when compared with Mick the potential knight's assumed lack of chivalry. Both McCartney and Elton John were in committed relationships, Paul to Linda and Elton in an openly gay but monogamous relationship with David Furnish. Mick Jagger, newly divorced at the time and linked to big-eyed, voluptuous model and writer Sophie Dahl, two decades his junior, was not exactly Sir Lancelot or Sir Perceval.

Unlike the other elder statesmen of pop, Mick had not grown out of his rock and roll lifestyle, gallivanting with models and party-hopping all over the world. The offer came in while he was on tour in 2002. Unlike McCartney and John, he was still the feline and lithe frontman, shaking his ass. Every night he went out there in front of thousands of people in sports arenas all over the world and sang about "tricks with fruit" that "keep your pussy clean" ("Star Star") and "Puerto Rican girls who are just dying to meet you" ("Miss You") from Hong Kong to Milan to Washington, D.C. Then there was his history. This was, unlike Paul McCartney, a former radical. When the Beatles became Members of the British Empire in 1965, the Stones were being groomed by

Andrew Loog Oldham as their polar opposites, committed bad boys who'd just as soon storm the palace. When John Lennon returned his M.B.E. medal in 1970, in protest of the Vietnam War (and "Cold Turkey" slipping in the charts), even Mick cheered in the press. "At last. He should have returned it as soon as he got it." But 1970 was a long time ago. There were still lines dividing the establishment and the outsiders. Or were there? Keith still saw them.

It presented an instant quandary. If Mick had declined, what measure of outrage would it have produced? Let's say he refused, citing England's alignment with Bush in Iraq, a partnership that would remove any of that new cool from Blair. Surely people would snipe that it was a publicity stunt and take him to task for his political opportunism. Yes there's a history of artists declining knighthood, including the writer Alan Bennett and the actor Albert Finney.

As expected, Mick's accepting the honor produced more angry letters from the establishment than refusing it might have. Subjects of the empire flooded the newspapers with angry letters and took to the Internet to express their outrage. "Perhaps he should go in for a bit of charity. What about unwed mothers?" said Charles Mosley of *Burke's Peerage and Baronetage*. "That's good charity. One that's very close to his heart."

Then there was the issue of what the other Stones and those close to the band would think. Predictably, the decision drew mixed reaction. Some, like Marshall Chess, were bemused. "Mick was always drawn to royalty. His biggest dream was becoming Sir Mick. Who knows what he had to do to get that? You have to work to get that." Charlie Watts was impressed by Mick's ability to charm the higher-ups and carry on caddishly. "Anybody else would be lynched: eighteen wives and twenty children and he's knighted, fantastic!" Charlie Watts laughed. The loudest gripes, of course, came not from the British establishment but from Keith Richards. Keith never forgot or forgave the Courts for putting him in Wormwood Scrubs in '67. "I thought it was ludicrous to take one of those gongs from the establishment when they did their very best to throw us in jail," Richards told *Uncut* magazine, adding, "I told Mick it's a paltry honor. It's not what the Stones is about, is it?" More than vexing Keith, Mick accepted in part, surely, because his father, Joe, was still alive. Mick's mother, Eva, had passed away at the age of eighty-seven in 2000. Joe was turning ninety. Mick was about to turn sixty. It would also be a chance to take his children to the palace. He shrugged off his bandmate's comments as sour grapes, telling reporters, "It's like being given an ice cream—one gets one and they all want one." He informed Blair that once he got off tour, he would happily accept the honor. He would become Sir Mick.

Ultimately, rebellion and revolution are two different things, and the latter is more focused and lasting. The idea of bringing the establishment to you, if that is what Mick did, is noble. It's imprinting your surroundings, opening the world up for the better; tearing away the unrealistic fantasy images of perfect leaders and heroes who only let you down when examined more closely. This was the rock and roll equivalent of progress.

Look at the leap from Bill Clinton saying he didn't inhale to Barack Obama admitting he smoked pot and did a little blow when he had the money. Never again will a good man be denied the presidency because of something he did when he was young and foolish and having fun. Knights were, since the Middle Ages, obliged to be chivalrous. What then of the author of "Under My Thumb," "Stupid Girl," and "Out of Time"? "I don't think the establishment as we knew it exists anymore," Mick keenly observed when pressed on what his knighthood would mean for the good fight, the one Keith was still fighting every day. When told that didn't make Keith happy, he quipped, "He's not a happy person." The attention might have been what Keith was envious of. What does a Keith mean if there's no establishment to rage against. It's like being a superhero without having an archenemy. Superman without Lex Luthor; Batman without the Joker.

Perhaps the more fascinating question is what did the monarchy gain by bestowing knighthood on Mick Jagger? Would it make the royal family's own scandalous behavior, the Diana situation, the carryings-on of the Duchess of York, Charles' affair with Camilla Parker Bowles, seem less outrageous by comparison? Mick Jagger would humanize the whole lot. Certain political pundits pointed out this very thing. "For exhibiting virtues of nobility," one said, "like my son Charles."

As it turned out, it was Charles, not the Queen, who did the honors. Her Majesty was, at the time, recovering from surgery. And so, on December 12, 2003, Mick Jagger, tax exile but otherwise loyal subject, woke up, put on his coat (black leather) and a suit and tie. In the company of two of his grown daughters, Karis (whose mother was Marsha Hunt) and Elizabeth (whose mother was Jerry Hall), and his father, he took a limo to the palace, and Sir Mick was born.

In the intervening years, Sir Mick has become something of an affectionate joke, and Jagger, unlike, say, Ben Kingsley, has never indicated that he's been affected one way or the other by the honor. Still, Keith has never let it go. It's now a permanent bête noire that he can point to, and in nearly a decade since has still not let it go; is still fighting the fight. "Sir Mick," Keith, who'd always found Mick's perceived class-consciousness tedious, told an interviewer. "Here's a guy who went to the London School of Economics for Christ's sake. He's not one for the hierarchy. I thought he should hang out for a Peerage. I thought it was a cheap shot. The damned knighthood. You should be lord. I thought it was a shoddy award—I wouldn't let that family near me with a sharp stick, let alone a sword." To date, the honor has not been extended to Sir Mick's partner.

21

"Who Wants Yesterday's Papers?"

Mick is perhaps the least sentimental of rock stars, and one gets the feeling that trafficking in nostalgia in any way is painful to his psyche, even as the Stones catalog only strengthens each year, from LPs to eight-tracks, to cassettes, CDs, and now digital downloads. "Mick's not a great lover of yesterday," Charlie Watts put it with typical succinctness. His sole reaction to Keith's memoir was to take it to task for wading into the past for mercenary purposes is implied. "Personally, I think it's really quite tedious tracking over the past. Mostly people only do it for the money." Jagger himself took a large advance some years back to tell his own story but decided against it. Popular opinion is that he found he couldn't remember anything, and even turned to Bill Wyman, the Rolling Stones' self-appointed archivist (and author of multiple interesting books on the band, including the memoir *Stone Alone*), only to be told where he can go.

Most likely, Mick didn't want to reckon with the past. It was tedious and painful, a constant reminder of mistakes and lost friends. Ahmet Ertegün had recently passed away after taking a tumble backstage at the Stones' show at the Beacon Theater in 2006 (during the concert that Scorsese filmed for his *Shine a Light* documentary). He was only the latest ally to depart. And yet, canny businessman that he is, he knows that it's the past that has the most currency. The Stones have released their share of compilations; a few of them, like *Hot Rocks* and *More Hot Rocks*, have taken on the patina of classics (that great *Hot Rocks* cover of the band stacked on top of each other in profile has become an icon). But going through the past darkly or otherwise seems anathema to Mick. So why, forty years on, did the Rolling Stones revisit the source of perhaps their greatest myth, their most legendary album, and get fully behind an *Exile on Main Street* media blitz of the spring and summer of 2010? What made looking back palatable, interesting, and new for someone as easily bored and dismissive of laurel resting as Mick Jagger?

In a word: technology. Digital recording, digital imaging, the new world of perception would allow machines to make the Rolling Stones look young, sound young, be young when, physically, they could no longer pull it off; their 2005 world tour in support of their last studio release to date, *A Bigger Bang*, the tacit bow for the Stones as we knew them, in their early sixties, but still fighting fit. Where to go from there? Into the virtual mystic. When the Stones appeared on the cover of *Rolling Stone* as part of the promotion of *A Bigger Bang*, they were weathered and old; it was a bit grim and not a great fit with the vital-sounding new material like "Rough Justice" and "Oh, No Not You Again."

When *Exile* redux was released, Mick and Keith appeared on the cover of *Rolling Stone* as their twenty-eight-year-old selves. They aged five years, and then de-aged thirty-five. By the way, the first time that Mick Jagger appears as his younger self on the cover of a magazine that could have easily run a photo of the current Mick was in 1989, when he appeared on *Spin's* December 1989 issue in a feature written by Lisa Robinson timed to the *Steel Wheels* juggernaut.

There's always been a weird ethic to just how much they will flog the old material. If they do a megatour, it's usually on the back of a new studio album (with few exceptions like 2002's *40 Licks*). "If we go out on tour, we gotta do a record," Mick has said. "It shows you are an actual functioning rock band. I don't want to be one of those bands that does hits. People say, 'I much prefer to hear "Brown Sugar" than some new song.' Well, I don't give a shit what you prefer." Perhaps it was the surprise critical response to *A Bigger Bang*, praised like no Stones album since 1983's *Undercover*, that freed Mick up to go to the vaults?

Or perhaps it was sensing a sort of pattern commercially, if not creatively. *A Bigger Bang*, despite deserved "it's their best album in years," didn't sell more than their last two albums. Like all of their post–*Steel Wheels* releases, it debuted high, provided an excuse for a mega-grossing tour, then fell off the charts without leaving behind a major hit single or selling much more than their standard million copies (ostensibly to hard-core Stones fans who are completists).

In 2006, the Stones switched record labels yet again, moving from Virgin to Universal, and taking their massive and highly lucrative back catalog with them.

They needed to do something to boost the catalog sales and turn kids on to the old stuff without covering themselves in dust and shoving themselves in the nostalgia closet. Again, technology came to the rescue. Universal was looking for marketing angles, eager to find one that might restart media interest in the Stones as musicians and not just a tabloid concern or a tired institution. They suggested a reissue of *Exile*, knowing that it might be distasteful to Mick. *Exile* was long identified as a "Keith" album. Mick had disparaged the sound quality in interviews in the past, "not just because of the vocals but because generally I think it sounds lousy." He much preferred the follow-up, *Goats Head Soup*, and pretty much stood alone there. *Goats Head Soup*, underrated as it is, has no myth. *Exile*'s myth was astronomical, one of rock and roll's most enduring and imitated. You can't know about the album without knowing where and under what conditions it was recorded: the Villa Nellcôte, the sixteen-bedroom mansion and former Nazi headquarters by the sea in the South of France. They'd been chased from England by the Labour Party and the tax man. Keith was a strung-out pirate, shooting Thai heroin and crafting a masterpiece from chaos, pulling riffs and soul out of the impossibly blue sky. Mick was . . . where was Mick anyway? The *Exile* myth is largely a Keith affair. Mick was off in Paris with Bianca. Now, four decades on, with the double album universally regarded as the Stones' masterwork, Mick was finally ready to insert himself into the story and not just the mix. He was ready to acknowledge the public opinion that this was the Stones' masterpiece, and a chance to put his take on it. He'd stopped, as he approached seventy, running from the past, and revisiting *Exile* would be the first offering from a man with a new sense of resolve.

Now it was the fans' turn to be agitated. Not since George Lucas tinkered with the *Star Wars* trilogy in the digital age had such a wave of worry been stirred up. *Exile* was holy. What on earth could the Stones be thinking? Were they so hubristic that they could fuck with their own legacy? This was far more mercenary and base than Pete Townsend unloading all his teenage wasteland anthems wholesale, or Brando rerecording his *Godfather* dialogue for a video game. Did they not know when to just up and walk away? They didn't look or sound anything like those rooster-haired, pouting, weary, rock and roll outlaws, on the run from the cops and the tax man, "partying in the face of tragedy," as Lester Bangs famously called it. This was tantamount to Sean Connery picking up his Walther PPK again.

"I'm a purist," says Liz Phair, who recorded her classic song-by-song response to the original back in 1993. "Not at all an audionerd. That's totally a boy thing and I don't want my dream world to be interrupted by some new conception. Don't come in and, like, fuck with my dream."

Nothing short of a time machine and a new lease at Villa Nellcôte, Keith and Anita Pallenberg's mansion on the Côte d'Azur, where much of the album was recorded, would do for fans like Phair. Messing with an acknowledged masterpiece was dangerous. Paul McCartney seized "Let It Be" from Phil Spector and had in 2003 released *Let It Be—Naked* to a sort of vaguely hostile indifference.

So why did Jagger come around? Largely, it was a surprise.

These up-in-arms Stones purists were genuinely shocked. If there's anything Jagger hates more than nostalgia, it's a pattern. Secondly, the myth of Nellcôte, a Keith myth, was also useful to Mick.

Finally, it was a challenge, one involving boxes and boxes of undated archives, but one that the Stones were uniquely qualified to take on, as they'd been picking and choosing from rapidly aging session tapes since the end of the '60s. Even the *Exile* stuff was not really *Exile* stuff. "We've used like, 'Sweet Virginia,' which was on *Exile on Main Street*," Jagger told *Creem* in 1982. "That was recorded from before *Beggars Banquet*. Know what I mean? And we've always done things like that and kept things because some things worked good sometimes and some things don't. But it doesn't really make any difference on anything because as long as it doesn't sound old." For this *Exile* reissue, sounding old but feeling new was the goal.

Mick commissioned the Stones' producer Don Was to investigate extra studio material from the period. "When Mick first called me about it," Was told the *New York Times*, "it was like he was asking me, 'Can you do me a favor, man? Can you take the garbage out?'" As they listened to hours and hours of tapes from the Stones archive, a place Was compared to the warehouse in the last scene of *Raiders of the Lost Ark*, they would narrow down an *Exile* period, tracks that had both the feel and the vintage. Some were obvious, like an alternate take on the album track "Loving Cup" or a version Keith sung of "Soul Survivor." Others fit the carbon-dating criteria but presented a challenge. There were no vocals. Mick decided to complete these tracks, some of which he'd recorded nearly forty years earlier. "I listened a bit to the regular album and just sort of copped the attitude a bit," Mick told *Rolling Stone* cryptically.

Eventually Mick got into the process; if nothing else, it was new and therefore interesting. When it leaked out gradually that the vocals were entirely new, the Stones camp were cagey, not because of the potential groan-factor but because they knew what would soon come to light: The experiment was succeeding. These songs sounded, against all probability, like great Rolling Stones songs. "I don't know if that takes away from them or not," Mick has said of his slightly tweaked vocals. "I mean I could have fibbed and you totally would have believed me."

The original *Exile on Main Street* producer, Jimmy Miller, passed away in '94, but mixer Andy Johns, who mixed the record in '72 at Los Angeles' Ocean Way, was on board, as was industry veteran Bob Clearmountain. Richards was brought in to add a little bit more guitar, and Mick Taylor, who left the band in 1974, met Mick in London to lay down some new solos, but really these tracks live or die by Jagger not only sounding like himself, but sounding newly engaged. "The strange thing is that 'Plundered My Soul' is very good," the *Times*' Ben Ratliff said of the album's first single. "[It's] the most soulful and energetic Stones track I can think of in almost thirty years." Rock's Peter Pan had finally found a way to stay young. So identifiable are the young Stones with this era that it's shocking to watch the documentary *Stones in Exile*, in which Mick and Charlie traipse through Olympic Studios as elderly men.

When the Stones appeared on the cover of *Rolling Stone* to promote the album, they were, indeed, young men, "lithe," as David Gates' cover story described them, their faces unlined, the future ahead. That same year, *Vanity Fair* ran no fewer than three cover stories featuring artists in their postcard prime: Marilyn Monroe, Grace Kelly, and Elizabeth Taylor (five if you count tribute issues to Michael Jackson and Farrah Fawcett). The Stones were a part of the zeitgeist once again.

The Robert Frank–shot *Exile* cover appeared on T-shirts and other merchandise, and while not everyone loved the record, it was, for a time in the spring of 2010, the biggest story in rock.

"Unlike the album proper, the bonus tracks are given a clean scrubbing, and it's blatantly obvious in places that Mick's vocals are circa 2009, not 1972," *Pitchfork* magazine groaned. "If allowing Jagger to touch up those vocals was the price to pay to allow *Exile* to receive the tribute it deserves, it's still a bargain." But Stones fans and kids interested in rock myths bought it. The album debuted at No. 2 in America and topped the charts in England, and for the first time in a long time, made us wonder . . . as they approach their golden anniversary in 2012, what are these guys going to do next? Who the fuck is Mick Jagger and what will he do next?

EPILOGUE

"Onstage with a Cane"

Mick Jagger is so imprinted on our pop culture DNA strands, as his *Bent* director Sean Mathias observed, that he doesn't really need to tour and record. It's hard to look at a fashion magazine today without seeing the Jagger-face in the form of his youngest daughter, Georgia May. His daughter with Jerry Hall, Elizabeth, posed for *Playboy* in the spring of 2011. His son James is in a band (Turbogeist). The fact that Mick now has children that are approaching the age when people first started wondering how long Mick could keep fronting the Stones (Karis, his first child with Marsha Hunt, and Jade, his child with Bianca, are now in their early forties) has once again turned the subject to age and, with that, professional vitality and, ultimately, mortality.

If you are going to be asked questions by dozens if not hundreds of reporters over fifty years, your take on the issue is bound to change. Most famously, Mick told *People* magazine in 1975, "I only meant to do it for two years. I guessed the band would disperse one day and say good-bye. I would continue to write and sing but I'd rather be dead than sing 'Satisfaction' when I'm forty-five." Two years earlier, he told urbane talk show host Dick Cavett that he could easily see himself doing it at sixty. "Going onstage with a cane," citing Marlene Dietrich, then playing cabaret shows to adoring cinema fans, as an example of the way it could be pulled off.

Back in 1966, he fretted, "I'm dreading [old age]. There are only a few very old people who are very happy. When their minds stop thinking about the present and future, and stay wrapped up in the past, they are awfully dull. I don't want old dears saying 'How old do you think I am? Forty-eight? No, I'm seventy-eight, and I watch all the pop shows and I've got all your records.' Then I think it's time to grow up."

The real question ultimately does not fall to Mick, especially since we, his fans and observers, have never vacillated from our opinion on the matter. Why have we not let this guy get old? Is it racism, as some have suggested? Are we not really used to our white rock stars up there playing at seventy (Chuck Berry played a New Years Eve 2011 gig at eighty-four)? Why can we never be truly comfortable, beloved as they remain, with our Old Stones? Lord knows, we've had plenty of time to prepare for this guy to turn seventy. Mick Jagger is so old that the Stones had a flashback to the '60s segment on their 1981 tour (photos of the band as kids flashed on the video screens while they played "Time Is on My Side"). So old that a 1993 *Esquire* cover story headline read: HAVE YOU SEEN YOUR GRANDFATHER, BABY? (a reference, of course, to the Stones' peerlessly fuzzy 1967 single, "Have You Seen Your Mother, Baby, Standing in the Shadows?") They are so old, a book about them called *Old Gods, Almost Dead* (by Stephen Davis) was released in 2001. They're so old, they inspired Motorhead's funniest lyric: "Blackhearted to the bone. Older than the Rolling Stones" (from "I'm So Bad [Baby I Don't Care]"), not to mention one of (peerlessly) lethargic stand-up comic Stephen Wright's most quoted lines: "The Stones, I love the Stones. I can't believe they're still doing it. I watch them whenever I can. Fred, Barney."

And what happens after seventy? If this purported world tour is marketed as a farewell tour, will Mick and Keith be out there, like Chuck Berry, at eighty-four? In a July 2010 article about the increased virility of septuagenarians, the *New York Times* singled out only Mick Jagger among the rock stars approaching their seventies with regard to their performance style. "Can he really strut like that when he's seventy-five?" the piece asked (Bob Dylan, also mentioned in the piece, would be dignified and old, touring at seventy-five).

Unlike Jones, Hendrix, Morrison, Joplin, and John Lennon, Mick, Keith, Paul McCartney, and Dylan are '60s figures who were fated to wrinkle. But unlike Dylan, only Mick was a symbol of sexual liberation, one who so deftly parodied the social mores of the middle-aged and middle class of '60s-era London ("What a drag it is getting old . . ."). As a young man, his beauty alone seemed revolutionary, neither fully male nor fully female, pretty or ugly, as the artist Cecil Beaton recorded with wonder in his since-published '60s diaries. Those who gazed on him then once saw possibility; they now see mortality.

"He was a good-looking boy in those days," says Keith Altham, who first interviewed the Stones in 1966. "Now he looks like a gargoyle who should be tacked on the side of Notre Dame cathedral." This does not help him solve the Brenda problem, the one he doesn't acknowledge. Yes, Mick did himself no favors with the "Satisfaction," quote, a durable sound bite. And typically, he has never issued a warm mea culpa on this subject or even a nice, bitchy retort: "Would you prefer I'd died?" putting us on the spot, on the defense, whereas Keith addressed the issue at length in his memoir, *Life*.

Instead, Mick simply absorbs the negativity. "A sexy black hole in space," the journalist Keith Altham has called him. Subsequently, we once again must fill the void. Each crag and thinning wisp on Keith is a big "Fuck you" to those who've been writing his obituary since 1973 (when the *N.M.E.* selected him as the next great rock icon to croak). Growing old for Mick is a great "I told you so" to those who were threatened by his youthful beauty and the perceived arrogance that went with it (and those jealous of his wealth and way with women, for sure). It's as if a certain faction of the pop media had been laying in wait for something to humanize him.

"You'll look funny when you're fifty," James Fox's on-the-lam gangster Chas comments when encountering Jagger as Turner in 1968's *Performance*. Jagger was only twenty-five at the time and already the line was poison-tipped and portentous. When Mick Jagger was fifty, by the way, he looked more fit than most people do at that age, freakishly so, which I suppose is "funny." Check the blue-lit sleeve photos for *Wandering Spirit*; on one he's even barechested. Let's just throw this out there as if we needed more evidence that the guy is a paradox: He has clearly had no cosmetic surgery. Look at his face compared with, say, Steven Tyler or

David Bowie or Madonna. It's as raw and lived in as Keith's: pride over vanity, soul over brain, perhaps. When I interviewed him for *Spin* back in 2002 (when he was just shy of the big 6-0) I addressed this.

> **MARC:** How do you think you're aging?
>
> **MICK:** It's a bit of a problem in rock music. You gotta keep your body together.
>
> **MARC:** Do you have a game plan for aging gracefully?
>
> **MICK:** No more than anyone else. Thank god for technology.

I didn't press it, and at the time of this writing, it looks like he still hasn't turned to it.

There is still time. There's longevity in the Jagger genes. His mother passed away at eighty-seven. His father lived to age ninety-three. If Mick's performance on the 53rd annual Grammy Awards in February of 2011 is any indicator, he can still shake his hips, hit the notes, and vie with musicians a third his age. He brought down the house with a tribute to the late Solomon Burke, releasing as he had with the Red Devils in the early '90s, his occasionally dormant inner record-collecting geek. Similarly, his version of Dylan's "Watching the River Flow," on the Ian Stewart tribute album *Boogie 4 Stu: A Tribute to Ian Stewart* (featuring the other Stones as well as founding bassist Bill Wyman) brought to mind a man half Mick's age. Connecting with the old blues and soul seems to bring out his best, and probably keeps him young. Mick and his fellow Rolling Stones have become like the old bluesmen they worshipped in their teens, but it's the model of Mick, displayed to such relieving and exhilarating effect on the Grammys, that really powers the Stones corporation. I would pay to see them play "Start Me Up" on a stool, but there are moments when even I ask, "Why do they want to play 'Start Me Up' on a stool?" When we think of "Brenda" we assume one thing: the money (when we think of Keith we assume: the glory). But perhaps it really is the search—the one that began when he played his very first Rolling Stones show there on Oxford Street, the Marquee stage, 1962.

"I feel he is himself," Cecil Beaton wrote candidly of Mick in his 1967 diary, later published. Beaton saw the singular Mick Jagger. Mick, a "lovely bunch of guys," as he's been referred to by Keith, Nick Kent, and dozens of others, is still looking for him. And so this book can only really end with informed predictions: He will make a solo album with Dave Stewart. He will make nice with Keith, get beyond the barbs and quips of *Life,* and record another Stones album in time for their fiftieth anniversary; or perhaps he will finally deliver his own version of the Stones saga. I doubt that will happen, as absolutes paint him into black corners. Mick is and will likely remain our most consistently misunderstood rock and roller, and I'm not sure if it isn't so by design. As long as we don't really get him, he is free to surprise, as he did at the Grammys and as he almost certainly will do well into his seventies.

Acknowledgments

I'm grateful to everyone who worked with me: James Fitzgerald, Lauren Marino, Cara Bedick, Hal Horowitz, Carrie Borzillo, Connor Raus, John Pelosi, Ray Lundgren, Julia Gilroy, Jessica Chun, Lisa Johnson, Anne Kosmoski, Bill Shinker, and everyone at Gotham. And to those who helped and bore with me and helped me complete this project: Elizabeth Goodman, Joni Mitchell and Jerry Orbach, Maureen Callahan, Alan Light, Josh Seftel, Christina Godfrey, Mr. Rob Sheffield, Ricki Josephberg, Al Josephberg, Eric Fitzgerald, Jesse Malin, Bryan Smith, Rob Gelardi, Tom Vaught and everyone at XOU (Exhile, Sticky Fingers, and Hot Rocks on the Jukebox), Richard, Omar, Johnny and everyone at black and white, Michael Bonner, Bill German, Michael Hogan, Carrie Thornton, Doug Brod, Brett Valley, Alisse Kingsley, James Burke, and Laura Coxson. And finally, thank you to the Rolling Stones and Sir Michael Phillip Jagger for all of the inspirational music.

Bibliography

INTERVIEWS

Tariq Ali, Keith Altham, Richard Ashcroft, Peter Asher, Steve Binder, Rollin Binzer, Marshall Chess, Rae Dawn Chong, Caroline Coon, Sam Cutler, Mick Farren, Bill German, Vivien Goldman, Robert Greenfield, Anthony Haden-Guest, Neil Innes, Nick Kent, Alan Light, Sean Mathias, Albert Maysles, Duff McKagan, Kris Needs, Chris O'Dell, Liz Phair, Vernon Reid, Peter Rudge, Rob Sheffield, Carly Simon, Paul Size, Dick Taylor, Gary Weiss, Peter Whitehead.

BOOKS

According to the Rolling Stones, the Rolling Stones. Chronicle Books, New York. 2009

The Americans, Robert Frank (introduction by Jack Kerouac). Steidl, National Gallery of Art, Washington, D.C. 2008

Angelina: An Unauthorized Biography, Andrew Morton. St. Martin's Press, New York. 2010

Arise Sir Mick: The True Story of Britain's Naughtiest Knight, Laura Jackson. Blake Publishing Ltd, London. 2003

The Armies of the Night, Norman Mailer. Signet Books, New York. 1968

Awopbopaloobop Alopbambloom: The Golden Age of Rock, Nik Cohn. Grove Press, New York. 2001 ed.

Beaton in the Sixties, Cecil Beaton (introduction by Hugo Vickers). Alfred A. Knopf, New York. 2004

Being Hal Ashby: Life of a Hollywood Rebel, Nick Dawson. University Press of Kentucky. 2009

Beyond Good and Evil, Friedrich Nietzsche. Tribeca Books, New York. 2011

Bill Graham Presents: My Life Inside Rock and Out, Bill Graham and Robert Greenfield. Da Capo, New York. 2004

Blown Away: The Rolling Stones and the Death of the 60s, A.E. Hotchner. Simon and Schuster, New York. 1994

Brian Jones: The Untold Life and Mysterious Death of a Rock Legend, Laura Jackson. Piatkus Books, London. 2009

Brian Jones: Who Killed Christopher Robin? The Murder of a Rolling Stone, Terry Rawlings. Helter Skelter Publishing, London. 2005

Can't Be Satisfied: The Life and Times of Muddy Waters, Robert Gordon. Back Bay Books/Little, Brown and Company, New York. 2002

Capote: A Biography, Gerald Clarke. Carroll and Graf Publishers, New York. 1988

Catch a Fire: The Life of Bob Marley, Timothy White. Holt and Co., New York. 1998 ed.

Clapton: The Autobiography, Eric Clapton. Broadway Books, New York. 2007

Conquest of the Useless: Reflections from the Making of Fitzcarraldo, Werner Herzog. Ecco, New York. 2010

Deep Blues, Robert Palmer. Penguin, New York. 1981

Dino: Living High in the Dirty Business of Dreams, Nick Tosches. Dell, New York. 1992

England's Dreaming, Jon Savage. St. Martin's Press, New York. 1992

Faithfull: An Autobiography, Marianne Faithfull with David Dalton. Little, Brown and Company, New York. 1994

Girls Like Us—Carole King, Joni Mitchell, Carly Simon, and the Journey of a Generation, Sheila Weller. Atria/Simon and Schuster, New York. 2008

Groovy Bob: The Life and Times of Robert Fraser, Harriet Vyner. Faber and Faber, New York. 2001

High on Arrival, Mackenzie Phillips. Simon Spotlight, New York. 2009

Howling at the Moon: The Odyssey of a Monstrous Music Mogul in the Age of Excess, Walter Yetnikoff with David Ritz. Broadway Books, New York. 2004

Jagger Unauthorized, Christopher P. Andersen. Delacorte Press, New York. 1993

James Brown: The Godfather of Soul, James Brown with Bruce Tucker. Macmillan, New York. 1986

Jerry Hall's Tall Tales, Jerry Hall and Christopher Hemphill. Elm Tree Books, London. 1985

The Kandy-Kolored Tangerine-Flake Streamline Baby, Tom Wolfe. Picador, New York. 2009 ed.

Keith Richards: Before They Make Me Run, Kris Needs. Plexus, London. 2004

Let It Bleed: The Rolling Stones, Altamont, and the End of the Sixties, Ethan Russell with Gerard Van Der Leun. Springboard Press, New York. 2009

Life, Keith Richards. Little, Brown, New York. 2010

The Lord of the Flies, William Golding. Faber and Faber, London. 1973

Machers and Rockers—Chess Records and the Business of Rock and Roll, Rich Cohen. W.W. Norton, New York. 2004

Mick Jagger: A Biography, Anthony Scaduto. W.H. Allen, London. 1974

Mick Jagger: The Unauthorised Biography, Alan Clayson. Sanctuary Publishing Ltd, London. 2005

Mick and Keith, Chris Salewicz. Orion, London. 2002

Miss O'Dell, Chris O'Dell with Katherine Ketcham. Touchstone/Simon and Schuster, New York. 2009

My Life in Pictures, Jerry Hall. Quadrille Publishing, London. 2010

Nankering with the Rolling Stones: The Untold Story of The Early Days, James Phelge. Chicago Review Press, Chicago. 2000

Now Dig This: The Unspeakable Writings of Terry Southern, 1950–1995. Review of Contemporary Fiction, London. 2002

Old Gods, Almost Dead, Stephen Davis. Broadway Books, New York. 2001

Ossie Clark: 1964/74, Judith Watt. V and A Publications, London. 2003

Pop Music and the Press, Steve Jones. Temple University Press, Philadelphia. 2002

Portraits and Observations: Essays of Truman Capote, Truman Capote. Modern Library, New York. 2007

The PR Strikes Back, Keith Altham. John Blake, London. 2001

Real Life, Marsha Hunt. Flamingo Books/Harper Collins, New York. 1986

Revolt into Style: The Pop Arts in the 50s and 60s, George Melly. Oxford University Press, London. 1989

Rock Wives, Victoria Balfour. William Morrow and Co., New York. 1987

The Rolling Stones, Robert Palmer. Sphere Books Limited, London. 1984

The Rolling Stones: In Their Own Words, David Dalton and Mick Farren. Putnam, New York. 1983

The Rolling Stones: A Life on the Road. Interviews by Jools Holland and Dora Loewenstein. Penguin Studio, New York. 1998

The Rolling Stone Interviews, Peter Herbst and Ben Fong-Torres. SMP Paperbacks, New York. 1989

The Rolling Stone Interviews. Back Bay Books/Little, Brown and Company, New York. 2007

The Rolling Stones on Tour, Annie Leibovitz and Terry Southern. Dragon's Dream Ltd, France. 1978

Rolling with the Stones. Bill Wyman with Richard Havers. DK Publishing, London. 2002

Ronnie, Ronnie Wood. St. Martin's Griffin, New York. 2007

Rotten: No Irish, No Blacks, No Dogs, Johnny Rotten with Keith and Kent Zimmerman. Picador, New York. 1995

The Sixties: Diaries 1960–1969, Christopher Isherwood. Harper, New York. 2010

Stoned, Andrew Loog Oldham. Vintage, New York. 2004

Stones: 365 Days, Simon Wells/Getty Images. Abrams, New York. 2006

The Stones, Phillip Norman. Penguin Books, London. 1993

S.T.P.: A Journey Through America with the Rolling Stones, Robert Greenfield. Da Capo, New York. 2002

True Adventures of the Rolling Stones, Stanley Booth. Chicago Review Press, Chicago. 2000

Truman Capote: In Which Various Friends, Enemies, Acquaintances and Detractors Recall His Turbulent Career, George Plimpton. Anchor Books, New York. 1998

Under Their Thumb, Bill German. Villard, New York. 2009

Up and Down with the Rolling Stones, Tony Sanchez. William Morrow, New York. 1979

White Bicycles: Making Music in the 1960s, Joe Boyd. Serpent's Tail, London. 2006

You Can't Always Get What You Want, Sam Cutler. ECW Press/Random House. 2010

MAGAZINES/WEB

Blender Magazine, September 2003, 50 Worst Artists in Music History

Classic Rock Magazine, February 2011

Creem Magazine, January 1982, by Ray Bonici

Daily Telegraph, October 21, 2010

The Economist, October 7, 2010

Entertainment Weekly, January 31, 1992, by Owen Gleiberman

The Guardian, October 16, 1999, by Jonathan Jones

Harper's Bazaar, October 15, 2010, by Christine Lennon

The Independent, March 22, 2008, by Susie Rushton

L.A. Examiner, September 22, 2009, by Phyllis Pollack

Life Magazine, July 14, 1972, by Thomas Thompson

London Evening Standard, March 4, 1966, by Maureen Cleave

Los Angeles Times, October 21, 1989, by Richard Cromelin

The Mirror, May 19, 2002, by Alan Rimmer

Mojo, October 2004, by David Dalton

Mojo, April 2008, by Peter Doggett

New York Observer, December 9, 2001, by Ron Rosenbaum

New Yorker, November 1, 2010, by David Remnick

New York Times, July 11, 2010, by Kate Zernike

New York Times, March 21, 2010, by Alan Light

New York Times, May 23, 2010, by Ben Ratliff

New York Times Style Magazine, December 5, 2010, by Zoë Heller

N.M.E., February 11, 1966

N.M.E., Summer Special 1966, by Keith Altham

N.M.E., April 2, 1966, by Keith Altham
N.M.E., February 4, 1967, by Keith Altham
N.M.E., September 16, 1967, by Keith Altham
N.M.E., December 21, 1968, by Keith Altham
N.M.E., August 10, 1974, by Roy Carr
People Magazine, June 9, 1975, Mick Jagger cover story by Jim Jerome
People Magazine, November 22, 1982, by Jim Jerome (reported by Linda
    Marx, John Dunn, and Jerene Jones)
Pitchfork, May 19, 2010, by Rob Mitchum
Playboy, November 1971, interview with Allen Klein by Craig Vetter
Q, February 1996, The Making of The Rutles "All You Need Is
    Cash"
Rave, December 1966, by Mike Grant
Rolling Stones, January 21, 1970 (Altamont package)
Rolling Stone, January 4, 1973, James Taylor/Carly Simon interview, by
    Stuart Werbin
Rolling Stone, October 20, 1977, by Charles M. Young
Rolling Stone, September 7, 1978, by Chet Flippo
Rolling Stone, August 21, 1980, by Chet Flippo
Rolling Stone, January 22, 1981, John Lennon tribute
Rolling Stone, November 24, 1983, Mick Jagger cover story by Kurt
    Loder
Rolling Stone, February 14, 1985, by Christopher Connelly
Rolling Stone, August 10, 1989, by Del James
Rolling Stone, December 14, 1995, by Jann S. Wenner
Rolling Stone, September 22, 2005, by David Fricke
Slate, November 5, 2010, by Bill Wyman
Spin, December 1989, Mick Jagger–Rolling Stones cover story by Lisa
    Robinson
Spin, July 1999, by Marc Spitz
Telegraph, August 13, 2006, by Dominic Sandbrook
Telegraph, November 14, 2006, by Adam Edwards
Time Magazine, February 8, 2007, by Josh Tyrangiel
Times of London, July 1, 1967, by William Reece Mogg
Uncut, January 2004, by John Wilde and Nigel Williamson
Uncut, April 2010, by David Cavanaugh

Uncut, The Ultimate Music Guide, The Rolling Stones, from the makers of *Uncut*, Winter 2010/2011

Vanity Fair, November 1986, by Bob Colacello

Vanity Fair, November 2000, by Robert Sam Anson

Vanity Fair, 2008, Carla Bruni cover story by Maureen Orth

Washington Post, January 18, 1992, by Hal Hinson

Index

Ali, Tariq, 106, 110, 118
Altamont Speedway, 2–5, 12–14,
    148–53, 193, 198
Altham, Keith, 4–6, 16, 38, 71,
    74–75, 77, 182, 289–90
Ashby, Hal, 261–62
Ashcroft, Richard, 273–74
Asher, Peter, 38, 40–41, 63,
    68–69, 77
"As Tears Go By," 61–70, 141
Avory, Mick, 35, 37

Bailey, David, 39–40
Baker, Ginger, 139
Bangs, Lester, 191, 233, 283
Barclay, Eddie, 160
Barger, Sonny, 193
The Beatles: breakup of, 162, 164;
    and drugs, 86–87, 94; and early
    Stones music, 40, 41–42; and
    Klein, 85; popularity of, 80;
    public image of, 47–48, 75,
    77–79; reissues of songs, 283;
    relationship with the Stones, 224;
    Rutles parody, 194–201; and
    social conflict, 106, 108, 118
Beaton, Cecil, 86, 176, 289, 292
Belli, Melvin, 149–50
Berry, Chuck, 23–24, 28, 39, 41, 50,
    52–53, 212, 288
Binder, Steve, 52, 59

The Black Crowes, 263, 265
Blair, Tony, 117–18, 272, 276
Blaise's nightclub, 81, 82, 88
Blind Faith, 139, 149
Blues Incorporated, 30
Booth, Stanley, 117, 150
Bowie, David, 105, 183, 188, 204–5,
    215, 228, 232–33, 255, 291
Boyd, Joe, 83
Brando, Marlon, 106, 126,
    127–28, 170
Bredahoff, Patti, 152–53
Breton, Michèle, 129, 131, 133
Brown, James, 51–60
Bruce, Lenny, 206, 246
Bruni, Carla, 218, 220, 221
Burroughs, William S., 133, 172
Bush, George W., 118, 272
Butler, Lester, 266, 270

Caine, Michael, 78, 158–59
Cammell, Donald, 126–28,
    128–33, 140–41, 158–59
Capote, Truman, 167, 169–79
CBGB, 156, 241–42
CBS Records, 230, 232, 234, 242
Charlie Is My Darling (1965), 198
Chess, Marshall, 25, 49, 159, 169,
    172, 174, 178, 275
Chess Records, 24–25, 49
Chong, Rae Dawn, 233–34

Clapton, Eric, 128, 139, 218, 220
Clarke, Gerald, 177
The Clash, 105
A *Clockwork Orange* (Burgess), 72, 126
Cocksucker Blues (unreleased film), 167, 172, 176, 178
Cohn, Nik, 76, 161
Colacello, Bob, 155
Cooder, Ry, 133
Cooke, Sam, 84–85
Coon, Caroline, 83, 90, 93, 98, 101–2
Cooper, Michael, 89, 91
The Crawdaddy Club, 37, 40
Cutler, Sam, 137, 147–48, 152, 154

Davies, Cyril, 30, 36
Decca Records, 42, 68
Def American, 263, 265
Des Barres, Pamela, 217
Devo, 205
Diddley, Bo, 39, 40, 46, 59
Dixon, Willie, 32, 50, 74
Donovan, 84, 98
Drakoulias, George, 266
The Dreamers (Bertolucci), 117
Dunbar, John, 63, 69, 143
Dylan, Bob, 71–72, 91, 98, 106, 289

Ealing Club, 30, 36
Ed Sullivan Show, 48, 195
Edwards, Bernard, 224
Epstein, Brian, 75, 77, 85, 195
Ertegun, Ahmet, 159–60, 169–71, 173, 269, 280
Estevez, Emilio, 257, 259
Everly Brothers, 20, 46

Faithfull, Marianne: affairs, 145; and "As Tears Go By," 63–70; and *Beggars Banquet* sessions, 115; and Bianca Jagger, 160; and drugs, 87, 90–93, 97, 98, 133, 140–44; and family life with Jagger, 124; on Jagger's image, 10; miscarriage, 140; musical influence of, 121; and *Performance* production, 128, 130, 132; public perception of, 206; and Rutles parody, 197–98; and social conflict, 109–10, 118–19
Farren, Mick, 12–13, 107, 112, 116, 117
Fellini, Federico, 121, 122–23
Ferry, Brian, 218–20
Fitzcarraldo (1982), 256
Forman, Milos, 214
Fox, James, 127–29, 133, 290
Frank, Robert, 167, 169, 172, 178–79, 286
Fraser, Robert, 88–91, 93–94, 96–97, 132
Freejack (1992), 257–59
Fry, Stephen, 88–89

Gates, David, 285–86
Gaye, Marvin, 51–52, 54–55, 188
Geldof, Bob, 273
German, Bill, 228–29, 253–54
Gibbs, Christopher, 91, 109
Gimme Shelter (1970), 12–14, 32, 149–50, 213
Ginsberg, Alan, 106, 123
Gleason, Ralph J., 150
Glover, Corey, 240–41, 242
Godard, Jean-Luc, 112–16
Goldman, Vivien, 211, 212
Gomelsky, Giorgio, 37
Goodwin, Clive, 93

Graham, Bill, 149, 151
Grammy Awards, 291–92
Grateful Dead, 151, 236
Greenfield, Robert, 168–70, 173, 175
Grossman, Albert, 72
Grundy, Bill, 208
Guns 'n' Roses, 246–51, 265
Guy, Buddy, 50, 238

Haden-Guest, Anthony, 156, 164
Hall, Daryl, 183
Hall, Jerry, 3, 134, 215, 217–21, 233, 272, 287
Hall and Oates, 234
Hamilton, Richard, 94
harmonica, 3–4, 30, 39
Harrison, George, 91, 195–96, 274
Hazel, Eddie, 238–39
Heller, Zoë, 6
Hells Angels, 4–5, 102, 148, 151–52, 176–77, 193, 198, 237
Hendrix, Jimi, 142, 159, 238–39
heroin, 128, 132, 135, 141, 163, 186, 207
Hilburn, Robert, 243
Hoffman, Abbie, 117
Holly, Buddy, 20
Holzer, "Baby" Jane, 47
Hopkins, Anthony, 257–59
Hopkins, Nicky, 111
Hopper, Dennis, 233–34
Howlin' Wolf, 23, 24, 45–46, 269
Hunt, Marsha, 144–45, 160, 161, 164
Hunter, Meredith, 3, 13–14, 149, 152–53, 193
Huston, Anjelica, 261

Idle, Eric, 194–95, 198
In Cold Blood (Capote), 173, 175

Innes, Neil, 194–95, 198
The Invocation of My Demon Brother (1969), 113
Isherwood, Christopher, 214

Jackson, Michael, 183, 230–32
Jagged Films, 253, 261
Jagger, Basil ("Joe"), 19, 22–23, 26, 36, 43, 276
Jagger, Bianca, 155–65, 198, 216, 220–21, 287
Jagger, Christopher, 19, 36
Jagger, Elizabeth, 277, 287
Jagger, Eva, 19, 36, 43, 276
Jagger, Georgia May, 287
Jagger, Jade, 164, 287
Jagger, Karis, 145–46, 161, 277, 287
Jagger, Mick: childhood, 17–23; and drugs, 91–104, 137–54; early television performances, 51–60; education, 20–21, 27; film career, 92, 120–35, 141, 143, 146, 163, 254–57, 257–59, 261, 290; harmonica playing, 3–4, 30, 39; indecency arrest, 71–80; knighthood, 271–78; marriages, 160, 162, 164–65, 184, 215, 217–18, 220–21, 272; mimicry skills, 26, 32, 34, 209, 211, 269; musical influences, 23–28, 29–43; public perception of, 1–16; and social conflict, 105–18
James Brown, The Godfather of Soul (Brown), 55–56
Jan and Dean, 53, 55, 57
Jefferson Airplane, 151, 237
Johansen, David, 258
John, Elton, 10, 168, 226, 273, 274
Johns, Andy, 285

Jolie, Angelina, 216–17, 221

Jones, Brian: and age issues, 289; ambition of, 41, 43; and *Beggars Banquet* sessions, 114–15; and Chess Records session, 50; death, 139–43; and drugs, 81–82, 87, 93–94, 123–24, 137–38; and Dylan, 72; and early Rolling Stones performances, 37, 39–40; and Faithfull, 64; and Jagger's role in the Stones, 3–5, 11; and Jagger's sexual relationships, 217; and "Jumpin' Jack Flash," 103; living arrangements, 34–35, 42; and the London blues scene, 30–31, 32; and Marquee Club gig, 36; musical influences, 62; and Pallenberg, 122, 123–24; and *Performance* production, 128, 129, 132; and *Shindig*, 45; and social conflict, 111; at the *T.A.M.I. Show*, 58; and the "we piss anywhere" incident, 75

Joplin, Janis, 142–43

Jujuj, Mohammed, 91

Keeley, Charles, 74–75

Kent, Nick, 6, 8–10, 121, 236, 292

Kerouac, Jack, 172

Keys, Bobby, 147, 174, 179, 224, 245

King, B. B., 238

King, Martin Luther, Jr., 46, 112

King King (club), 265–66, 270

Kingsley, Ben, 277–78

Klein, Allen, 84–85, 138, 195, 273, 274

knighthood of Jagger, 271–78

Korine, Harmony, 120

Korner, Alexis, 30, 36, 38

Kramer, Nicky, 91–92

Kray brothers, 92, 107, 128

Kristofferson, Kris, 183, 254

Led Zeppelin, 157, 168, 204, 241

Lee, Spike, 244

Lennon, John: and copyright issues, 274; criticisms of the Stones, 223–24; and drugs, 82, 87, 128; and early Stones songs, 42; film roles, 126; leadership, 98; political protest, 275; on popularity of the Beatles, 80; and public image, 64, 78, 164; and Rolling Stones drug trial, 96; and social conflict, 106–8, 111–12, 117–18; songs with Jagger, 182–83, 269; withdrawal from public, 204

Letts, Don, 210

Life (Richards), 8, 11, 134, 135, 290, 292

Light, Alan, 241, 244, 267

Little Boy Blue and the Blue Boys, 27, 30–31

Live Aid, 234–35

Living Colour, 238–43, 245, 247–51

Living Theatre, 123

Loder, Kurt, 240, 255

Lofgren, Nils, 15–16

London School of Economics, 27, 33–36, 41–42, 65, 107–10

Lord of the Flies (Golding), 122–24, 134–35

Love, Mike, 55, 59

Lowenstein, Rupert, 5, 153–54, 159, 164, 262

LSD, 82–83, 85–87, 90, 97, 99, 124, 152

The Man from Elysian Fields (2001), 260–61
Marley, Bob, 211, 212
Marquand, Christian, 89, 126
Marquee (club), 36, 37
Mason, Dave, 231
Mathias, Sean, 260–61, 287
Maysles, Albert, 12–14
Maysles, David, 12–13
McCartney, Paul: and age issues, 289; and drugs, 86; and early Stones songs, 42; and Fraser, 89; and Jackson duet, 231; knighthood, 273, 274; and leadership, 98; post-Beatles music, 204; and public image, 47, 64, 77; and reissue of Beatles songs, 283; and Rolling Stones drug trial, 96; and videos, 226
McKagan, Duff, 247–48
McLaren, Malcolm, 206, 209
Melly, George, 31
Mercury, Freddie, 204, 231–32
Michaels, Lorne, 194–95, 199
Miller, Jimmy, 103, 111, 285
Mogg, William Reece, 99–101
Moon, Keith, 95, 204
Morad, Luciana, 221
Morrison, Jim, 112, 143
Morton, Andrew, 216–17
Mosley, Charles, 275
MTV, 226–29, 231–36
Murphy, Eddie, 200
Murphy, Geoff, 257
The Muses Are Heard (Capote), 167, 171, 174, 178

Nankering with the Stones (Phelge), 35–36
Ned Kelly (2003), 143, 146, 254–57
Needs, Kris, 207, 210, 219
New Musical Express, 22, 72, 74, 77, 107, 290
News of the World, 83, 88, 90–91, 93, 95
New Yorker, 167, 170, 171
New York Times, 185, 253, 289
Nilsson, Harry, 189
Nitzsche, Jack, 132–33
N.W.A., 244, 246, 247

Ochs, Phil, 106
O'Dell, Chris, 163, 185, 188
Oldham, Andrew Loog: and "As Tears Go By," 62, 65–67; and drugs, 85; and early Stones shows, 40–42; and Faithfull, 63–64; and Jagger's film career, 126; and management changes, 84, 102–3; and McLaren, 209; musical influence of, 121; and public image, 76–77, 204, 275; and Stewart's demotion, 16; and the "we piss anywhere" incident, 72–73, 75–76, 79–80
Ono, Yoko, 128, 164
Orton, Joe, 206
Other Voices, Other Rooms (Capote), 176

Page, Jimmy, 217
Pallenberg, Anita, 82, 115, 118–35, 162, 165, 217
Palmer, Robert, 24, 187
Parson, Gram, 163, 186–87
Passaro, Alan, 153

Performance (1970), 92, 120–35, 141, 163, 255–56, 261, 290

Perry, Richard, 189

Phair, Liz, 215–16, 283

Phelge, James, 35–36

Phillips, John, 182–83, 213–14

Phillips, Mackenzie, 213–14

Plant, Robert, 226

Plummer, Amanda, 258

Powell, Enoch, 112

Presley, Elvis, 71, 126, 162, 168, 208–9

Primitive Cool (Jagger), 235–36, 238, 242, 264

Prince, 227–28, 237, 239

Public Enemy, 244–45

punk music, 203–12

Radziwill, Lee, 171

Ramone, Dee Dee, 56

The Ramones, 56, 206, 209, 241

Ratliff, Ben, 285

Real Life (Hunt), 144

The Red Devils, 266, 267–70, 291

The Red Hot Chili Peppers, 264

Reed, Lou, 10

Reid, Vernon, 238, 240–42, 246–49

The Residents, 205

Revolt into Style (Melly), 31

Rhodes, Bernie, 206

Richards, Bert, 18, 19

Richards, Doris, 18

Richards, Keith: and age issues, 236, 289–90; and Altamont, 14; and "Angie," 191; and "As Tears Go By," 61, 67; and *Beggars Banquet* sessions, 115; and Bianca Jagger, 157–58, 162–63, 165; and Brown, 52; and Capote, 174; and Chess Records session, 49–50;

childhood, 17–28; competitiveness, 39; criticisms of Jagger, 5–8; and drugs, 87, 93–98, 100–101, 132–33, 135, 138, 186, 207; and Dylan, 72; and *Exile on Main Street* reissue, 284–85; and Faithfull, 64; film roles, 262; and formation of the Rolling Stones, 37; and future of the Rolling Stones, 292; on harmonica playing, 4; and Jagger's film work, 254; and Jagger's knighthood, 273–74, 276, 277, 278; on Jagger's sexual relationships, 215–16; and Jagger's solo work, 233, 234–35; and Jones' demotion, 81–82; and "Jumpin' Jack Flash," 103–4; and Lennon, 224; living arrangements, 34–35; and Living Colour, 243–44, 249; and London blues, 29, 33, 35; musical influences, 28; and new-wave music, 227–30; and the 1972 U.S tour, 179; and Pallenberg, 121–22, 124–25; and *Performance*, 128, 131–34; and Phillips, 182–83; and post-punk, 225; and public image, 15, 173, 204; and Rubin, 264; and social conflict, 111; songwriting, 134–35, 187; and Stones parodies, 2, 200; at the *T.A.M.I. Show*, 58; and videos, 226, 230

Richardson, Tony, 143

Robards, Jason, 256–57

Robinson, Smokey, 51–52, 54, 211

Rodgers, Nile, 232

Roeg, Nicolas, 131
Rolling Stones Records, 25, 159, 171–72, 211
Rose, Axl, 246, 248–49, 250
Rosenbaum, Ron, 7
Rotten, Johnny, 157, 207–8, 210
Rubin, Rick, 239, 263–70
Rudge, Peter, 5, 157, 162, 168, 170, 173–74
Russo, Rene, 257, 259
The Rutles: All You Need Is Cash (1978), 42, 194–201

Sanchez, Tony, 91, 121–22
Saturday Night Live, 1, 194–97, 199–200, 211, 245
Savage, Jon, 205
Schifrino, Mariano, 145
Schneiderman, David, 91–92
Scorsese, Martin, 69–70, 253, 261
Scully, Rock, 151, 153
The Sex Pistols, 205–8, 219
Sharpton, Al, 264
Sheffield, Rob, 220, 231–32
Sherman, Martin, 259–60
Shrimpton, Chrissie, 39–40, 65, 69, 72, 85, 215, 220
Simon, Carly, 181–91
Simon, Paul, 196
Sinatra, Frank, 48, 126
Size, Paul, 266–70
Skillings, Muzz, 241, 249
Slash, 247–48, 250
Slick, Grace, 152
Smith, Patti, 57–58, 157
Smokey Robinson and the Miracles, 54
Solanis, Valerie, 207
Some Girls (Rolling Stones), 187, 203, 209–10
Southern, Terry, 126, 172

Spector, Phil, 17, 133, 283
Spector, Ronnie, 52
Steel Wheels tour, 218, 245–51
Stewart, Dave, 235, 292
Stewart, Ian: and Chess Records sessions, 49; demotion, 78, 82; and early gigs, 30–32, 35; on Jagger's identity, 16; and Stones debut, 37–38; tribute record, 291
Stewart, Rod, 225–26
Stills, Stephen, 146–47
Straight Outta Compton (N.W.A.), 244
The Strand, 205
Studio 54, 156, 157
"Sympathy for the Devil," 113–15

Talk is Cheap (Richards), 245
T.A.M.I. Show, 51, 53–60, 133
Tate, Sharon, 193
Tattoo You (Rolling Stones), 226, 256–57
Taylor, Dick, 20–21, 23–29, 35, 37
Taylor, James, 184, 185, 190
Taylor, Mick, 6, 138, 147, 191, 204, 285
Temple, Julien, 206, 233
Their Satanic Majesties Request (Rolling Stones), 102
Times of London, 99–101
Tosh, Peter, 210–11, 211–12
Townsend, Pete, 204
Trudeau, Margaret, 217–18
Trudeau, Pierre, 217–18
True Adventures of the Rolling Stones (Booth), 117, 150
Turner, Tina, 213, 234, 238
Two-Lane Blacktop (Hellman), 184
"2,000 Light Years from Home," 98–99, 102
Tyler, Steven, 290–91

Under Their Thumb (German), 228
*Up and Down with the Rolling
    Stones* (Sanchez), 91, 121–22

Vadim, Roger, 125
Verhoeven, Paul, 258
The Verve, 5, 273–74
Vicious, Sid, 209, 212
Victory (Jackson), 230
videos, 225–26, 228–36
Vietnam War, 109, 275
Vivid (Living Colour), 242–46
Voorman, Klaus, 181–82

Walter, Little, 31
Wandering Spirit (Jagger), 265,
    267–69, 290
Ward, Stephen, 100
Warhol, Andy, 5, 123, 156, 170–71,
    176, 178
Warner, David, 124
Was, Don, 284
Waters, Muddy, 28, 30, 36–37,
    49–50
Watts, Charlie: addition to the
    Stones, 38; and "Angie," 191;
    and drugs, 91, 138; and
    Jagger's knighthood, 275–76;
    on Jagger's lack of nostalgia,
    279; and Jagger's solo work,
    233; Lennon on, 224;
    marriage, 162; and public
    image, 204; and the Steel
    Wheels tour, 245; and "Street
    Fighting Man," 111; and the
    T.A.M.I. Show, 58; and videos,
    226, 230

Weiss, Gary, 196–97, 198
Wenner, Jann, 6, 102, 167
Westwood, Vivienne, 206
Wexler, Haskell, 116
White, Jack, 238, 264–65
White Bicycles (Boyd), 83
Whitehead, Peter, 78–79, 96, 198
The Who, 95, 149
Wiazemsky, Anne, 115
Wilde, Oscar, 88–89, 96, 103
Williamson, Sonny Boy, 31
Wilson, Brian, 53–60
Wimbish, Doug, 240–41
Winwood, Steve, 32, 139
Wobble, Jay, 210
Wolfe, Tom, 47
Wonder, Stevie, 139, 168, 177,
    188, 228
Wood, Ron, 182–83, 198, 204, 226
Wyman, Bill: addition to the
    Stones, 38; and *Beggars
    Banquet* sessions, 114; and
    Boogie 4 Stu tribute, 291;
    marriage, 162; and public
    image, 204; as Rolling Stones
    archivist, 279; and *Slate*
    article, 8; and the *T.A.M.I.
    Show*, 58; and *Their Satanic
    Majesties Request*, 103; and the
    "we piss anywhere" incident,
    74, 75

Yetnikoff, Walter, 230
Young, Charles M., 208
"You're So Vain," 181–82, 186–91

Zwerin, Charlotte, 12